FOREIGN DIRECT INVESTMENT IN LESS DEVELOPED COUNTRIES

FOREIGN DIRECT INVESTMENT IN LESS DEVELOPED COUNTRIES

The Role of ICSID and MIGA

James C. Baker

Q

QUORUM BOOKS
Westport, Connecticut • London

Library of Congress Cataloging-in-Publication Data

Baker, James Calvin, 1935–
    Foreign direct investment in less developed countries : the role
of ICSID and MIGA / James C. Baker.
      p.   cm.
    Includes bibliographical references and index.
    ISBN 1–56720–312–4 (alk. paper)
    1. Investments, Foreign—Developing countries. 2. International
Centre for Settlement of Investment Disputes. 3. Multilateral
Investment Guarantee Agency. 4. Economic development—International
cooperation. I. Title.
HG5993.B34   1999
332.67'3'091724—dc21   99–10384

British Library Cataloguing in Publication Data is available.

Library of Congress Catalog Card Number: 99–10384
ISBN: 1–56720–312–4

First published in 1999

Quorum Books, 88 Post Road West, Westport, CT 06881
An imprint of Greenwood Publishing Group, Inc.
www.quorumbooks.com

Printed in the United States of America

The paper used in this book complies with the
Permanent Paper Standard issued by the National
Information Standards Organization (Z39.48–1984).

10 9 8 7 6 5 4 3 2 1

Copyright Acknowledgment

The author and publisher gratefully acknowledge permission to reprint material from the
Multilateral Investment Guarantee Agency as cited in the illustrations in chapters 8 and
9.

To Stefan Robock
who planted the seeds of
international business
and
economic development

Contents

II: INTERNATIONAL CENTRE FOR SETTLEMENT OF INVESTMENT DISPUTES

IV: CONCLUSIONS

Illustrations

TABLES

FIGURES

Preface

In 1972, I was an attendee of the Hague Academy of International Law at the International Court of Justice. During this three-week program, Aron Broches presented five lectures and two seminars about the operations of an obscure six-year-old institution called the International Centre for Settlement of Investment Disputes (ICSID). Thus, I first became aware of this small agency that has now completed three decades of dispute resolution in a very narrow area of jurisdiction. The late Mr. Broches was the first secretary-general of ICSID and his lectures and seminars excited me and another attendee and colleague, John K. Ryans, Jr., now Bridgestone Professor of International Business at Kent State University, to place this organization on our research agenda. Our articles about ICSID in the 1970s were the first about this institution to appear in the business academic literature. Since then, ICSID has remained a subject of my research interests.

After that initial encounter, the subject of international financial management became a major teaching interest to me. Foreign investment and political risk are important topics in this course. As a result, methods to reduce the loss from political risks developed into another research interest.

One such major method is foreign investment insurance against loss from political risks. In the latter part of the 1980s, another international agency was established and became another major research interest for me. The Multilateral Investment Guarantee Agency (MIGA) was that institution. This organization is the first fully global investment insurer and has just finished its tenth year of full-time operations.

Thus, ICSID and MIGA have developed into the major topics of this book. The history of their evolution and analysis of their operations precedes a discussion of representative cases handled by each institution. Their problems are analyzed and a look at their future reveals agencies whose significance in the improvement of the global foreign investment environment of less developed countries has been fully achieved.

Acknowledgments

I am indebted to many who have contributed to this book. The late Aron Broches planted the seed in those Hague lectures and seminars and furnished further help with studies in the 1970s. Christophe Bellinger, an officer of the Multilateral Investment Guarantee Agency (MIGA), furnished contemporaneous information on the agency's guarantees and funding. My colleagues, John Ryans and Lois Yoder Beier of Kent State University's College of Business Administration, have collaborated with me on a number of writing projects about the International Centre for Settlement of Investment Disputes (ICSID). Improvements have been suggested by a number of anonymous reviewers of papers on the subject of ICSID and MIGA by the author, which were presented at International Finance and Trade Association, Academy of International Business, and Association for Global Business conferences in recent years. Numerous graduate research assistants have mined the literature on ICSID and MIGA during the past 20 years. Some of these should be singled out for their diligence in gathering research materials on these agencies. They are Susan Edwards, Rossitsa Yalamova, Constantin Ogloblin, and Scott Meisel, all doctoral students in business at Kent State University. Others have reviewed various stages of this manuscript. Finally, the final edition of this book has been improved greatly by the editorial assistance of Alan M. Sturmer and his staff at Greenwood Publishing Group, Inc. I appreciate their patience and advice.

As with any writing project, many have assisted me. However, I remain solely responsible for any errors or omissions in this book. As with country risk, such mistakes come with the territory.

Acronyms

AAA	American Arbitration Association
AAPL	Asian Agricultural Products Limited
ACE	ACE Insurance Company, Ltd. of Bermuda
ADB	Asian Development Bank
AfDB	African Development Bank
AID	U.S. Agency for International Development
AIG	American International Group
Amco	Amco Asia Corporation
CEPSA	Compañia Española de Petroleos, S.A.
COFACE	Compagnie Française d'Assurance pour le Commerce Extérieur
CUP	Cooperative Underwriting Program
DAG	Definitive Application for Guarantee
EBRD	European Bank for Reconstruction and Development
ECGD	Export Credit Guarantee Department
ECOSOC	United Nations Economic and Social Council
FDI	foreign direct investment
FIAS	Foreign Investment Advisory Service
GDP	gross domestic product
GE	General Electric Company
IACAC	Inter-American Commercial Arbitration Commission
IAIGC	Inter-Arab Investment Guarantee Corporation

ICC   International Chamber of Commerce
ICSID   International Centre for Settlement of Investment
                 Disputes
IDA   International Development Association
IDB   Inter-American Development Bank
IFC   International Finance Corporation
IIGC   International Investment Guarantee Corporation
ILO   International Labour Organization
IMF   International Monetary Fund
ING   Internationale Nederlanden Bank, N.V.
IPA   investment promotion agency
IPAnet   Investment Promotion Agency Network
ITS   Investor Tracking System
JCAA   Japan Commercial Arbitration Association
KAFCO   Karnaphuli Fertilizer Company Limited
KCAB   Korean Commercial Arbitation Board
LDCs   less developed countries
MIGA   Multilateral Investment Guarantee Agency
MINE   Maritime International Nominees Establishment
MITI   Ministry of International Trade and Industry
MNC   multinational corporation
NAFTA   North American Free Trade Agreement
OECD   Organisation for Economic Co-operation and Develop-
                 ment
OPIC   Overseas Private Investment Corporation
PA   Preliminary Application
PAS   Policy and Advisory Services
PCA   Permanent Court of Arbitration
PLO   Palestine Liberation Organization
ROA   return on assets
UCC   Union Carbide Corporation
UNCITRAL   United Nations Commission on International Trade Law
UNCTAD   United Nations Conference on Trade and Development
UNIDO   United Nations Industrial Development Organization

I

INTRODUCTION

1

Foreign Investors and Less Developed Countries

Foreign direct investment (FDI) is considered the most important means of bringing goods and services to foreign markets. It is the principal way to link national economies. In 1992, world sales of the foreign affiliates of international companies amounted to $5.2 trillion, whereas world exports were $4.8 trillion. The investment stock that generated these sales was estimated to be $2.4 trillion, with more than $200 billion added to this stock annually. The United Nations estimates that 40,000 multinational corporations (MNCs) with 250,000 affiliates conduct this global business.[1]

The bulk of the FDI flows into developed countries. These nations hold approximately 75 percent of the global foreign investment stock and attract 60 percent of the investment flows. The plight of less developed countries (LDCs) since 1980 has been quite dismal, except for Asia, which attracts most of the FDI going into developing countries — about 70 percent or $60 billion in 1994, with similar amounts of inflows estimated for subsequent years.[2] Because sovereign debt in Mexico was rescheduled in 1982, many LDCs have had to reschedule their burgeoning external debt, totaling more than $1.2 trillion at present, or declared temporary moratoriums on their loan or interest payments. Although world energy prices have declined somewhat — except for the price spike caused by the Persian Gulf war — and interest rates have declined since the early 1980s, real prices have remained relatively high, and industrialized nations have not increased significantly their imports of LDC goods and services. Thus, the economies of LDCs have remained, with a few exceptions, relatively weak. FDI could greatly benefit these countries. However, general political and economic conditions in most of these nations discourage increased flows of FDI.

Although a study of trends in private investment in 30 LDCs revealed that total investment, public and private, as a percentage of gross domestic product (GDP) increased steadily during the 1970s, this trend was reversed in the 1980s.[3] The private share is higher on average than the public share of total investment, according to this study, and started rising as a percentage of GDP by 1986–87, although such investment fell in four of the countries surveyed: Bangladesh, Malaysia, the Philippines, and Tunisia.

These general trends show that most FDI flows into developed countries. LDCs need such investment more than do developed countries. Many reasons can be cited for the shortfall of FDI into LDCs. These reasons will be analyzed in the following sections of this chapter. The relatively small amounts of FDI directed at LDCs can be attributed primarily to the political risk prevalent in these countries. These risks will also be discussed in this chapter, as a prelude to the discussion of the need for institutionalized investment insurance on a global basis.

FOREIGN DIRECT INVESTMENT FLOWS TO LESS DEVELOPED COUNTRIES

One important source of private investment is FDI. However, LDCs' share of FDI generally has been about 30 percent of the total.[4] In some regions of the world, both private investment and FDI are at paltry levels. For example, in Africa, private investment has hovered at only 5 percent of GDP. FDI has been nearly nonexistent — about 0.5 percent of GDP, one-third of the level of FDI in all LDCs. The global level of FDI in LDCs, about 1.5 percent of GDP annually, has been abysmally low.

Although global FDI increased by 40 percent in 1995 over the previous year, the bulk of this investment stemmed from projects located in the developed world that were financed by MNCs.[5] Nearly 90 percent of the overall increase from 1994 to 1995 was made by MNCs into other countries in the industrialized world. Cross-border mergers and acquisitions in the pharmaceutical, telecommunications, financial services, and entertainment sectors accounted for much of this investment increase. Only one of the five largest foreign acquisitions took place in the developing countries.

BENEFITS OF FOREIGN DIRECT INVESTMENT
TO LESS DEVELOPED COUNTRIES

FDI benefits the host LDCs by providing additional equity capital, transfer of patented technologies, access to scarce managerial skills, creation of new jobs, access to overseas market networks and marketing expertise, reduced flight of domestic capital abroad, more rigorous appraisal of investment proposals, diffusion of improved techniques, long-term commitment to successful FDI projects, and catalytic effects leading to associated lending for specific projects.[6]

Home countries also benefit from FDI. These benefits include overcoming trade barriers to foreign markets, securing raw materials supplies, cost reduction in component supplies and finished goods that require labor-intensive operations, and the reinforcement of global marketing strategies of their principal exporters.

A specific benefit from FDI according to Frank Carlucci, the president of Sears World Trade, is that the private sector generates nearly three-quarters of the GDP of a developing country. Thus, any significant increases in output emanate from the private sector.[7]

PROBLEMS FOR FOREIGN INVESTORS
IN LESS DEVELOPED COUNTRIES

Despite the benefits that accrue to the host LDC from FDI, these countries often have environments that restrict foreign investors, resulting in extreme paucity of FDI in many regions. Several of these factors have been identified in a study conducted by the U.S. Agency for International Development.[8] For example, many LDCs place controls on ownership, limiting foreign investors to some maximum percentage or requiring the foreign investor to divest his interest within a certain period of time, as in the Andean Pact countries. Bureaucratic snafus in the project approval process are prevalent in many LDCs. Contract disputes, which arise between foreign investors and host states, often are difficult to resolve, although the International Centre for Settlement of Investment Disputes (ICSID), a major subject of this book, was created by the World Bank to facilitate resolution of such disputes.[9]

Other host country practices, which inhibit FDI, include quotas that require employment of a certain proportion of local nationals, regardless of their qualifications, or the imposition of residency requirements, which limits expatriate employment. Some LDCs impose performance requirements, including local content or the offsetting of imports with exports, countertrade, barter, or devotion of some production to exports. LDCs often impose exchange controls, restrictions on repatriation of capital, investment incentives that can distort efficient allocation of resources, and tax policies that discriminate against foreign firms.

In addition, local political conditions can increase the risk of operations significantly. Threats from political turmoil and strife inhibit FDI, as does the instability of the local political regime. Labor unrest can reduce productivity of projects financed by foreign investors.

Other, more specific obstacles to FDI are present in some LDCs.[10] For example, internal political pressures can lead to price controls. Contractual obligations might not be respected. Local governments might grant preferences to large prestige projects, especially if cronies of the presidents are involved. LDCs often practice excessive legalism or have legal texts that are imprecise. Decisions by government also can be slow or arbitrary, making it difficult for foreign investors to implement their decisions in a sufficiently prompt manner.

In addition to political obstacles, financial restraints inhibit FDI in many LDCs.[11] Inadequate investment funds and working capital inhibit development of the private sector. Financial restraints include restrictive financial regulations, inadequate financial intermediaries that can efficiently mobilize and allocate project funds, insufficient foreign exchange reserves, the public sector crowding out the private sector for funds, heavy taxation that squeezes corporate profits and reduces private sector incentive, and public sector monopolization of foreign loans and grants.

The Most Recent Past

Several countries have struggled in their encouragement of foreign private investment, which furnishes the catalyst for economic development in LDCs. The recent plight of the Asian nations and the ongoing problems in Africa, especially sub-Saharan Africa, provide excellent examples of the problems that face foreign investors in LDCs. These regions and their problems are discussed in the following sections.

The 1990–96 period has been much better for LDCs than the previous decade. Private capital flows to these countries have increased fivefold to $244 billion in 1996, according to the Multilateral Investment Guarantee Agency (MIGA).[12] More than 80 percent of these flows were from private sources with FDI into LDCs increasing from $25 billion in 1990 to $110 billion in 1996, whereas aid from official sources remained at $40–50 billion.

What is the explanation for this increase in private sector capital flows to LDCs? Four trends can be identified in the LDCs that deviate from the restrictions discussed above. Many LDCs have moved toward democratic governments with market economies. Macroeconomic management in many of these nations has improved. Their banking systems have been strengthened. The investment environment in many of these countries has been liberalized. The ensuing FDI into LDCs has resulted in more global integration among developed and developing nations. At the same time, capital and labor markets have been linked more closely, and productivity and economic growth in LDCs have increased. Much of this improvement in the economic environment of the LDCs can be attributed to several multilateral agencies established since the end of World War II to foster growth in these nations.

Asia

Despite these improvements, several of the developing countries with the highest economic growth rates have incurred problems with their economies. The most severe example is that of the Asian countries, which suffered declining foreign exchange rates and stock market prices in 1997. The most extreme examples are Thailand, Indonesia, South Korea, Malaysia, and the Philippines. The economic crisis could spread to Japan, China, and Malaysia by means of systemic risk in their banking systems and financial markets.

Because of the magnitude of the crisis in that region, one of the most complex financial reorganizations is being orchestrated. This reorganization involves the International Monetary Fund (IMF), the World Bank, the U.S. Treasury, the Asian nations whose economies are in crisis, private investment bankers, and multinational banks. Early estimates of the bailout of the most affected nations total $103 billion.[13]

Analysts attribute the cause of the Asian financial crisis to several factors. These countries have had large, average growth rates for several years, and the markets for the products they export could have reached saturation points. Most of the governments in these countries are fraught with corruption, and many government officials have committed high-cost projects to their political cronies and relatives. Many of these projects have driven up the budget deficits in these nations with concomitant high inflation, high interest rates, and falling foreign exchange rates for their currencies. Real estate and other financial values have fallen, causing a collapse of many of the banks in these countries.

Such a financial collapse can be felt in other parts of a world, which is now a global economy. This financial crisis caused a severe decline of share prices on the stock exchanges of these nations as well as those in Hong Kong and Singapore. In late October 1997, the contagion was felt on the stock markets in Tokyo, Europe, and the United States. On one day, October 27, 1997, the Dow-Jones Industrial Average in New York fell 544 points, the largest single-point decline in the history of that average.

The financial rescue coalition seemed to focus on Indonesia. Regulators found that Indonesian companies had borrowed billions in U.S. dollar-denominated debt but had never reported it. The extremely high rates of interest, meant to prop up the Indonesian currency, will damage economic growth there. Big companies moved capital offshore to avoid financial and political problems. The political unrest that stems from the Suharto regime will make an orderly succession difficult.

In South Korea, large companies — *chaebol* — have incurred extremely high debt-to-equity ratios by borrowing too much to finance their growth rates. These companies have debt that amounts to 3–10 times their equity. With slower growth predicted in South Korea, these companies will not be able to grow their way out of this debt problem. Resulting bankruptcies have moved Korean bankers to tighten credit, and government bureaucrats have slowed the growth in government spending. Bribery scandals have arisen in this country.

Africa

As mentioned earlier, private foreign capital has been very slow in flowing into Africa, especially sub-Saharan Africa. Private investment flows to this area peaked in 1982 at $5.5 billion.[14] The share of long-term private capital — the sum of private loans (bank loans plus bond finance), portfolio equity flows, and FDI — that flows to sub-Saharan Africa is lower, as a percentage of GDP, than that of all other developing areas except South Asia. In fact, total private investment flows, including unrequited transfers, to this region are lower than for all other developing areas.[15]

For most of the period since, and particularly in the 1990s, annual long-term private capital flows have been less than half the 1982 peak amount. From 1965 to 1987, the average annual growth rate of GDP per capita was 1.1 percent for all of Africa and 0.4 percent for sub-Saharan Africa — actually 0.1 percent if Nigeria is excluded. From 1986 to 1991, real GDP declined by 0.7 percent annually, including North Africa but excluding South Africa. The performance of sub-Saharan Africa was the worst among all LDCs. Black Africa's GDP per capita fell by an average 1.2 percent, whereas East Asia during this period grew by 6.2 percent and South Asia grew by 3 percent.[16]

Some of the reasons for the slowdown in capital flows to this region in Africa can be attributed to aid fatigue and fiscal pressures felt by the industrialized nations. The elite leadership in sub-Saharan Africa, however, blamed external causes for the plight of this area. These causes included Western colonialism and imperialism, effects of the slave trade, exploitation by MNCs, the injustice of the international economic system with its negative terms of trade, and inadequate flows of foreign aid.[17]

However, internal problems in sub-Saharan African nations have more to do with the paucity of private capital flows to this region, and the new generation of leadership has agreed with this analysis. These countries suffer from: civil strife, macroeconomic instability, slow economic growth and small domestic markets, inward orientation and burdensome regulations, slow progress on privatization, poor infrastructure, high wage and production costs, as well as misguided leadership, political corruption, senseless civil wars, human rights violations, and military vandalism.

A demographic analysis of Africa reveals many of these problems.[18] In the early 1990s, African democracies increased from only four in 1990 to 15 in 1995. However, two of these, Congo-Brazzaville and Sierra Leone, were taken over by military regimes in 1996. Other countries have failed in moving from a dictatorship to a democracy. In Nigeria, the military seized power in a January 1996 coup. Violence erupted in the January 1998 elections in Kenya when President Daniel arap Moi accused the country's election commission, whose chairman he appointed, of rigging the votes in the election to favor the opposition. The violence, centered at first on the coastal areas, moved to the interior where atrocities were committed in late January 1998.

Economic reform has not been effective in Africa in recent years. Africa's GDP grew by 5 percent in 1996, but the population growth rate of 3 percent caused per capita GDP to grow by only 2 percent. In a continent with vast mineral wealth, Africa could probably grow by 12 percent annually if it had better leadership. The large countries of Algeria, Angola, Congo, Kenya, Nigeria, Sudan, and Zimbabwe are dragging down the continent's overall economy. Several thousand people have been killed by Algeria's violence in the late 1990s.

It has been suggested that several changes will have to be made in these countries if they are to overcome the restrictions on private foreign investment.[19] These changes include improvement of infrastructure, strengthening of the banking systems, development of capital markets by accelerating the pace of privatization and broadening the domestic investor base, formulation of an appropriate regulatory framework and imposition of a more liberal investment regime, introduction of competitive labor market policies while creating and maintaining institutions for upgrading human capital, and reform of the judiciary system and containment of corruption.

Currently, domestic investors do not have faith in Africa. According to the Index of Economic Freedom, published by the Heritage Foundation and *The Wall Street Journal*, Africa is the least economically free continent. It is plagued by all of the problems mentioned above.

Nigeria is a strong example of the problems of Africa. Between mid-1992 and January 1994, as many as 12 or more foreign partners pulled out of the country. The Nigerian Institute of Social and Economic Research produced a 1995 study that blamed these losses on a weak currency, poor infrastructure, lack of safety and security of life and property, high tariffs, and political instability. The Manufacturing Association of Nigeria has had more than 40 percent of its members close their businesses since 1987.

Other countries in Africa have few key institutions. They do not have an independent central bank, judiciary, or media, nor does a neutral and professional military and police force exist in many of these countries. Thus, corruption and cronyism are prevalent. Commercial and personal properties are seized arbitrarily by drunken soldiers. Dissidents frequently vanish. Senseless civil wars are fought for long periods. Many of the countries essentially are governed, if that is the word, by gangsters and scoundrels who use the government to enrich themselves and their cronies.

Bureaucracy is prevalent and burgeoning in many African countries. Guinea was reported to have 50,000 civil servants in 1996 who consumed 51 percent of the nation's wealth. Some of the governments have too many ministers at the top as witnessed in Ghana, which had 88 cabinet and deputy ministers in 1995, and in Zimbabwe, where 54 officials held ministerial offices.

In contrast, some African nations have attracted foreign investment in recent years and appear to be favorable targets for foreign business firms. In addition to South Africa, which attracts a large portion of FDI in Africa, other countries such as Zimbabwe, Kenya, Botswana, and Cote d'Ivoire provide attractive investment environments, although Kenya has encountered political problems as a result of the 1998 elections.[20] See Table 1.1 for a breakdown of U.S. FDI into sub-Saharan African nations.

TABLE 1.1
U.S. Foreign Direct Investment in Sub-Saharan Africa
(in $millions)

Country	1993	1994	1995
South Africa	900	1,013	1,269
Nigeria	478	322	595
Cameroon	253	228	158
Liberia	181	197	229
Kenya	104	134	190
Ghana	117	143	170
Zimbabwe	127	144	150

Source: G. Alisha Davis, "Africa's New Dawn," *International Business* 10 (February 1997): 8.

Latin America

Latin American countries have had two distinct periods during the past two decades when foreign investment faced crises of one kind or another. During the early 1980s, a massive international debt crisis emerged from defaults by several Latin American governments on jumbo loans made by the international banking community. The first of these defaults occurred in 1982 when Mexico notified a syndicate of international banks that the government would not be able to meet the payment schedule on a jumbo loan made to Mexico by the syndicate. The announcement took the international financial community by surprise because it came just prior to the final arrangements for another large loan to Mexico.

During that period, loans to more than 20 countries, most in Latin America, had to be rescheduled. These were, technically speaking, defaults but the payment schedules and interest rates were rescheduled by the international banking community. Two of the largest loans rescheduled had been made to Argentina and Brazil. Interest rates, whether U.S. prime rate or Euromoney LIBOR, were extremely high. Loans made during the 1970s had presumably been made for specific projects in these countries. However, when the loans became non-performing in the 1980s, it was discovered that most of these loans were merely balance of payments loans, that is, loans to pay off previous loans in order to improve the balance of payments of these countries. It was this crisis, along with the earlier Cuban expropriations of foreign investment, which was instrumental in moving the World Bank to accelerate plans to establish a multilateral agency to insure foreign investments in developing countries. This agency, MIGA, is one of the two major topics of this book.

The international debt crisis of the 1980s appears to have ended — except for some similarities in the current Asian crisis — as a result of several actions. The rescheduling of many of these loans gave these countries time to enact changes in their economies. The IMF demanded economic policy changes in some these countries. Several proposals were enacted to change the character of these loans, including Brady bonds, and the security of many of the loans. However, the key factors that alleviated the crisis have been the decline in international inflation, interest rates, and oil prices. These actions in the global economy reduced the cost of these loans, most of which were made on a floating-rate basis, and the cost of energy, because most of these countries were petroleum-importing nations.

The second major crisis during the immediate past, which dampened foreign investment interest in LDCs, was the Mexican peso currency crisis during 1994–95.[21] As a result of political turmoil in Mexico in 1994, foreign investment inflows into the country slowed and the country's official reserves declined, causing a flight from pesos. The peso foreign exchange rate declined 45 percent during that year and early 1995. Much of these funds had been invested in Mexican mutual funds. Much of the $45 billion invested in such funds was pulled out of the Mexican economy and the Mexico City Stock Exchange.

The crisis was alleviated by loans from the international economic community. The U.S. Government put together a $49.8 billion loan guarantee package. This guarantee was coupled with a $10 billion loan from the IMF in addition to $7.8 billion already promised by this agency. Other funds were made available on a short-term basis from other countries through the Bank for International Settlements and the U.S. Federal Reserve System. The IMF assistance required Mexico to make certain changes in the nation's economic policies, including tightened monetary policy to shore up the peso, aggressive deregulation, and tax cuts for small and mid-sized entrepreneurs for development projects.

This crisis occurred during the year after the North American Free Trade Agreement was negotiated and put into effect. The monetary crisis in Mexico placed a great deal of strain on the North American Free Trade Agreement, but the economic relief by the international financial community and the policy changes made by the Mexican Government have strengthened the Mexican economy and ended the crisis.

POLITICAL RISK

The problems found in many of the LDCs, especially sub-Saharan Africa, stem from the political risk that permeates the economic environments of these nations and their governments. Investors can incur losses in their investments in host states from any of four major political risks. Political risk affects foreign investment projects as a result of government action in the form of laws, decrees, policies, actions, and regulations and is manifested by five major risks: violence or war, currency restrictions, contract interference, expropriation, and unfair regulatory environment. These risks are discussed in the following sections.

Violence or War

Foreign investors can encounter violence from civil war, insurrection, coups, and terrorism in the host state. The violence can be either organized or unorganized. For example, it can stem from the failure of the host government to negotiate a peaceful settlement of a dispute with factions within the country and, thus, can result in civil war. This was true of the conflict in 1994 in Bosnia, when Serbians, Moslems, and Bosnians engaged in a bloody war. Such violence has occurred during the past decade in Sri Lanka, Pakistan, India, Algeria, Liberia, Chad, Burundi, Rwanda, and various other nations. Violence also can occur in industrialized nations as it did with the 1993 World Trade Center bombing in New York City, the Federal Building bombing in Oklahoma City, and the Irish Republican Army terrorism in Great Britain.

Currency Restrictions

Government policies in many LDCs can restrict the ability of foreign investors to convert local currency into their home currency or the currency of some third country for repatriation of capital or remittance of earnings from a project in the host state. The flow of funds from the host state can be restricted or blocked entirely by local currency regulations. Banks and foreign exchange brokers can be licensed by the host state to handle foreign exchange and, thus, the amount of foreign exchange available for commercial transactions can be rationed. In many LDCs, this has led to corruption and bribing of public officials.

Contract Interference

Actions on the part of the host state can result in interference with a contract or agreement between foreign investors and local business firms or between foreign investors and the host state government. For example, when the Korean jetliner 007 was shot down by a Soviet military plane, the Canadian Government ended cultural exchanges with the Soviet Union. A tour of Canada by a Moscow circus had to be cancelled as a result of the suspension of cultural relations — an act of a government that caused a contract to be repudiated. After the invasion of Kuwait by the Iraqis, which led to the Desert Storm war, on-demand bonds had to be called. Such bonds were required by foreign construction companies to guarantee performance on construction projects in Kuwait. The U.S.-imposed embargo against Iraq also caused the cancellation of performance bonds.

Expropriation

A government has a sovereign right to expropriate or take over private property, whether domestically owned or foreign owned. This is called the right to eminent domain and can even happen in the United States. However, government expropriation should be compensated. In many cases, investors are not compensated at all or, if they are, the compensation can be inadequate. Such occurred in the takeover of foreign property by the Castro regime after the Cuban Revolution, in the nationalization of foreign copper companies by the Chilean Government, and in the expropriation of French assets by Tunisia. In these cases, no compensation was offered by the host governments. Even if the investor is compensated, the amount could be considered inadequate, resulting in a dispute that could necessitate arbitration by a third party.

Unfair Regulatory Environment

A foreign company operating in a host state can be discriminated against in many ways because of an unfair regulatory environment in that country. For example, the firm can encounter national treatment inconsistencies such as discriminatory capital requirements, tax structures that are different from those faced by domestic firms, limitations on access to necessary materials and components needed in the production process, or limitations of access to local distribution systems.[22]

TOOLS TO FACILITATE FOREIGN DIRECT INVESTMENT FLOWS INTO LESS DEVELOPED COUNTRIES

Since 1955, multilateral agencies have been established to facilitate the flow of FDI into LDCs. These institutions are, in addition to the World Bank, the International Development Association, Inter-American Development Bank, African Development Bank, Asian Development Bank, and other financial agencies that lend to developing countries for social infrastructure projects. These agencies will be discussed in Chapter 2. The primary agencies established to assist the private sectors in LDCs are the International Finance Corporation (IFC), ICSID, and MIGA. The major focus of this book is on the latter two agencies. First, however, a few words should mentioned about IFC.

The IFC was established in 1955 to make loans and, later, equity investments in private sector projects in LDCs that are members of the World Bank. Such investments are made *without government guarantee.*[23] This latter qualification makes IFC unique among the multilateral financial institutions. A total of 172 nations are members of this World Bank affiliate. IFC, during its first 40 years of operations, has made cumulative commitments of more than $21.2 billion in loans and equity investments to more than 1,850 private companies in 129 countries.[24]

During the past five fiscal years, 1993–97, IFC has set records for its support of private sector projects in LDCs.[25] During this period, IFC financed 1,169 projects with a record 276 financed in FY1997. Total financing by IFC during this period amounted to $28.53 billion, with a record $8.118 billion financed by IFC in FY1996. Total cost of the projects financed by IFC during these five years amounted to $90.191 billion. After FY1997, IFC had committed 1,046 firms to its investment portfolio, which amounted to $18.992 billion. At the end of FY1997, the agency's borrowings amounted to $10.123 billion and its paid-in capital amounted to $2.229 billion, up from $100 million at its inception in 1956.

In addition to its private sector investments in LDCs, IFC has facilitated the flow of FDI into LDCs in the following ways:

Its investments in LDCs represent approximately 25 percent of the total project costs — thus, total book value of the projects supported by IFC is approximately $80 billion.

Its loan syndications have encouraged more than 380 international financial institutions to participate in some 450 projects in 70 LDCs.

Its capital markets function has assisted the establishment of stock exchanges in several LDCs as well as the mobilization of $6.2 billion in investment funds and $4.5 billion in securities underwriting and placement in LDCs.

It has assisted the establishment of several country fund closed-end investment companies that invest in the companies of a given LDC, for example, Hungary Fund and Korea Fund.

Its advisory services have assisted several LDCs in such areas as privatization of government-owned enterprises as well as land in the former Soviet Union.

Its recent work in environmentally sustainable development in LDCs, for example, investments in water and waste-water treatment plants in Brazil and Argentina and environmental benchmarking in east and central European transition economies.

SUMMARY AND CONCLUSIONS

In this introductory chapter, an overview of the flows of FDI into LDCs has been discussed. In addition, the benefits of FDI for LDCs were analyzed. Reasons for the relatively low amount of FDI into LDCs were discussed, including the restrictions generally posed by governments of these LDCs.

Three multilateral financial agencies, IFC, ICSID, and MIGA, have been formed to facilitate the flows of FDI into LDCs and to make these countries more amenable to foreign private investors. The remainder of this book is devoted to a discussion of the evolution, organization, and operations of ICSID and MIGA. These two rather obscure, relatively small agencies have played significant roles in fostering FDI into LDCs — in the case of ICSID for more than 30 years and the case of MIGA for the past decade.

NOTES

1.   Karl P. Sauvant, "FDI and the Asia Pacific Region," *News from ICSID* 12 (Summer 1995): 3.

2.   Ibid.

3.   Guy P. Pfefferman and Andrea Madarassy, *Trends in Private Investment in Thirty Developing Countries* (Washington, D.C.: International Finance Corporation, 1989).

4.   I.F.I. Shihata, "Increasing Private Capital Flows to LDCs," *Finance & Development* 29 (December 1984): 6.

5.   Fred R. Bleakley, "Foreign Investment by Multinationals Grew 40% in 1995, Lifted by Mergers," *The Wall Street Journal*, September 25, 1996, p. A2.

6. Keith Marsden, "The Role of Foreign Direct Investment," extract from FIAS Background Paper on the Private Investment Climate in Sub-Saharan Africa at International Finance Corporation, Washington, D.C., August 1989.

7. Dennis Holden, "More Debt — or Investment?" *United States Banker* 96 (October 1985): 76.

8. Ibid.

9. James C. Baker, "Settling Foreign Investment Disputes Via ICSID," *Business* 40 (July–August–September 1990): 43–44.

10. K. Marsden and T. Bélot, *Private Enterprise in Africa: Creating a Better Environment* (Washington, D.C.: World Bank, 1987), pp. viii–ix.

11. Ibid., p. ix.

12. Multilateral Investment Guarantee Agency, *Annual Report 1997* (Washington, D.C.: Multilateral Investment Guarantee Agency), p. 12.

13. Brian Bremner, Michael Shari, Ihlwan Moon, Mike McNamee, and Kerry Capell, "Rescuing Asia," *Business Week,* November 17, 1997, pp. 116–22.

14. Amar Bhattacharya, Peter J. Montiel, and Sunil Sharma, "How Can Sub-Saharan Africa Attract More Private Capital Flows," *Finance & Development* 34 (June 1997): 3–6.

15. Ibid., p. 3.

16. George B. N. Ayittey, "How Africa Ruined Itself," *The Wall Street Journal,* December 9, 1992, p. A20.

17. Ibid.

18. George B. N. Aytittey, "African Thugs Keep Their Continent Poor," *The Wall Street Journal,* January 2, 1998, p. 8.

19. Bhattacharya, Montiel, and Sharma, "How Can Sub-Saharan Africa Attract More Private Capital Flows," p. 6.

20. G. Alisha Davis, "Africa's New Dawn," *International Business* 10 (February 1997): 10.

21. James C. Baker, *International Finance: Management, Markets, and Institutions* (Upper Saddle River, N.J.: Prentice-Hall, 1998), pp. 43–45.

22. Frederick Schroath, "The Political Risk Environment for Risk and Insurance," In Harold D. Shipper, Jr. (ed.), *International Risk and Insurance: An Environmental-Managerial Approach* (Burr Ridge, Ill.: Irwin McGraw-Hill, 1998), pp. 193–94.

23. See James C. Baker, *International Business Expansion into Less-Developed Countries: The International Finance Corporation and its Operations* (Binghamton, N.Y.: The Haworth Press, Inc., 1993), for a detailed history of the evolution, organization, and operations of the International Finance Corporation.

24. International Finance Corporation, *IFC Annual Report 1996* (Washington, D.C.: International Finance Corporation, 1996).

25. International Finance Corporation, *IFC Annual Report 1997* (Washington, D.C.: International Finance Corporation, 1997).

2

International Institutions and Foreign Direct Investment in Less Developed Countries

Since the establishment of the International Monetary Fund (IMF) and World Bank at the Bretton Woods, New Hampshire, conference at the end of World War II and the formation of the United Nations, several institutions, both national and multilateral, have been created to assist the development and industrialization of low income countries. The national institutions work on a bilateral basis. They are funded by the home government and work on a country-to-country basis, usually with two objectives of increasing opportunities for citizens or companies of the home country and economic growth of the foreign country. The multilateral economic development agencies cater to global memberships of both developed and developing countries but concentrate their efforts on the developing country members. The advantages and disadvantages of the two types of institutions, bilateral and multilateral, will be discussed and analyzed in this chapter.

BILATERAL VERSUS MULTILATERAL INSTITUTIONS: PROS AND CONS

The benefits of foreign private investment, particularly foreign direct investment (FDI), to less developed countries (LDCs) were discussed in Chapter 1. Several agencies and institutions have been established since the end of World War II to facilitate the economic development of LDCs.

Nearly all industrialized nations have one or more national government-owned and -operated financial institutions that are responsible for economic assistance to these countries. Selected examples include the U.S. Agency for International Development, the Canadian International Development Agency, the Kreditanstalt für Wiederaufbau in Germany, the Ministere de la Cooperation in France, the Department for International Development in the United Kingdom, as well as the Japan International Cooperation Agency, the Norwegian Development Agency, the Swedish International Development Authority, and the Finnish International Development Agency. These are bilateral agencies because they represent a nation-to-nation flow of funds for loans or grants from the sponsoring government to the recipient government.

More than 30 national governments have some type of export and/or import financing agency, for example, the U.S. Export-Import Bank, the Japan Import-Export Bank, the Korean Export-Import Bank, Compagnie Française d'Assurance pour le Commerce Extérieur (COFACE) in France, Export Credit Guarantee Department (ECGD) in Great Britain, the Ministry of International Trade & Industry in Japan, and Hermes in Germany.[1] These are also bilateral agencies because they are involved only in the financing of exports and/or imports for the country whose government sponsors the agency.

Several multilateral economic development or financial assistance agencies have been established whose primary goal is to assist the development of the LDCs. These include the World Bank and International Development Association (IDA), institutions that only make government-guaranteed loans to LDC governments for social infrastructure projects. Three other institutions, the Inter-American Development Bank (IDB), the African Development Bank (AfDB), and the Asian Development Bank (ADB) are comprised of member countries world-wide but disseminate development loans for public and private enterprise projects that are located in a specific region of the world. The European Bank for Reconstruction and Development (EBRD) is a relatively new institution that makes loans similar to those of the World Bank and IDA but to projects located in the former communist countries of Eastern Europe and the former Union of Soviet Socialist Republics, now the Commonwealth of Independent States. One multilateral financial institution, the World Bank affiliate, International Finance Corporation (IFC), is devoted to financing private sector projects *without government guarantee* and was discussed in Chapter 1.

Multilateral financial institutions have a major advantage over bilateral agencies because they represent many governments and make their services available to many countries, whereas bilateral agencies generally are tied to the philosophy of one nation and often politicize their economic assistance. Multilateral institutions generally do not promote any one political philosophy. Multilateral financial institutions also usually have greater financial resources than do bilateral agencies that are tied to the budget policies of one country.

Bilateral institutions have a major disadvantage because their economic assistance usually carries with it some political agenda. The assisting country is the developed nation and, in some cases, the nation being assisted is a former colony of the assisting country. This has been the case in foreign aid from the Netherlands to its former colony, Indonesia, from Belgium to the Congo region in Africa, and from France to its former West African colonies. The recipient country generally feels tied to the economic assistance. Much of U.S. economic assistance has been to countries involved in a political struggle between capitalism and communism during the days of the U.S.–Russian "iron curtain" conflict.

WORK OF MULTILATERAL INSTITUTIONS

Multilateral Financial Institutions

In this section, an overview is presented of multilateral financial institutions, which have global country membership and which finance development projects either on a global basis or on a regional basis. The World Bank Group — World Bank, the IDA, and the IFC — represent those institutions that finance projects in LDCs around the world. Those institutions that focus on development projects in regional areas are represented by the IDB, the ADB, the AfDB, and the EBRD. The operations of these institutions will be discussed in the following sections.

The International Monetary Fund

The IMF was established at a United Nations conference in Bretton Woods, New Hampshire, in 1944. This agency was established for the following purposes:[2]

to promote international monetary cooperation through a permanent institution that provides the machinery for consultation and collaboration on international monetary problems;

to facilitate the expansion and balanced growth of international trade, and to contribute thereby to the promotion and maintenance of high levels of employment and real income and to the development of the productive resources of all members as primary objectives of economic policy;

to promote exchange stability, to maintain orderly exchange arrangements among members, and to avoid competitive exchange depreciation;

to assist in the establishment of a multilateral system of payments in respect to current transactions between members and in the elimination of foreign exchange restrictions that hamper the growth of world trade;

to give confidence to members by making the general resources of the IMF temporarily available to them under adequate safeguards, thus providing them with the opportunity to correct maladjustments in their balance of payments without resorting to measures destructive of national or international prosperity; and

in accordance with the above, to shorten the duration and lessen the degree of disequilibrium in the international balances of payments of members.

The IMF, headquartered in Washington, D. C., has more than 150 member nations and total available resources that amount to more than $123.4 billion. The agency has provided more than 2,000 credits totaling nearly $55 billion to 86 countries. Occasionally even an industrialized nation such as the United States has drawn funds from the IMF to alleviate short-term balance of payment shortfalls.

One of the IMF's major functions in recent years has been to establish economic stability programs mandated for developing countries with severe currency crises. For example, during the 1997–98 Asian currency crisis, the IMF imposed severe economic restrictions on some of the countries whose financial systems were in jeopardy. The IMF imposes these restrictions in return for the massive funds it advances to a country to alleviate its financial crisis.

The World Bank Group

The World Bank Group, headquartered in Washington, D.C., is comprised of five multilateral economic assistance institutions. The primary agency is the World Bank, or International Bank for Reconstruction and Development, formed at the same Bretton Woods, New Hampshire, conference at which the IMF was established in 1944 to operate as one of the United Nations' global financial agencies. Since then, other agencies have been established to achieve specific objectives related to economic development of the LDCs. These agencies include, in addition to the World Bank, the IDA, the IFC, International Centre for Settlement of Investment Disputes (ICSID), and the Multilateral Investment Guarantee Agency

(MIGA). These latter two multilateral agencies have been instrumental in promoting increased flows of foreign private investment into LDCs. They are the central focus of this book.

World Bank

The World Bank was established at the Bretton Woods, New Hampshire, conference in 1944, which also spawned the IMF and is one of the three major agencies, along with the IDA and IFC, which make up the World Bank Group. The original objectives of the World Bank, originally named the International Bank for Reconstruction and Development, were to assist the reconstruction of war-torn areas after World War II and economic development of low-income nations.[3] For more than four decades, the Bank has focussed on development assistance only. Member nations had to be members of the United Nations and subscribed capital in the beginning amounted to $10 billion. At the end of FY1997, the World Bank had 180 member countries. During FY1997, the Bank made commitments totaling $14,525 million for 141 projects, including $3,080.9 million to the poorest countries — those with per capita gross national product of $785 or less.[4]

The World Bank makes loans to LDC member countries for social infrastructure projects that must be guaranteed by the host government. These loans are considered "hard term" loans because they have relatively short maturities, that is, 15 years, and relatively high variable interest rates. Some of the Bank's loans are fixed-interest rate loans but most are made on a variable-rate basis. During the July 1, 1997, to December 31, 1997, period, the interest rate on its variable-rate loans averaged 6.54 percent.

The Bank's financial resources for its loans are comprised of principal and interest on existing loans, funds borrowed in the international bond markets with securities that are rated AAA, and sales of investments that the Bank holds in its portfolio. A favorite practice of the World Bank is to syndicate some of its loans to international banks, which then participate in the development process. This allows the Bank to achieve one of its charter objectives: to encourage private sector international banks to participate in the development process. The World Bank has loaned a total of more than $400 billion since its inception more than 50 years ago.

International Development Association

The IDA is an affiliate of the World Bank Group and was established in 1960 with subscribed capital of $1 billion to make "soft term" loans to LDCs. IDA's loans, for example, carry no interest, have a 10-year grace period before the first payment, and have maturities of 50 years. A small service fee on the unpaid balance is payable annually. IDA makes the same type loans as does the World Bank, for social infrastructure projects with government guarantee, but to the lowest income LDCs. Loan recipients must be members of the World Bank.

One of IDA's most glaring problems stems from its payment schedule. For its first ten years, no payments of principal were due. It has constantly run short of funds and has had to have its capital replenished by member contributions on at least nine occasions. As the industrialized member countries look more inwardly to improve their own budget problems, it increasingly has become more difficult for IDA to obtain the replenishment level of capital desired by IDA officials.

The World Bank and IDA work closely in their economic assistance programs. They even report their operations in the same annual report. During FY1997, IDA made 100 commitments of funds totalling $4,622 million. The World Bank has begun to place some emphasis on aid to the poorest countries by assisting LDCs with per capita gross national product of $785 or less, as mentioned previously. In FY1997, the World Bank's assistance to these countries totalled $3,080.9 million, whereas the bulk of IDA's loans, $4,362 million, were made to such countries.[5]

IDA's members must be members of the World Bank. At the end of FY1997, IDA had 159 members. Membership action was pending for Barbados, Ukraine, Venezuela, and the Federal Republic of Yugoslavia — the regions of Serbia and Montenegro.

International Finance Corporation

As discussed in Chapter 1, the IFC began operations in 1956 as a World Bank affiliate whose major objective has been to support private sector projects in member country LDCs *without government guarantee* with loans and equity investments. Today, IFC is the largest source of multilateral loans and equity financing for private sector projects in LDCs. IFC has invested more than $21.2 billion in more than 1,850 companies in 129 LDCs. This is a book value figure. The present market value of these projects can amount to many times the $21 billion invested by IFC.

During FY1997, IFC invested $6.7 billion in 276 projects in 84 countries and regions. IFC mobilized $3.4 billion of these funds from more than 120 financial institutions from 28 countries that participated in IFC's syndicated loan program. Since its inception, IFC has placed participations in its investments with some 380 financial institutions totaling $14 billion. Its own loan portfolio totaled $8.5 billion at the end of FY1997. IFC invested in infrastructure projects as well as those in the agribusiness, capital markets, extractives, chemicals, and petrochemicals industries in FY1997.

In addition to the financing activities covered in Chapter 1, IFC has several advisory operations that assist governments in the creation of improved conditions that increase the flow of domestic and foreign private savings and investment. Much of this advisory work is carried out by IFC's Foreign Investment Advisory Service (FIAS) formed in 1986. In addition, IFC has assisted the development of several financial markets and instruments including the Korea Stock Exchange and Korea Fund — a closed-end investment company that invests in Korean company shares. IFC tracks the operations of more than 40 stock markets in LDCs through its Emerging Markets Data Base, formed in 1981 and launched commercially in 1987.

IFC is now permitted by the World Bank to borrow funds in the international debt markets. Its borrowings have been rated AAA by U.S. bond rating agencies. When IFC began operations in 1956, its subscribed capital was only $100 million. Today, its total capitalization amounts to more than $13 billion, including $2.1 billion in paid-in capital and more than $8 billion in borrowings.

Regional Development Banks

Inter-American Development Bank

The IDB was established in 1959 to assist economic and social development in Latin America and the Caribbean. IDB is headquartered in Washington, D.C., and has 46 member nations. Between 1976 and 1993, 18 nonregional countries joined IDB, established to promote the economic development of its regional countries by financing small and medium-scale private enterprises. IDB has become a major catalyst in mobilizing development finance resources for the Latin American region.

Its charter requires this institution to use its own capital, funds it has raised in financial markets, and other available resources to finance the development of borrowing member countries. IDB can also supplement private investment in the Latin American and Caribbean region when private capital is unavailable with reasonable terms and conditions. IDB also furnishes technical assistance for the preparation, financing, and implementation of development plans and projects in this region.

The total investments by IDB amount to more than $206 billion, and its annual lending has grown from $294 million in 1961 to $6.7 billion in 1996. Its current lending is focussed on poverty reduction and social equity, modernization and integration, and the environment of Latin American and Caribbean borrowing member countries. To supplement its investment income and member-subscribed capital, IDB has borrowed funds for its lending from the European, Japanese, Latin American, Caribbean, and U.S. capital markets. Its debt issues are rated AAA by the three major rating services in the United States.

Asian Development Bank

The ADB, headquartered in Manila, the Philippines, was established in 1966 to promote economic and social progress of its developing member countries in the Asian and Pacific Region. The ADB has 55 member countries, both developing and developed. Of these, 40 are regional members and 15 are non-regional. The regional members own 63.3 percent of the agency's shares. Total debt for the ADB amounted to $14.1 billion on September 30, 1997, and disbursements by the ADB during the first nine months of 1997 amounted to $3,034.26 million. Of this total, project loans amounted to 70.7 percent of the total loans, sector loans amounted to 18.7 percent of the total, and the remainder was for program loans and private sector loans.[6]

The principal functions of the ADB[7] are to make loans and equity investments for the economic and social advancement of developing member countries; provide technical assistance for the preparation and execution of development projects and programs and advisory services; promote investment of private and public capital for development purposes; and respond to requests for assistance in coordinating development policies and plans of member countries.

African Development Bank

The AfDB was established in 1964 and began operations July 1, 1966, with headquarters in Abidjan, Ivory Coast. The AfDB has 53 regional member countries and 24 non-regional member countries. Its loans and grants are restricted to the member nations of the regional area of Africa. Its principal functions are to make loans and equity investments for the economic and social advancement of the regional member countries; to provide technical assistance for the preparation and execution of development projects and programs; to promote investment of public and private capital for development purposes; and to respond to requests for assistance in coordinating development policies and plans of regional member countries.

Two-thirds of the subscribed capital of the AfDB is held by regional member countries and one-third by non-regional member countries. Its authorized capital amounted to $23.29 billion at the end of 1996. Financial resources of the AfDB stem from ordinary capital comprised of subscribed capital, reserves, funds raised from borrowings, and accumulated net income.[8]

In 1997, the AfDB focussed on five sectors for its lending: agriculture (24 percent), public utilities (22 percent), transport (17 percent), industry (16 percent), and multisector (11 percent). The Bank's planned lending for 1997 amounted to $2.5 billion. It is expected that 25 percent of the AfDB's resources will be loaned directly to the private sector.[9]

European Bank for Reconstruction and Development

The EBRD was established in 1991 to assist the transition of central and eastern European countries to market-oriented economies and to promote private and entrepreneurial initiatives within these countries, when such nations are committed to and apply the fundamental principles of multiparty democracy, pluralism, and market economics.[10] Its headquarters are located in London.

The EBRD has 60 members, including the European Community and the European Investment Bank, with 26 of these member nations in central and Eastern Europe and the Commonwealth of Independent States. The subscribed capital is ECU 20 billion, and other financial resources are borrowed in various currencies on global capital markets. Its financing consists of loans, equity investments, and guarantees, tailored to fit specific projects. By the end of 1996, the EBRD had approved 450 projects that involved ECU 9.96 billion of its own funds and have mobilized an additional ECU 20.1 billion.[11] Nearly three-fourths of the total approved funding was invested in private sector projects.[12]

In order to increase the scope of its own resources, the EBRD encourages co-financing and FDI from the private and public sectors, assists in the mobilization of domestic capital in European countries, and provides technical cooperation in relevant investment areas. It cooperates with other multilateral financial institutions including the World Bank.

Non-Financial Global Institutions

ICSID and MIGA are the central topics of this book. Obviously ICSID, established in 1966, and MIGA, established in 1988, as World Bank affiliates, are vastly different institutions and have broad objectives designed to facilitate and encourage the flow of foreign private investment into LDCs. ICSID assists in the arbitration or conciliation of investment disputes that arise between foreign private investors and host state governments, when both the investor's home country and the host government are signatories of the ICSID Convention. MIGA's major activity is the insurance of foreign private investment projects in LDCs against political risk resulting from actions by the host state government. The remainder of this book will focus on these two agencies, ICSID and MIGA.

CONCLUSIONS

The advantages stemming from the operations of the multilateral financial institutions offset the advantages found among the bilateral or national economic assistance agencies. However, some of the activities of the bilateral and multilateral institutions are intertwined. An increasing amount of national foreign aid appropriations are being made to support the multilateral financial institutions. For example, the United States pays $1 billion to the World Bank annually for its upkeep. Although the multilateral institutions have espoused, by the rhetoric of their top officials, free enterprise in the LDCs, they still lend large sums to governments of LDCs to the disadvantage of the private sector in these countries.[13]

The IMF has assisted several countries in recent years and is approaching the status as a lender of last resort. Its cooperation in the bailout of Mexico during Mexico's currency crisis of 1994–95, its assistance to the former Soviet bloc countries in their transition to market economies, and its quick fix of liquidity advanced to the Asian countries during the 1997–98 Asian currency crisis are examples of what has become increasingly necessary in a world of volatile currency trading of more than a trillion dollars every day.

The four decades of financing private sector projects in LDCs without government guarantees by the IFC have shown that such a multilateral institution can result in broad successes in the developing world. A recent U.S. General Accounting Office survey of private financiers showed that 90 percent of the respondents believed that the IFC "enhanced the environment for private investment in developing countries."[14]

The advent of the two agencies, which are the subjects of this book, has also enhanced the environment for FDI flows into LDCs. ICSID, with its major function of facilitating the arbitration or conciliation of investment contract disputes between foreign investors and host state governments and MIGA, with its investment project insurance against major political risks in LDCs, are agencies whose benefits to developing countries can be measured in many ways. These agencies and their benefits are the major topics of the following chapters.

NOTES

1.   Daniel Wagner, "A New World For Political Risk Investment Insurance," *Risk Management* 41 (October 1994): 32.

2.   James C. Baker, *International Business Expansion into Less-Developed Countries: The International Finance Corporation and Its Operations* (Binghamton, N.Y.: Haworth Press, 1993), pp. 3–4.

3.   Ibid., p. 6.

4.   http://www.worldbank.org/html/extpb/annrep97/overview.htm (November 17, 1997, p. 8).

5.   Ibid.

6.   http://www.asiandevbank.org/glance/regmem.html (November 17, 1997, p. 1).

7.   Baker, *International Business Expansion into Less-Developed Countries*, p. 14.

8.   http://www.africandevelopmentbank.com/BOARD.HTM (November 17, 1997, p. 1).

9.   http://www.africandevelopmentbank.com/BROCHUR.HTM (November 17, 1997, p. 1).

10.   http://www.ebrd.com/inro/contact/g01.htm (November 17, 1997, p. 1).

11.   An ECU is the European Currency Unit, a portfolio currency used by the European Monetary System as an average exchange rate for the European Union. It is used as a currency of denomination for lending, borrowing, and trade.

12.   http://www.ebrd.com/inro/contact/g01.htm (November 17, 1997, pp. 1–2).

13.   G. Pascal Zachary, "Development Banks Face Brave New World," *The Wall Street Journal*, December 2, 1996, p. A1.

14.   Ibid.

II

INTERNATIONAL CENTRE FOR SETTLEMENT OF INVESTMENT DISPUTES

3

Arbitration by Private Institutions and by ICSID

The major activity of the International Centre for Settlement of Investment Disputes (ICSID) is its arbitration of disputes between foreign investors from signatory nations and host state signatory governments. Arbitration of usual business contract disputes, that is, those where both parties to the dispute are private parties, generally is handled by a variety of private institutions. Among these are the American Arbitration Association (AAA), International Chamber of Commerce (ICC), and those arbitration agencies in Japan and Korea. In addition, some governmental agencies were established to deal with dispute arbitration between private parties and state governments. These include the Permanent Court of Arbitration (PCA) and the United Nations Commission on International Trade Law (UNCITRAL). The work of these institutions will be discussed in this chapter as a prelude to the introduction of ICSID's arbitral operations.

SETTLEMENT OF FOREIGN DIRECT INVESTMENT DISPUTES

International disputes are settled in a manner similar to the way in which domestic disputes are settled.[1] Diplomacy and negotiations between the parties are tried and, if unsuccessful, such cases can be settled in the courts. Disputes between state governments or intergovernmental organizations can be settled in an international tribunal such as the International Court of Justice. Finally, if the dispute is between private investors or between private investors and a state government, the dispute can be settled by arbitration or by a municipal court.

Foreign investment is fraught with examples of disputes between the parties, foreign and domestic, over the agreement to develop a project. Of the many reasons that can be cited for these disputes, the most obvious one is that the parties are from different cultures. They will have different political beliefs, practice different financial and accounting procedures, interpret the project contract provisions using different legal definitions and philosophies, and operate from different moral standards. Sometimes the local government implements legislation or regulations that cause the contract to be repudiated or to have its provisions changed with adverse results for one of the parties.

The bulk of foreign project contract disputes are between private parties—the foreign investor and a local company, individual, or institution. These disputes can be resolved in several ways: either amicably by the parties themselves, in the court system of one the nations from which the parties come, or by some private sector organization or agency designed to settle private investment disputes.

In many cases involving investment disputes, individual professional arbitrators, conciliators, or mediators are involved in resolving the dispute. However, international arbitration institutions play a significant role in the facilitation of the dispute resolution. Such institutions differ in the management of the dispute resolution. They can have different objectives, they can differ in the type of disputant to which they cater, and they can differ in the administrative resources and services that they make available.

The use of dispute resolution institutions by investors has advantages and disadvantages.[2] Some advantages are that

the procedure can be governed by the institution's own rules — quite useful if one party withholds cooperation and default procedures become operable;

the process momentum can be maintained;

the arbitrator's administrative tasks can be eased;

the award rendered by the institution carries its authority — a fact that can be useful during the enforcement stage; and

the arbitrator can maintain a level of conscientiousness and diligence.

Some disadvantages that can accrue from the use of institutional arbitration are:

the cost can be higher because the institution can charge its own administrative costs in addition to the arbitrator's fee;

the process can be slower; and

institutional time limits can be imposed that are too short for some classes of disputants such as governmental parties because bureaucratic constraints can slow decision-making.

Finally, the laws or rules governing the arbitration of investment disputes can create problems, especially in the area of jurisdiction, depending on whether the dispute being resolved is one between sovereign states or whether it is a dispute arising in the area of international commercial activities. International arbitration of a dispute between sovereign states is governed by public international law.[3] Public international law is based on a body of agreements, conventions, usage, and equitable principles. The arbitrators of such disputes have a monopoly on the dispute and form the only forum to hear the dispute. No higher court is available to monitor their procedures or review their decisions.

On the other hand, arbitration of international commercial disputes is not covered by international public law. The various systems of conflict of laws among the sovereign states in which investment disputes arise govern the procedures. These systems tend toward uniformity, which has been facilitated by multilateral conventions. These conventions introduced international arbitration agreements into the equation, replacing individual agreements between any two international parties.

Such an international arbitration agreement was first defined in Article 1 of the Geneva Protocol on Arbitration Clauses signed in Geneva, Switzerland, in 1923.[4] This article stated that:

Each of the contracting states recognizes the validity of an agreement whether relating to existing or future differences between the parties subject respectively to the jurisdiction of different contracting states by which the parties to a contract agree to submit to arbitration all or any differences that may arise in connection with such contract relating to commercial matters or to other matters capable of settlement by arbitration, whether or not the arbitration is to take place in a country to whose jurisdiction none of the parties is subject.

The parties to an international commercial agreement are subject to the jurisdiction of two different states. Although the venue can be held in any number of different major cities, for example, London, Paris, New York, Tokyo, and so forth, it is not the venue that makes the arbitration international, it is the jurisdiction of a different state over a different party to an arbitration that makes commercial arbitration international in nature. Jurisdiction will be a significant factor when one of the major subjects, the ICSID, is discussed in the next chapter.

Private Arbitration Institutions

Among the commercial arbitration agencies, the AAA, the Korean Commercial Arbitration Board (KCAB), the Japan Commercial Arbitration Association (JCAA), and the ICC are the most important dispute resolution institutions. The procedures of these private organizations are discussed in the following sections.

American Arbitration Association

The AAA is one of the most important private organizations to which private business disputes are brought for settlement. Most such disputes are settled by arbitration by some private organization whose rules are supported and enforced by the courts. The bulk of international commercial disputes are of a private nature and, thus, are addressed by these private arbitration associations. Commercial Arbitration Rules, rules that are used in conjunction with Supplementary Procedures for International Commercial Arbitration and the International Arbitration Rules, are used by AAA in the arbitration of these international commercial disputes, including those involving contract disputes arising from a foreign private investment. These rules provide arbitrators with broad authority to order measures that are incorporated into a judicially enforceable award.[5] The power of arbitrators would be pointless if their findings and awards judicially could not be enforced immediately.

The AAA procedures allow the parties to agree to arbitration at the time of the dispute or in anticipation of a future dispute, similar to the Japan method, but opposed to the ICC method, both to be discussed in subsequent sections. AAA requires the petitioning party to give written notice to the other party at the time of filing the arbitration request. It also employs rules for preliminary hearings and mediation conferences in addition to procedures that will expedite resolution of smaller claims. AAA maintains a panel of more than 3,000 arbitrators qualified for international cases.

One major difference between the procedure of the AAA and that of Korea, Japan, and others is its adversarial attitude. Because this system is similar to the U.S. court system, it promotes an adversarial attitude. Such an attitude fosters protracted hearings and costly enforcement measures. The Japanese system, discussed below, attempts, by cultural philosophy, to preserve harmony in the proceedings, awards, and enforcement. Thus, its procedures can be speedier and less costly, although as discussed later, there have been exceptions.

Korean Commercial Arbitration Board

Another arbitration body that has become a significant force in dispute resolution is the KCAB. The Korea Arbitration Act governs arbitration in Korea and, under this law, the KCAB is the only body that can offer institutional commercial arbitration in Korea.[6] KCAB is governed by rules that it has promulgated based on Korea law and the Korea Arbitration Act. Under these rules, for example, no person with a personal interest in the outcome of the arbitration can be an arbitrator in such a case. The parties to the dispute can determine the number of arbitrators and, if they are unable to do so, the KCAB Secretariat will select one or three arbitrators.

The Korea Arbitration Act requires that an award be rendered within three months of the beginning of the arbitration proceedings unless otherwise stipulated by the parties. Once the award is decided, it can be enforced in Korea only after a court has issued an enforcement judgment. This usually does not present a problem to the parties to the dispute. Appeals can be made to higher courts. After the award has been made and enforced by the Korean courts, it can be enforced in any member country of the United Nations Convention on the Recognition and Enforcement of Foreign Arbitral Awards of 1958.[7]

Japan Commercial Arbitration Association

The JCAA was established in 1953 by the Ministry of International Trade and Industry with the primary objective of arbitrating international commercial disputes in international trade.[8] The concept of arbitration in Japan stems from the Code of Civil Procedure of 1890. This code was influenced by the German Code of Civil Procedure of 1887. Although the 1890 Code does not address international arbitration, it does provide a framework of guidelines useful in the regulation of the Japanese arbitration process. The German influence in the Japanese code created a conflict between the written laws and normal Japanese social practices. These social practices included, for example, the reverence for harmony. Thus, conflicts such as international commercial disputes disturb harmony, and the public recognition of a dispute is considered a dishonorable disturbance. As a result, Japanese arbitration rules have been developed that preserve the use of informal dispute settlement procedures. This concept is referred to as *hanashi-ai*, or amicable negotiation. Harmony can be preserved by this form of negotiation, and the process is less costly and results in a faster resolution than litigation.

As with AAA resolution procedures, JCAA arbitration can be agreed to at the time of the dispute or in anticipation of a future dispute. This is contrary to the procedure used by the ICC, discussed in the following section. However, JCAA does not consider an arbitration agreement valid unless the parties can effect a compromise regarding the subject matter of the dispute, and the matter could have been submitted to litigation in a court. This is in keeping with the desire to avoid disturbing harmony. Thus, some matters are considered outside the possibility of arbitration, including disputes about bankruptcy, intangible property rights, and antitrust.

An arbitration proceeding is initiated when a party submits a written request to the JCAA that identifies the parties and the dispute conflict. If the documents are written in a foreign language, a Japanese translation must be attached unless such is waived by the arbitration tribunal. The Japanese procedure does not require that either party notify the other party of the procedure. If such has not been done by the claimant party, JCAA will notify the other party(ies). JCAA maintains a panel of nearly 200 arbitrators qualified to serve in international dispute cases. The parties can spell out the arbitrator selection process.

The JCAA has developed its own set of rules for its hearings. Its arbitration tribunal determines the date, time, and place of the hearing. These hearings must proceed with the least amount of delay. JCAA arbitrators are not bound by any specific substantive law or rules of evidence. The Japanese concept of justice is similar to the French concept of *amiable compositeur* under which arbitrators can make decisions regardless of the rule of law.[9] Upon deposit of an arbitration award with the court, JCAA considers its work finished. Such awards are written in Japanese unless a request has been made for an English translation.

Some problems have arisen with the JCAA procedures.[10] Although its rules require speedy resolution of disputes, some arbitrations have not begun for two years. Issues were not framed early on in these procedures and insignificant briefs were exchanged by the parties. Another problem involved the taking of evidence in the traditional Japanese procedure in which the arbitrator heard evidence from one or two witnesses for a few days and then adjourned the arbitration for a month or more to allow for preparation for cross-examination. In some of these cases, no official record was kept of these preliminary proceedings and no real evidentiary rules were applied. When parties did not agree on all matters, the Japanese norm was used — to maintain harmony — and the arbitration tribunal became reluctant to enter an order that might have expedited the matter. Finally in these cases, when all of the evidence was submitted, the tribunal, before deliberating on the evidence, made it clear to the parties that it preferred that they negotiated a settlement.

Another cultural problem has been encountered by some foreign business parties to an arbitration proceeding by the JCAA. Although its rules do not require that a foreign party to a dispute must use Japanese lawyers, the practice is common. Language and residency requirements often are imposed on arbitrators and counsel. Thus, tribunal lawyers are often Japanese. In addition, these Japanese lawyers also must be *bengoshi*, or graduates of the Japanese Training Institute.[11]

International Chamber of Commerce

The ICC was established in 1919 to promote international commerce and its headquarters are located in Paris. The ICC established an international arbitration system in 1923[12] because of the many problems inherent in cross-border contracts between and among investors and host state governments. These problems included dealing in a foreign language; different cultural backgrounds, customs, laws, and business practices; and foreign lawyers hired in disputes with local individuals or institutions, who might not be totally independent or neutral. This move was popular in the commercial world because disputes needed to be solved quickly, at a reasonable cost, in an independent manner, with confidentiality respected and with a system that would permit the parties to a dispute to select their own arbitrators.

It has been the experience of the ICC that arbitration generally is used to avoid having the law applied by the courts of the country of the other party and not to avoid the application of national law. Thus, the ICC rules state that "In the absence of any indication by the parties of the applicable law, the arbitrator shall apply the law designated as the proper law by the rule of conflict which he deems appropriate."[13] In addition, the ICC's experience shows that agreements between parties to a dispute are impossible to arbitrate after the dispute has arisen. Thus, in a significant number of ICC cases acted upon, arbitration clauses had been included in the contracts, which stated the parties had agreed to submit *future* disputes to arbitration.

The ICC Court of Arbitration receives more requests for arbitration than do all comparable arbitration agencies combined. At any given time, the ICC is considering 650–700 cases with most claims ranging from $1 million to $10 million, although a handful of claims involve amounts less than $50,000. Nearly half of ICC's cases involve disputes by parties in sales of goods and construction. In recent years, there has been a marked increase in cases involving licensing, technology transfer, and high-tech business. A significant number of the parties to ICC arbitrations are governmental or quasi-governmental agencies.

The ICC arbitration system has the widest coverage of the private institutions.[14] It covers any type of international dispute, including those of public, semi-public, and private parties from any country. It addresses any system of law, including civil, common, and Islamic laws, and can use any language. Its rules and practice permit parties complete freedom in selecting their counsel, arbitrators, the place of arbitration, the governing law, the language, and the procedural law. The ICC Court of Arbitration does not have judicial power and does not render an award in the dispute resolution. Parties to the dispute do not appear before the court. The ICC Court's function is to organize the arbitration tribunal and to supervise the proceedings.

Because ICC rules do not exclude multi-party arbitration, the ICC system has more flexibility in its dispute resolution.[15] However, ICC's current practice requires multiple parties to agree on a single arbitrator. If they are unable to select an arbitrator, the ICC Court of Arbitration will appoint one on their behalf.

Problems

The settlement of international commercial disputes, particularly by the courts, historically has been fraught with many difficulties. First, most commercial conflicts concern issues of fact rather than of law, and the judge or jury often are unable to determine an equitable solution to the problem. Second, since law and procedure vary from country to country, the adjudication of a dispute can change from country to country. The differences between English common law and Napoleonic civil law, for example, are quite significant. Finally, no treaties required contracting states to recognize the jurisdiction of institutions such as the AAA, ICC, or the PCA over disputes between sovereign states and foreign nationals. Some other institution was needed to fill this gap.

History of the Evolution of ICSID

Having noted these difficulties, it is easy to understand why the International Court of Justice has not had a particularly outstanding record in handling complex commercial disputes. Although arbitration has a long history as a vehicle for resolving disputes, the practice of arbitration has not been adopted widely in the Western Hemisphere. The Treaty of International Procedural Law of 1888, signed in Montevideo, Uruguay, and referred to as the Montevideo Treaty of 1888, gave "the same force to judgments or decisions by arbitration in the territory of others that they have in the issuing country." This treaty was ratified in only four countries.[16]

After the end of World War I, the work of the League of Nations and the ICC resulted in two multilateral treaties that dealt with arbitration. These were the Geneva Protocol on Arbitration Clauses of 1923 and the Geneva Convention on the Execution of Foreign Awards of 1927.[17]

The 7th International Conference of American States then adopted a resolution to create a multinational agency for the establishment of an inter-American system of arbitration. This resulted in the development of the Inter-American Commercial Arbitration Commission (IACAC) in 1934 under the guidance of the AAA.

One major roadblock in the development of widespread use of the IACAC was its inability to enforce the decisions handed down. Although foreign arbitration awards or judgments are generally enforceable in foreign courts, the parties generally resort to a voluntary cooperation approach instead of the coercive twist of adjudication.

An attempt to draft an international code on foreign investments was made in 1947.[18] The United Nations Economic and Social Council through its Economic and Employment Commission began a feasibility study for such a code. Later a progress report was published based on this study, which examined the problem of protecting foreign investments. In this report, a proposal for the arbitration of disputes between states and private investors on a voluntary basis was discussed. This study, after 10 years of research, produced a resolution overwhelmingly approved by the U.N. General Assembly in 1962 on the Permanent Sovereignty over Natural Resources. This resolution addressed several problems concerning the role of foreign capital in less developed countries (LDCs). Among these were investment insurance by the investor's state under national legislation and mechanisms for the speedy amicable settlement of disputes between investors and host states. These proposals were the forerunners of the Multilateral Investment Guarantee Agency (MIGA) and ICSID.

By this time, the Castro revolution in Cuba had ended and a large amount of foreign investment had been expropriated by the Cuban Government. A crisis of confidence had materialized between foreign investors and host state governments in the developing world. Dag Hammerskjold, Secretary-General of the United Nations, told the attendees of an American Bankers' Association conference: "It is becoming apparent that, if a system commanding wide acceptance in the United Nations could be set up for the arbitration of disputes arising between government and private foreign investors in connection with such matters as the amount of compensation in the case of appropriation, the investment climate would be considerably improved."[19] Most efforts at that time to create some type of arbitral mechanism were undertaken by the United Nations. However, the presence of the Communist bloc in that body thwarted its efforts to furnish a solution for dispute resolution.

The next step in the evolution of an ICSID-type agency was designed to overcome the inadequate enforcement of the treaties discussed above. Collaboration between the ICC and the United Nations Economic and Social Council resulted in the United Nations Conference on International Commercial Arbitration in 1958. This New York conference adopted the Convention on Recognition and Enforcement of Foreign Arbitral Awards of 1958 (New York Convention), a convention that significantly improved international commercial arbitration.

During the 1950s and 1960s, several international incidents, which resulted in serious contract disputes between foreign investors and host states, confronted the World Bank and other multilateral development agencies. The Cuban nationalization of foreign investments mentioned earlier was one example. Another example occurred when, on May 10, 1964, the Tunisian National Assembly passed legislation that nationalized all farmland owned by foreigners. More than one million acres of land and other assets were seized, most of which had been owned by large French corporations. The President of Tunisia, Habib Bourguiba, publicly stated that this action would be inconsequential to the French but was "a question of life or death" to Tunisians. The country had received its independence from France in 1956. French reaction resulted in the suspension of financial aid to Tunisia. Fears of a resumption of war between France and Tunisia were widespread, and holders of expropriated property appealed to multilateral institutions such as the World Bank. These agencies were not equipped to handle such a situation. Businessmen who had lost property appealed to the French Government, and the financial crisis became a political crisis. This and other such occurrences, including the Chilean takeover of foreign copper companies, were catalysts in the World Bank's move to draft the ICSID Convention and to create ICSID, and later MIGA.

Latin American nations prepared a draft convention on International Commercial Arbitration in 1967, which culminated in 1975 with the Inter-American Convention on International Commercial Arbitration at the

Inter-American Specialized Conference on Private International Law in Panama. This Convention adopted and combined parts of both the Juridical Committee's 1967 Draft Convention and the New York Convention of 1958, each of which required that disputes should be submitted to arbitration rather than to the courts. When an award is made under these conventions, it is enforceable by the courts of the countries that adopted these conventions. By 1988, 79 countries had ratified or acceded to the New York Convention, whereas, by 1985, nine had ratifed the Inter-American Convention. Sixteen countries had ratified one convention but not the other, whereas eight countries had ratified neither.

These conventions require that disputes should be submitted to arbitration rather than to the courts, especially for the reasons cited above. Furthermore, once an award is made, it is enforceable by the courts of the countries that have adopted these conventions. However, problems have arisen from the implementation of these conventions. The major shortcoming of these conventions is that they do not apply to arbitration of an investment dispute in cases where one of the parties is a state government.

The other problem in the development of the use of arbitration under these conventions includes the reluctance of investors to use local courts and judges, particularly in Latin America, to show their good faith in the legal structure of the country. This stems from the widespread adoption of the Calvo Clause doctrine of law by Latin American nations toward foreign investors. This concept of international law, although inconclusive, concerns any part of a contract between an alien and a government and forbids the alien from requesting assistance from his government for protection in any legal issue arising from the contract. It requires the exhaustion of local legal remedies. Latin American countries are relatively volatile politically but have great potential for foreign investment. The Calvo Clause and its implications for ICSID will be covered in more detail in Chapter 6.

Finally, investors often have been unaware of the availability of the arbitration process or do not know about the IACAC. It seems clear that, if it is to have any significant impact, any institution established to facilitate the arbitration or conciliation of foreign investment disputes must have a jurisdiction that is quite clear to investors.

One area of investment disputes not covered by the institutions discussed in the preceding sections relates to those disagreements that arise between governments and private foreign investors. An increasing number of contracts have been formulated between host state governments and private foreign investors during the past three decades. These disputes involve agreements between a country and an investor who can be either a company or an individual. As previously mentioned, the New York and Latin American Conventions do not cover arbitration of disputes in which one party is a state government.

Governmental Arbitration Institutions

In addition to the private dispute resolution institutions discussed in this chapter, two governmental institutions are also significant agencies in this field. They are the PCA and UNCITRAL, both of which engage in the resolution of international commercial disputes.[20]

The PCA is an intergovernmental body that was established by the Hague Conventions of 1899 and 1907. More than 60 nations have approved these conventions, and its headquarters is in the Netherlands. Although not a court, the PCA is a bureau that administers a panel of international arbitrators. In 1962, the PCA established its Rules of Arbitration and Conciliation for Settlement of International Disputes between Two Parties, when one is a state. The latter must be a treaty member to the Hague Conventions. The PCA handles very few arbitrations.

UNCITRAL was established in 1966, and its primary objective is to harmonize and unify world trade. Through its promotion of the New York Convention of 1958, it adopted arbitration rules in 1976. These rules were designed to be used in ad hoc arbitrations, and its awards are meant to be appropriate for enforcement under the New York Convention. UNCITRAL does not administer arbitrations but its rules are used by other arbitration institutions. UNCITRAL has also adopted conciliation rules.

ESTABLISHMENT OF ICSID

The World Bank did not desire to become involved in the mediation or conciliation of these disputes. The Bank's Board of Governors initiated a study of this problem in 1962 to determine the feasibility of establishing an agency that could facilitate the arbitration or conciliation of investment disputes between private foreign investors and host state governments.

Certain types of contract disputes do not apply to the institutions and their procedures discussed in the preceding sections.[21] Tribunals organized by private institutions such as the AAA, IACAC, and the ICC were unacceptable to several governments in the settlement of investment disputes. The PCA, the sole public international arbitral institution, was unavailable to private investors.

This study resulted in the creation of the Convention on the Settlement of Investment Disputes between States and Nationals of Other States

(Convention), submitted to World Bank members for ratification in March 1965 and that became effective in October 1966. The Convention, thus, established the ICSID. Advocates of this World Bank affiliate believed that the work of such an institution could facilitate the promotion of an increase in international investment, particularly foreign private investment, into LDCs. Thus, ICSID was created to furnish a neutral institution that would arbitrate disputes and that would be accepted as impartial in its procedures by both foreign investors and host governments.

ICSID, an autonomous international organization with close ties to the World Bank, was established when World Bank members ratified the Convention. At the end of FY1997, 141 countries had signed the Convention, and 127 of these had become members of ICSID. Since then, Colombia and Latvia have joined, bringing ICSID membership to 129. A nation must be a member of the World Bank in order to become a member of ICSID.

Regional Acceptance of ICSID

The Convention to establish ICSID was accepted rather quickly by large numbers of both capital-exporting and capital-importing nations. In Asia, the only glaring examples of initial opposition to ICSID were India and Indonesia, two of the most important developing nations in that region. Most other countries in the region ratified the Convention at first or within a few years. Indonesia has since become a signatory state. At the end of FY1997, India still had not become an ICSID signatory state. The Communist bloc countries were nearly unanimously opposed to ICSID when it was established. Only Yugoslavia ratified the Convention. At the present time, at least 17 countries from the Communist bloc have ratified or initiated the ratification process. These include East European and former U.S.S.R. nations, including the Russian Federation and China. Most African nations have become signatories of the Convention. Latin American countries voiced opposition to ICSID until the last decade. Most of this opposition stemmed from the so-called Calvo Doctrine, a concept that will be discussed in more detail in Chapter 6. During the past 10 years, several Latin American nations have signed the Convention. Brazil and Mexico are the only major countries in that region that have not become signatories.

Thus, by the end of FY1997, ICSID and the Convention had been well-accepted by capital-exporting and capital-importing nations in all regions of the world. The major nations that have yet to initiate ratification procedures are Brazil, India, and Mexico, three of the most important developing nations.[22]

The Case of Canada

The most glaring example of a country that has not become a signatory of the ICSID Convention is Canada. Until 1991, three major industrialized nations had not ratified the Convention. These were Australia, Canada, and Spain. Australia and Spain have ratified the Convention during the 1990s. Canada remains the only industrialized country in the Organisation for Economic Co-operation and Development that has not ratified the Convention.

Five reasons can be offered for the delay in ratification of the Convention by Canada.[23] First, some government officials in Canada believe that ratification of ICSID would constrain Canada's policies toward foreign investment into Canada. However, the business community believes this concern to be unfounded, especially because Investment Canada, which replaced the Foreign Investment Review Agency, was established to encourage and facilitate investment into Canada. Second, some believe that provincial legislation is required to ratify the Convention. The Canadian Council of the ICC has argued that provincial legislation is not required. Even if such legislation is required, it would be only one step toward Convention ratification. Third, the argument that ICSID was of limited geographic value because no Latin American countries were members is, at present, not valid because Mexico and Brazil are the only major Latin American countries that have not ratified the Convention during the past decade. This issue will be discussed in more detail in Chapter 6. Fourth, the issue of few disputes submitted to ICSID is becoming less of a problem because the number of cases submitted to ICSID, 45 overall at the present time, is growing at a significant rate. Finally, it has been argued in Canada that nonratification has not harmed the country, and that little business support exists for ratification. However, one Canadian company did not proceed with an investment in Africa because Canada was not a signatory of the Convention. Another Canadian company, which had invested in Latin America, was prejudiced in the conclusion of the dispute settlement mechanism because Canada was not a member of ICSID. In another case, a Canadian company was placed at a competitive disadvantage with a U.S. company whose dispute was resolved with the aid of an ICSID contract clause. In fact, the Canadian business community clearly has expressed its support of ICSID to the federal government on several occasions.

ICSID'S OPERATIONS AND ITS BENEFITS

ICSID provides conciliation and arbitration facilities to ICSID-member host state governments and private foreign investors from an ICSID-member state when investment disputes arise between such parties. A detailed discussion and analysis of such conciliation and arbitration operations will follow in Chapter 4. Private sector organizations such as the AAA, the ICC, and similar agencies in Japan and Korea do not offer mediation services when the investment dispute involves a host state government on the one side and a private foreign investor on the other. If such disputes are not settled amicably between the parties, a legal remedy can be sought by one of the parties. Such a remedy is generally very expensive and can take a long time to resolve, especially when the case deals with parties from different nations with private international legal and conflict of laws principles involved. Thus, the services offered by ICSID can represent the easiest and least expensive method of solving international investment disputes between host state governments and foreign investors.

Arbitration and Conciliation

The most important functions performed by ICSID are concerned with the arbitration or conciliation of investment disputes of a certain nature. Arbitration is a process that is used to reconcile differences of parties to a dispute. The parties submit their differences to an impartial third person, group, or tribunal selected by mutual consent of the parties, and this person, group, or tribunal makes a judgment about the merits of the case. Conciliation differs from arbitration in that the impartial third party makes an independent investigation of the dispute and suggests a solution. The parties then can accept or decline the solution.

ICSID does not engage in arbitration or conciliation itself but furnishes a format and a process to facilitate such activities. Its jurisdiction is limited to disputes between foreign investors from countries that have ratified the Convention and host state governments that are also signatory nations. These disputes arise from agreements that a foreign investor signs with the host state government. The procedure will be discussed in more detail in Chapter 4.

Contracts in which ICSID can be of value in dispute resolution include economic development or cooperation agreements between LDCs and foreign investors.[24] These can include petroleum and mineral concessions as well as industrial processing and manufacturing activities. The foreign investor in these agreements needs to be assured that the terms of such contracts will not be unilaterally changed by the host government.

Investment Treaties and Laws

ICSID assists LDCs in the formulation of treaties and laws that encourage and ease foreign investment into such countries. At the end of ICSID's FY1997, nearly 1,200 investment treaties had been consummated and 75 percent of these provide for the settlement of investment disputes by ICSID arbitration culminating from investments covered by these treaties. Several investment laws written in LDCs in recent years also make reference to the use of ICSID arbitration procedures. These and other activities of ICSID will be discussed in more detail in Chapter 4.

Advantages to the Private Investor

The ICSID Convention and ICSID arbitration and conciliation offer several advantages to the private foreign investor.[25] Among these are its direct access, its exclusive remedy, and the supranational character of the registration of an arbitral award made by the ICSID procedure.

The private foreign investor from a signatory state has direct access to the ICSID facilities. Refusal by a contracting state to comply with an award made by an ICSID tribunal is considered a breach of a treaty obligation. Either party to ICSID proceedings cannot frustrate the proceedings by refusing to appear before the proceedings or unilaterally withdraw its consent from ICSID's jurisdiction — although a case involving a signatory host state that withdrew from the proceedings will be discussed in Chapter 5.

The ICSID Convention provides that ICSID will be the exclusive remedy for resolution of the dispute between the parties. The courts of either party to the dispute do not need to become involved although the Convention allows the possibility for the parties to agree to subsequent court hearings. In addition, the Convention offers one of the few forums to private persons for litigating a dispute with a foreign government.

Parties to proceedings voluntarily abide by the terms of an arbitration decision by the tribunal, and, thus, the arbitral award is generally accepted by any signatory state in the ideal sense. However, if the investor needs to execute an arbitral award in a state that does not recognize the award as a domestic judgment, the investor might have to run a gauntlet of other remedies. Article 54 of the ICSID Convention offers a remedy to this problem in cases resolved by the ICSID procedure. The Convention holds that signatory states are bound by an ICSID arbitral award and must enforce any resulting pecuniary obligation as though it were a domestic court judgment. This registration of an arbitral award by an ICSID tribunal gives the award a supranational standing and, thus, the state that does not recognize the award faces the international stigma of such supranational registrations. In other words, repudiation of the principal agreement by the host state government cannot deprive the investor of his remedy in court.

Advantages to Signatory States

The ICSID Convention and arbitral procedures offer the LDC a means to facilitate the increased flow of foreign direct investment (FDI) into the country. The Convention permits the host state to nominate members to a panel of arbitrators and to consent in writing to ICSID's jurisdiction to arbitration of a dispute involving that state before any action can be rendered against it. The signatory state can name at least one of the members of the arbitral tribunal and if a tribunal's decision requires the World Bank to become involved, the host state, a developing country, can usually count on the objectivity of the World Bank in facilitating a decision. The Convention also permits a state party to stipulate that the private foreign investor must first exhaust local remedies offered by the state before ICSID will exercise jurisdiction over the dispute. In other words, the investor's own state cannot give him diplomatic protection or bring an international claim on his behalf. Thus, affairs of the host state are minimized by outside interference.

Mutual Advantages for the
Host State and the Foreign Investor

The ICSID Convention also offers some advantages that are mutually beneficial to both the host signatory state and the foreign investor national from a signatory state.[26] For example, the wide recognition given to an ICSID award and the enforceability of their provisions should be of benefit to both parties. Both parties will benefit because any proceeding that ICSID institutes under its jurisdiction will actually take place and, sooner or later, either a conciliation report or an arbitral award will be rendered. Such a certainty can reduce some of the differences between the parties.

Advantages for the Investor's State

Some of the above-mentioned advantages also can accrue to the investor's own state. The ICSID Convention and its procedures enable the investor's state to avoid any intergovernmental embarrassment from a foreign investment conflict, which might be exacerbated by petty parochial domestic pressures in one state or the other. The investor's state can rely on ICSID to resolve the differences without being involved.

SUMMARY AND CONCLUSIONS

This chapter introduced the settlement of FDI disputes and the institutions that offer this function to investors. These include the private arbitration institutions of the AAA, KCAB, JCAA, and the ICC, and the public arbitration agencies of the PCA and the UNCITRAL. The institutions arbitrate disputes between private businesses in the case of the private institutions and between foreign investors and host state governments or between states in the case of the public agencies.

The evolution of ICSID was discussed as well as the regional acceptance of this concept. Most countries now have become signatories of the Convention that established ICSID. Among Latin American nations, Brazil and Mexico are the most important non-signatory states. India is the most important Asian state to remain a non-member. Canada is the most significant capital-exporting nation that has not signed the Convention.

The chapter concluded with a discussion of the benefits offered by ICSID arbitration and conciliation. ICSID provides direct access to foreign private investors from a signatory host state and is an exclusive remedy to dispute resolution for such investors. ICSID resolution of FDI disputes can facilitate an increased flow of foreign investment into LDCs. Finally, ICSID awards have wide enforceability within signatory nations.

NOTES

1. See Ray August, *International Business Law: Text, Cases, and Readings* (Englewood Cliffs, N.J.: Prentice-Hall, 1993), pp. 92–147.

2. Alastair Hirst, "How the Major Arbitration Institutions Work in Practice, and How They Compare," *Middle East Executive Reports* 18 (May, 1995): 1.

3. V. S. Deshpande, "International Commercial Arbitration: Uniformity of Jurisdiction," *Journal of International Arbitration* 5 (June 1988): 115.

4. Ibid., pp. 115–16.

5. Michael F. Hoellering, "Conservatory and Provisional Measures in International Arbitration: AAA's Experience," *Arbitration Journal* 16 (December 1992): 40–45.

6. Duck-Soon Chang, "Arbitration in Korea," *East Asian Executive Reports* 14 (January 1992): 21–22.

7. Ibid., p. 22.

8. Michelle L. D. Hanlon, "The Japan Commercial Arbitration Association: Arbitration with the Flavor of Conciliation," *Law & Policy in International Business* 22 (1991): 619.

9. Ibid., p. 603.

10. Charles R. Ragan, "Arbitration in Japan: Using Alternative Methods of Resolving Disputes," *East Asian Executive Reports* 14 (October 1992): 18.

11. Hanlon, "The Japan Commercial ArbitrationAssociation," p. 625.

12. For a concise analysis of the international arbitration procedures of the International Chamber of Commerce, see Stephen R. Bond, "Arbitration of International Commercial Disputes under the Auspices of the International Chamber of Commerce," *International Journal of Technology Management* 4 (1989): 489–511.

13. Ibid., p. 491.

14. Ibid., p. 495.

15. Christopher R. Seppala and Daniel Gogek, "Multi-party Arbitration Under ICC Rules," *International Financial Law Review* 8 (November 1989): 32–34.

16. James C. Baker and Lois J. Yoder, "ICSID Arbitration and the U.S. Multinational Corporation," *Journal of International Arbitration* 5 (December 1988): 83.

17. Ibid.

18. C. W. Pinto, "Settlement of Investment Disputes: The World Bank's Convention," *Howard Law Journal* 13 (Spring 1967): 338–41.

19. Address by Dag Hammerskjold to the American Bankers' Association Meeting, March 22, 1960, in United Nations Press Release S.G. 904,5.

20. Hirst, "How the Major Arbitration Institutions Work in Practice," p. 1.

21. Joy Cherian, "Foreign Investment Arbitration: The Role of the International Center for Settlement of Investment Disputes." In *Foreign Investment in the Light of the New International Economic Order* (Windsor: Third World Legal Studies: 1983), p. 174.

22. Thomas Kuchenberg, "The World Bank: Arbiter Extraordinaire," *The Journal of Law and Economic Development* 2 (1968): 278–79.

23. T. C. Drucker, "The Perspective of Canadian Investors on Accession to ICSID," *News from ICSID* 7 (Winter 1990): 6.

24. Aaron Broches, "Choice-of-Law Provisions in Contracts with Governments," *Record of the Association of the Bar of the City of New York* 26 (January 1971): 51.

    25.   Michael M. Moore, "International Arbitration Between States and Foreign Investors — the World Bank Convention," *Stanford Law Review* 18 (June 1966): 1372–74.

    26.   Paul C. Szasz, "A Practical Guide to the Convention on Settlement of Investment Disputes," *Cornell International Law Journal* 1 (1968): 3.

4

ICSID's Operations

The International Centre for Settlement of Investment Disputes (ICSID) has filled a gap that has become more important in global investment and flows of foreign direct investment (FDI) into less developed countries (LDCs).[1] The narrow but growing area of investment projects in LDCs covered by agreements between investors from a foreign state and the host state government has become more prevalent in the developing world. ICSID facilitates the resolution of contract disputes of agreements between foreign investors from states that are signatories of the ICSID Convention and host state signatories of the Convention.

During its more than 30 years of operations, the agency slowly has built a body of rules, procedures, and decisions resulting in a system of arbitration or conciliation of disputes in this narrow area of jurisdiction. It slowly has become recognized as one of the preeminent arbitration institutions by the international investment community, particularly the community involved in FDI projects in LDCs.

The Convention, which makes ICSID operable, is a treaty that, when ratified by state governments, signifies the acceptance of the terms of this treaty. In a court decision concerning one of the cases discussed in Chapter 5, Maritime International Nominees Establishment v. the Republic of Guinea, the Court of Appeals for the District of Columbia, in reversing a lower court decision, held that ICSID is a unique and distinct international body that is governed by the rules of the ICSID treaty, the Convention, thus preventing any type of domestic intervention until an ICSID arbitral award is made.[2]

In the following sections of this chapter, several ICSID functions will be discussed. Among these are the adoption of an arbitration and conciliation procedure, construction of model contract clauses, various publications, compilation of the investment laws of the world, assistance in the development of investment treaties, and the organization of conferences concerned with arbitration, investment law, and other means to promote the flow of FDI into LDCs.

ICSID'S ARBITRATION AND CONCILIATION PROCEDURE

ICSID serves as a permanent structure with a predetermined procedure of conflict resolution in contractual disputes between foreign investors from nations that have signed the ICSID Convention and host state governments that are also signatory nations.[3] This facility and its organization are discussed in the following sections.

Panel of Conciliators and Arbitrators

ICSID maintains a list of experts in finance, law, and arbitration, most of whom are designated by contracting states, that is, ICSID member countries. This is referred to as the ICSID Panel of Conciliators and Arbitrators. Each signatory state can place up to four names on this list and the ICSID Secretary-General can appoint as many as 10 persons to this panel. Article 14(1) of the ICSID Convention describes the required characteristics of those persons who make up the panel. Those individuals nominated to the panel must be "persons of high moral character and recognized competence in the fields of law, commerce, industry or finance, who can be relied upon to exercise independent judgment." The article embodies a general statement of the standards of integrity, competence, and ability to exercise independent judgment that any ICSID conciliator or arbitrator should meet. Parties to a dispute can select arbitrators or conciliators from outside the panel. Such selections must have the qualities required by Article 14(1) for members listed on the panel.[4]

When a dispute arises between such parties and is referred to ICSID, the latter facilitates the process of arbitration or conciliation by organizing an arbitration panel or conciliation commission. ICSID, itself, does not engage in the arbitration or conciliation of the case but merely facilitates the process.[5]

Procedural Framework of ICSID Arbitration

Various rules govern the ICSID arbitral proceedings.[6] The ICSID Convention provides the basic format for the rules. Details and regulations concerning these rules are formulated by the Administrative Council of ICSID and include the process that governs submission to and registration by ICSID of arbitration requests. This system of rules governs a procedural regime that is more complex than that used by any major international arbitration institution. However, the rules and regulations that govern ICSID arbitration procedures are sufficiently flexible to permit the parties to a dispute to formulate changes in some of the rules during the proceedings.

The ICSID arbitration rules provide for a preliminary procedural consultation between the parties and the president of an established ICSID tribunal as soon after its constitution as possible. The selection and organization of the tribunal will be discussed below. This preliminary procedural consultation has the objective of seeking answers to several relevant questions concerning the dispute, such as:

the number of members of the tribunal required to constitute a quorum at its sittings;
the language or languages to be used in the proceeding;
the number and sequence of the pleadings and the time limits within which they are to be filed;
the number of copies desired by each party of instruments filed by the other;
dispensing with the written or the oral procedure;
the manner in which the cost of the proceeding is to be apportioned; and
the manner in which the record of the hearings shall be kept.

The decisions on some of these queries can be postponed until the first session of the tribunal, to be held within 60 days of its constitution.

The Choice of Law for ICSID Arbitral Tribunals

The choice of law is an important part of any arbitration proceeding. In the case of ICSID arbitration proceedings, they are governed by public international procedural law. The ICSID Convention in Article 42 offers directives to the arbitral tribunal that resolve the choice of law problem.[7] These directives are as follows:

1. The tribunal shall decide a dispute in accordance with such rules of law as can be agreed by the parties. In the absence of such agreement, the tribunal

shall apply the law of the contracting state party to the dispute (including its rules on the conflict of laws) and such rules of international law as can be applicable.

2. The tribunal cannot bring in a finding of *non liquet* on the grounds of silence or obscurity of the law. (*Non liquet* is the legal phrase used by a tribunal when it cannot render a verdict because the available legal rules are insufficient, uncertain, or lack clarity.)

3. The provision of paragraphs (1) and (2) shall not prejudice the power of the tribunal to decide a dispute *ex aequo et bono* if the parties so agree. (To decide a dispute *ex aequo et bono* is to decide it in accordance with what is just and equitable in certain circumstances instead of by the application of the rules of law.)

It has been suggested that arbitration *ex aequo et bono* permits a flexible interpretation of complex long-term investment agreements between host countries and foreign investors.[8] Once the rule of law to be used by the arbitral tribunal has been decided, the ICSID process will then proceed until an award is rendered or until the case has been discontinued.

The Process

Consent of both parties to the settlement process is of central importance in an ICSID procedure. Once both parties have consented to the process, neither can withdraw unilaterally from such an agreement, according to the Convention. The latter contains provisions that are designed to prevent refusal of a party to cooperate after it has agreed to enter the ICSID process.[9]

The dispute is first screened by the Secretary-General of ICSID to determine if it is indeed within the agency's jurisdiction. Under Article 36(3) of the Convention, the Secretary-General can refuse to register the dispute if "he finds, on the basis of the information contained in the request, that the dispute is manifestly outside the jurisdiction of the Centre."[10] The Secretary-General makes his decision based on information solicited from the party requesting the services of ICSID. Most of these requests are screened in a very short time, sometimes in one day, on the basis of the information furnished. On occasion, more information is necessary, especially in cases where the nationality of a corporation is in doubt for any reason. If the Secretary-General refuses to register a dispute, ICSID facilities cannot be utilized because no appeal from such a decision is possible.

The dispute must be a legal dispute, which arises from an investment by a foreign investor whose home country is a signatory of the ICSID Convention and a host state signatory government, and such parties must have given their consent for the dispute to be resolved by the ICSID procedure. After a dispute has been screened by and registered with ICSID, an arbitration or conciliation tribunal is constituted as soon as possible. Generally, each party to the dispute selects one person from the Panel of Conciliators and Arbitrators. The parties are free to agree on the number of arbitrators as long as the number of members is uneven.

These two party-appointed arbitrators will select a third member of the tribunal who will be the chair. If they are unable to select the third member, the Secretary-General of ICSID will make the appointment. If the parties are unable to form a tribunal within certain time limits, usually 90 days, the Chairman of the ICSID Administrative Council will select the arbitrator or arbitrators not yet named. These selections then make up the arbitration or conciliation tribunal. ICSID then facilitates the process by organizing the meeting times and places of the tribunal's discussions and deliberations. The place of the meetings is held at the convenience of the tribunal members but neutrality must be regarded in the selection of meeting sites. Usually, these meetings are held at the Permanent Court of Arbitration at The Hague or in arbitration centers located in Cairo, Kuala Lumpur, Melbourne, and Sydney, or at ICSID headquarters. Other locations require the permission of ICSID.

Composition of ICSID Arbitral Tribunals

All ICSID tribunals thus far have been comprised of three members.[11] The makeup of these tribunals has been quite diversified. In a majority of the cases, at least one member of the tribunal has been a national from a developing country. In at least nine proceedings, all members of the tribunal were nationals of developed countries. In three proceedings, two of the three arbitrators were nationals from LDCs. In the remaining cases, two of the three tribunal members were nationals from industrialized nations.

Other operational procedures include the language of the proceedings and the fees charged. The language of the proceedings will be either English, French, or Spanish. If two of these languages are chosen by the parties, translation machinery will be furnished. ICSID has its own schedule of fees and the Secretariat's administrative charges are limited to reimbursement of its out-of-pocket expenses for the proceedings, which would include equipment for bilingual translation of the proceedings as well as travel and secretarial services. Such an administrative charge structure is basically different from the International Chamber of Commerce (ICC) and the American Arbitration Association. Essentially, ICSID subsidizes the process because arbitration costs and the cost of legal counsel, born by the parties to the dispute, would overwhelm the ICSID Secretariat costs.

An advantage of the ICSID procedures is that each dispute proceeding is different, and ICSID can facilitate the process by customization of the procedures. By using Secretariat staff to organize the tribunals and their deliberations, administrative costs can be reduced.

Rights of ICSID Arbitrators

ICSID arbitrators have certain rights meant to protect their independence while conducting a proceeding.[12] They have the right to security of tenure and are immune from legal process with respect to acts performed by them during the exercise of their functions as members of the tribunal. Furthermore, membership on the ICSID panels of arbitrators and conciliators is permanent during the term of their appointment. They can only be replaced in the event of death or resignation. Compensation for their ICSID activities cannot be taxed by signatory states. They are provided with extensive administrative support during the proceedings by ICSID. Arbitrators receive a daily fee of about $900 for their services.

Conciliation Commissions

The ICSID Convention allows for conciliation as well as for arbitration. The Convention does not make recourse to conciliation a prerequisite to recourse to arbitration as does the 1974 Convention on the Settlement of Investment Disputes between Host States of Arab Investments and Nationals of Other Arab States, the multilateral treaty discussed in Chapter 2. However, the parties to a dispute are not barred by the Convention from resorting first to conciliation and, if a settlement is not reached, then to institute arbitration proceedings.

The parties to a dispute select the members of a conciliation commission in the same manner as they do the members of an arbitration tribunal. The panel of conciliators is appointed in the same manner as is the panel of arbitrators. The panel members serve for renewable six-year terms. The ICSID Administrative Council Chairman can appoint 10 members and each ICSID signatory state can appoint four members to the panel.

The request for conciliation of a dispute must be submitted in writing to the Secretary-General and should contain information concerning the issues raised in the dispute. If the jurisdictional requirements are met, the request is registered, the parties are notified, and the Conciliation

Commission then attempts to mediate the dispute and encourage the disputants to accept the mediation results. The World Bank's experience in the mediation of prior international disputes resulted in the adoption of a conciliation process in the ICSID Convention. The Bank had mediated such disputes as the Pakistan-India Indus River resolution in the 1950s and the Suez Canal crisis of 1956.[13]

The Convention bars any person who has acted as a conciliator in a conciliation proceeding from being appointed as a member to a subsequent arbitral tribunal. It is necessary that an arbitrator come to the arbitration proceeding without a preconception that might have been formed by participation in a conciliation proceeding.

In the case of an ICSID conciliation, the Commission's decision is not binding on the parties, as is an arbitral award, although the parties must agree to give the Commission's recommendations serious consideration.[14] The ICSID Conciliation Commission is only required to clarify the issues of the dispute between the parties and to attempt to bring the parties to a mutual acceptance of the terms of the agreement. The Commission then drafts a report showing that the parties have reached agreement, that no agreement can be reached, or that one party has failed to participate in the proceedings.[15] Almost all other areas of the procedures for ICSID conciliation and ICSID arbitration are identical.

The differences between conciliation and arbitration under the Convention reflect the principal difference between the two procedures in that conciliation seeks to bring the parties to an agreed settlement, whereas arbitration leads to a binding enforceable resolution of the dispute.[16] Conciliation results in merely a recommendation to the parties for a settlement of their dispute. These recommendations can be made at any time during the proceedings, whereas an arbitral award is made at the end of the proceeding.

Another difference between the ICSID arbitration proceedings and conciliation proceedings is that witnesses and experts are obliged to make solemn declarations upon their honor and conscience before giving their evidence and statements in an arbitral case, whereas witnesses and experts in a conciliation proceeding are not required to make such a declaration. In the conciliation proceeding, fees and expenses of members of a conciliation commission as well as for the use of the ICSID facilities are shared equally by the parties to the dispute. In the arbitration proceeding, the tribunal decides how and by whom the fees and costs will be paid. As mentioned earlier, parties to a conciliation proceeding are not bound by the commission's recommendations, whereas the parties to an arbitral proceeding are bound by the tribunal's award.

Awards

Final awards by these tribunals are binding on both parties and enforceable under the rules of international law. Once an award has been made by an arbitration panel or conciliation commission by a majority vote of the members, the award is binding on the parties under international law and, thus, enforceable as such. The ICSID signatory state is required by the Convention to recognize the award as binding and to enforce any pecuniary obligation imposed by the tribunal whether the government or its agents were parties to the proceedings. In addition, the finding should prevent any further conflict between the government hosting the foreign investment and the investor's state government.[17] Some have estimated that parties voluntarily comply with 85 percent of arbitral awards. No provision in international law was available before the ICSID Convention to force a state to arbitrate a dispute with a private individual or to compel a state to enforce an arbitral award against itself.[18]

The binding nature of an ICSID award differs from a court judgment to enforce an award of a private institution made in a commercial dispute between private parties. In private arbitration procedures, obtaining recognition and enforcement is uncertain and difficult, especially for an American judgment by a foreign tribunal, and vice versa. No multilateral treaty between the United States and foreign countries is presently in force that requires reciprocal recognition of judgments.[19] However, an arbitral award of such commercial disputes is different but similar to the ICSID award enforcement procedure. Most arbitral awards involving parties to a dispute from different countries are enforceable internationally. As discussed earlier, the enforcement of these awards is governed by the New York Convention signed by 90 nations including the United States. For example, a U.S. company, which has won an award against a company located in the Netherlands as a result of arbitration proceedings held in Belgium or Great Britain, will be able to have a Netherlands court, or a court in a third signatory country in which the Netherlands company has assets, enforce the arbitral award.[20]

If a signatory state refuses to honor the award of the ICSID Tribunal, such action would amount to a breach of the Convention's provisions to which the state is a signatory. The private investor then could obtain the assistance of his government to legally pursue the claim through diplomatic channels or multilateral avenues of relief such as the International Court of Justice. However, Article 55 of the Convention states that the provisions of Article 54 requiring the award to be recognized by the host state should not alter the laws of any signatory state. Thus, it would appear that any signatory state against which an award has been rendered could plead the rules of sovereign immunity from execution of the judgment of the award.[21]

An issue related to ICSID awards is whether the Convention permits parties to ICSID arbitration to seek provisional measures such as attachments from national courts even if the relevant arbitration agreement does not specifically provide for recourse to the courts for this purpose. Article 26 of the Convention provides that ICSID arbitration, which has the consent of both parties, will be to the exclusion of any other remedies. During the 1984–86 period, the courts of France, Belgium, and Switzerland vacated attachments obtained by arbitration parties from lower courts to secure their ICSID claims. The decisions were rendered on the basis that Article 26 precluded courts from ordering such attachments. The French Cour de cassation decided otherwise in that the Convention does not prohibit parties from requesting national courts to order provisional measures that would guarantee the execution of a future award. In addition, this court determined that the power of the courts to order such measures could only be excluded by express agreement of the parties. In 1984, the ICSID Administrative Council amended the ICSID Arbitration Rules to provide that the parties to a dispute registered with the agency are free to request any judicial authority to order provisional measures, if the parties have so stipulated in the agreement recording their consent.[22]

Appeals of the Award

Although the award is binding on the parties, a party to the proceeding can, within a specified number of days, appeal to the arbitral tribunal to consider issues omitted or clerical or arithmetical errors in the award.[23] Either party can request revision of the award on the grounds of newly discovered evidence, if 90 days since the initial award have not elapsed. The tribunal can stay the award pending determination of such an application. This is usually done during the annulment proceeding discussed in the next section. Corruption and improper procedure are available as grounds for setting aside an award.

Annulment

The Convention enables the party against which an award is rendered to file for an annulment of the award. A request for an annulment can be made on one or more of the following grounds:[24]

the tribunal was not properly constituted;
the tribunal manifestly exceeded its powers;

there was corruption on the part of a member of the tribunal;

there was a serious departure from a fundamental rule of procedure; and

the award failed to state the reasons on which it was based.

Thus, the principal objective of the ICSID annulment process is to protect the parties against procedural injustice.[25]

In Chapter 5, the case of Maritime International Nominees Establishment v. Republic of Guinea will be discussed as an example of a case in which an annulment proceeding was heard by ICSID. Of the 45 cases registered by ICSID for arbitration or conciliation proceedings, annulment proceedings have been requested in only four of these cases. None of the annulment requests has been fully granted, and some of the cases have had annulment requests resubmitted, only to have the original annulment award reversed. Annulment of an ICSID award is very difficult.

When an annulment proceeding is requested, the ad hoc committee appointed to hear the case has the discretion to rule on the application for annulment. The ad hoc committee can order a stay of enforcement of the award while the annulment request is being heard. This occurred in the cases of Amco Asia et al. v. Republic of Indonesia in the first annulment proceeding and in Maritime International Nominees Establishment v. Republic of Guinea. In the Amco case, the ad hoc committee required the signatory host state, Indonesia, to provide a bank guarantee to protect Amco against possible steps to delay or frustrate enforcement if annulment were to be refused. In the Maritime International Nominees Establishment case, the stay of enforcement was ordered but Guinea was not required to provide security. These cases are discussed in more detail in Chapter 5.

It has been argued that the party against which an award has been ordered should be required by ICSID to post a performance bond until the annulment proceeding has been completed.[26] Broches argues that the ICSID awards are immediately enforceable "except to the extent that enforcement shall have been stayed pursuant to the relevant provisions of this Convention" (Article 53(1))[27] and, therefore, no performance bond is necessary.

An annulment procedure has only occurred in four of the 45 cases registered with ICSID, and it is expected to be a rare event in the future. The Convention does not offer an appeals process to parties. It is feared that, if dispute parties are dissatisfied with awards and annulment proceedings become regularly utilized, the advantages of the ICSID arbitration process, that is, its speed, relatively low cost, and effectiveness, will be lessened.[28]

Subrogation

A feature, which is becoming a standard addition to foreign investment contracts, is that the guarantor will succeed or be subrogated to some or all of the investor's loss-related rights and claims upon indemnification under any insurance or guarantee policy. Such a right or claim often represents a claim against the host government. The question that arises in these cases is whether the subrogated government can take advantage of this right as the indemnified investor might have to pursue ICSID arbitration proceedings against the host government in respect to the covered loss. Article 25(1) of the Convention provides that the ICSID proceedings shall only be available for investment disputes between an ICSID signatory state or designated subdivision or agency of that state and a national of another signatory state. If the subrogee is a private insurer and a national of another signatory state, the subrogee can appear as a party in an ICSID proceeding, provided that the host state gives its consent to the subrogation. In cases in which the subrogee is a governmental or intergovernmental entity and, therefore, not a national of another signatory state, such an entity cannot avail itself of the investor's right to ICSID arbitration against the host signatory state.[29]

ICSID'S ADDITIONAL FACILITY

ICSID established an Additional Facility in 1978 to administer certain types of proceedings between states and foreign nationals that fall outside the scope of the ICSID Convention.[30] Under this Additional Facility, ICSID offers conciliation and arbitration proceedings to disputes in which either the state party or home state of the foreign investor is not a signatory of the ICSID Convention. The Additional Facility also extends ICSID's jurisdiction to cases in which the dispute is not an investment dispute but relates to a transaction having characteristics that distinguish it from an ordinary commercial transaction. The ICSID Additional Facility also can administer proceedings that are not provided in the Convention. For example, fact-finding proceedings can be held by ICSID to which any state or foreign national can have recourse if either wishes to institute an inquiry to gather and report on facts relevant to their case.

ICSID MODEL CLAUSES

ICSID further facilitates international resolution of investment disputes by its work in the design of model clauses to be included in investment agreements between foreign investors and host state governments, both of which are signatories to the ICSID Convention. These clauses were issued by ICSID in 1968 and were designed for insertion into bilateral investment contracts. Such clauses enable parties to trigger the use of the ICSID facilities including arbitration/conciliation of investment disputes.[31] The following represents an example of an ICSID model clause:

The (Government)/(*name of constituent subdivision or agency*) of *name of Contracting State* (hereinafter the "Host State") and *name of investor* (hereinafter the "Investor") hereby consent to submit to the jurisdiction of the International Centre for Settlement of Investment Disputes (hereinafter called the "Centre") all disputes arising out of this agreement (or relating to any investment made under it), for settlement by (conciliation)/(arbitration) (conciliation followed, if the dispute remains unresolved with *time limit* of the communication of the report of the Conciliation Commission to the parties, by arbitration) pursuant to the convention on the Settlement of Investment Disputes between States and Nationals of Other States (hereinafter the "Convention").[32]

The development of model clauses by ICSID has been one of the institution's most successful activities. It has been estimated that more than 1,000 of these arbitration clauses have been included in contracts between foreign investors and host state governments. The investments protected by these clauses amount to more than $2 billion.[33]

In 1969, ICSID also introduced a set of model treaty clauses.[34] These were designed to be inserted into bilateral intergovernmental agreements for the protection and promotion of foreign investments. In addition, ICSID also occasionally formulates and makes available to signatory states other types of model clauses, including those for multipartite proceedings and for legislation.

ICSID PUBLICATIONS

ICSID produces several publications that are available to the public. Among these are a journal, *ICSID Review — Foreign Investment Law Journal*, a newsletter, *News from ICSID*, occasional publications such as *ICSID Bibliography* and *ICSID Cases*, its annual report, the annual meeting minutes of its administrative council, and press releases. In addition, major works have been published by ICSID including its collection of

Investment Treaties in six volumes and its 10-volume set of *Investment Laws of the World*. The agency occasionally sponsors the publication of other studies. For example, in FY1995, a book on bilateral investment treaties, coauthored by Rudolf Dolzer and Margrete Stevens, was published by ICSID.

The Journal

ICSID began publication of its semiannual journal, *ICSID Review — Foreign Investment Law Journal* (hereafter *Journal*) in 1986. This journal is a scholarly law review that concentrates on ICSID cases and foreign investment law and endeavors to fill a gap in the existing literature on the law and practice relating to foreign investments. Articles have covered legal aspects of ICSID procedures, detailed analyses of ICSID cases with discussion of theories supporting the awards, analyses of states' economic reforms or investment laws, coverage of other arbitration institutions, investment laws, and treaties, the negotiation and performance of investment agreements, the resolution of investment disputes, and legal aspects of cooperative ventures with other multilateral financial institutions. The *Journal* also includes a section on documents relevant to investment laws and arbitration and bibliographies concerned with arbitration. The *Journal* can be subscribed to through ICSID or the World Bank Publications Office.

ICSID Bibliography

ICSID publishes a detailed reference booklet, *ICSID Bibliography*, containing a bibliography of publications about ICSID, its cases, and related activities. The latest edition was published in 1997.[35] The latest version contains texts of the ICSID Convention and a list of publications of the Centre, a bibliography of articles and books by authors outside ICSID, and a bibliography of references that contain decisions and discussion of ICSID cases and their disposition. This is a very valuable resource for scholars of the ICSID arbitration process.

ICSID Cases

For several years, ICSID has published a brochure, *ICSID Cases*. Decisions and awards have been rendered in several ICSID cases. This brochure contains references to these decisions as well as any national court proceedings that have concerned ICSID cases. Each case submitted to ICSID is covered in this brochure with disposition, dates when the cases were registered, dates of any continuances, names and nationalities of the parties, and current status of the cases. This document is a very valuable resource for students of the specific ICSID cases and is available to the public from ICSID.

Miscellaneous Publications

In addition to press releases concerning its cases, ICSID also publishes two informational documents. These are *News from ICSID* and the minutes of the annual meeting of its administrative council. *News from ICSID* is published semiannually and contains up-to-date news about ICSID cases, membership, and arbitration/conciliation panel lists as well as brief articles about investment dispute settlement and foreign investment and announcements about special conferences pertinent to these subjects. The minutes of the administrative council contain a report about ICSID operations as of the date of the meeting.

Investment Laws of the World

One of the earliest non-arbitration services performed by ICSID was the compilation, in one publication, of the investment laws of member countries. During the agency's fourth fiscal year, it began a pilot project for the collection, classification, and dissemination of national legislation and international agreements relating to foreign investments to help signatory states compare investment promotion instruments in various parts of the world.[36] These have been published as *Investment Laws of the World* by Oceana Publications in New York. The latest edition is in ten volumes and contains the text of the basic investment laws of 126 countries. The newest release of this publication, also published by Oceana Publications, includes the texts of the basic investment legislation of Lithuania, the Maldives, Moldova, Myanmar, and Papua New Guinea, as well as supplements related to investment laws of Mexico, Morocco, the Philippines, and Ukraine.[37]

Some of these investment laws refer to the possibility of settling disputes by ICSID arbitration. Some of these laws contain advance consents by the state concerned with ICSID arbitration or conciliation, whereas others defer any such consents to individual ICSID clauses. Some of them provide for the possible submission of such disputes to ad hoc arbitration under the Arbitration Rules of the United Nations Commission on International Trade Law. The ICSID Secretary-General has been designated in these laws as the appointing authority of arbitrators. Examples of such laws include those of the Central African Republic adopted in 1988 and of the former government of Yugoslavia adopted in 1989.[38] The Central African Republic's Investment Code contains a provision that refers to both the ICSID Convention and the ICSID Additional Facility, whereas Yugoslavia's Law on Foreign Investment deferred to an individual ICSID clause.

During ICSID's FY1996, the Organisation for Economic Co-operation and Development worked on a Multilateral Agreement on Investment, concluded in 1997, that contained provisions referring to ICSID arbitration.

Investment Promotion Treaties

ICSID has participated in the formulation of bilateral investment promotion and protection treaties. These treaties provide dispute settlement procedures based on ICSID rules and regulations. The following represent examples of these treaties:[39]

Treaty Between the United States and the Arab Republic of Egypt concerning the Reciprocal Encouragement and Protections of Investments, signed on September 29, 1982, in which Article VII concerns "Settlement of Legal Investment Disputes Between One Party and a National or Company Of the Other Party."

Treaty Between the United States of America and the Republic of Panama Concerning the Treatment and Protection of Investments, signed on October 27, 1982. At the time this treaty was signed, Panama was not a member of ICSID but Article VII of the treaty provided that such disputes might be settled pursuant to the Additional Facility Rules administered by ICSID.

Agreement Between the Government of the United Kingdom of Great Britain and Northern Ireland and the Government of Belize for the Promotion and Protection of Investments, which was signed and entered into force on April 30, 1982. Belize was not then a member of ICSID; thus, the agreement's Article 8 referred to the Additional Facility of ICSID to settle relevant disputes.

Bilateral Agreement between Tunisia and the United States, signed in 1993, which guarantees 1) that foreign investments will not be treated less favorably than domestic investments, 2) that international law standards for expropriation and compensation will be recognized, and 3) that disputes will be settled through the auspices of ICSID.

ICSID has also compiled a seven-volume collection, *Investment Treaties*. This compilation contains the texts of 640 bilateral investment treaties concluded by 140 countries, of the more than 1,000 treaties of this kind. The collection is supplemented about every five years with the most recent investment treaties. For example, the 1997 release contains texts for 85 bilateral treaties concluded by 76 countries during 1991–95.[40] In FY1992, ICSID was involved in a major research study for a report requested by the Development Committee of the Boards of Governors of the World Bank and International Monetary Fund. This study examined the legal framework for the treatment of foreign investment. ICSID also prepared background studies and bibliographies for the report.[41]

ICSID CONFERENCES

ICSID has promoted international investment in the LDCs by sponsoring or cosponsoring conferences on arbitration and other topics. For example, ICSID cosponsored two arbitration conferences in FY1997.[42] The first was the 13th joint ICSID/American Arbitration Association/ICC International Court of Arbitration colloquium on international arbitration held in New York on November 15, 1996. The fourteenth such colloquium was held at the World Bank in Washington, D.C., and the theme was concerned with institutional arbitration and its uniformity and diversity. The major topic at this conference concerned the role of party autonomy in international arbitration. The second conference was cosponsored by ICSID, the ICC International Court of Arbitration, and the London Court of International Arbitration. The conference dealt with the resolution of international trade and investment disputes in Africa and was held in Johannesburg on March 6–8, 1997.

The Secretariat of ICSID also participates in conferences dealing with international investment and dispute resolution. Three such meetings in FY1997 were attended by the Secretariat. These included meetings of the Expert Group convened by the Organisation for Economic Co-operation and Development to assist the development of the dispute-settlement provisions of the projected Multilateral Agreement on Investment. Other meetings attended by the Secretariat included the 5th Meeting of the Free Trade Area of the Americas Working Group on Investment in San José, Costa Rica, and a Meeting on Funding of and Access to International Courts and Dispute Settlement Bodies in London.

ICSID also has been a major topic at conferences that are not sponsored or organized by the agency. For example, at the 7th Annual International Trade Law Seminar held in Ottawa in 1989, one major topic concerned the ICSID system and Canada's reluctance to sign the Convention. Major speakers included Ibrahim F. I. Shihata, the Secretary-General of ICSID.

T. C. Drucker, General Counsel of Bata Ltd., gave an address, "The Perspective of Canadian Investors on Accession to ICSID" in which he outlined the reasons why Canada had not yet become a signatory to the Convention.

SUMMARY AND CONCLUSIONS

ICSID's operations primarily are concerned with the arbitration or conciliation of investment contract disputes between investors from a signatory nation and host states that are signatories. The agency has developed a procedure to implement this objective. This chapter has contained a discussion of that procedure.

The procedure involves the designation of a panel of conciliators and arbitrators — successful businessmen, lawyers, or financiers from signatory nations who have arbitrator skills. The composition of arbitral tribunals and conciliation commissions and the members' rights were discussed. Arbitral awards and the appeals and annulment processes were also discussed.

Three lesser functions performed by ICSID were also covered in this chapter: the generation of model clauses that can be included in foreign investors' contracts and that can trigger the ICSID procedures for arbitration or conciliation; the sponsorship of several publications including a semiannual journal that covers foreign investment law and ICSID cases, a compilation of investment treaties of countries around the world, and a bibliography of books and articles about ICSID; and the promotion of conferences, seminars, and symposia to cover ICSID procedures and means to increase FDI flows into LDCs that are ICSID signatories.

The analysis of the ICSID operations reveals arbitration procedures that are more flexible than those of other public and private agencies, although its jurisdiction is quite narrow. Its publication of investment laws and treaties has become a classic in the area of international legal literature.

NOTES

1. The operations of ICSID, which are discussed in this chapter, are based on the authority derived from International Centre for Settlement of Investment Disputes, *Convention on the Settlement of Investment Disputes between States and Nationals of Other States* (Washington, D.C.: International Bank for Reconstruction and Development, October 14, 1966) and International Centre for Settlement of Investment Disputes, *Additional Facility for the Administration of*

Conciliation, Arbitration and Fact-Finding Proceedings, Document ICSID/11 (Washington, D.C.: International Centre for Settlement of Investment Disputes, September 1978).

2.   David A. Soley, "ICSID Implementation: An Effective Alternative to International Conflict," *The International Lawyer* 19 (Spring 1985): 533.

3.   See, for example, John K. Ryans, Jr., and James C. Baker, "The International Centre for Settlement of Investment Disputes (ICSID)," *Journal of World Trade Law* 10 (January/February 1976): 66–67.

4.   Ibrahim F. I. Shihata, "The Experience of ICSID in the Selection of Arbitrators," remarks at the Sixth Joint American Arbitration Association/International Chamber of Commerce/ICSID Colloquium and reprinted in *News from ICSID* 6 (Winter 1989): 5.

5.   The administration of the ICSID process is spelled out in Alejandro A. Escobar, "Three Aspects of ICSID's Administration of Arbitration Proceedings," *News from ICSID* 14 (Summer 1997): 4–8.

6.   Bertrand P. Marchais, "Setting up the Initial Procedural Framework in ICSID Arbitration," *News from ICSID* 5 (Winter 1988): 5–9.

7.   Joy Cherian, "Foreign Investment Arbitration: The Role of the International Center for Settlement of Investment Disputes," in Third World Legal Studies, *Foreign Investment in the Light of the New International Economic Order* (Windsor, Ontario: Third World Legal Studies, 1983), p. 177.

8.   Aron Broches, "Introductory Remarks," 1972 Administrative Council Annual Meeting (Washington, D.C.: International Centre for Settlement of Investment Disputes, 1972), p. 3.

9.   Aron Broches, "The Convention on the Settlement of Investment Disputes: Some Observations on Jurisdiction," *Columbia Journal of Transnational Law* 5 (1968): 264–65.

10.   Georges R. Delaume, "ICSID Arbitration Proceedings: Practical Aspects," *Pace Law Review* 5 (Spring 1985): 568.

11.   Bertrand P. Marchais, "Composition of ICSID Tribunals," *News from ICSID* 4 (Summer 1987): 5.

12.   A. R. Parra, "The Rights and Duties of ICSID Arbitrators," *News from ICSID* 13 (Winter 1996): 6–7.

13.   Michael M. Moore, "International Arbitration Between States and Foreign Investors — The World Bank Convention," *Stanford Law Review* 18 (June 1966): 1361.

14.   Patrick O'Hare, "The Convention on the Settlement of Investment Disputes," *Stanford Journal of International Studies* 6 (1971): 150.

15.   Chong Su Yun, "The Convention on the Settlement of Investment Disputes — Commentary and Forecast," *Malaya Law Review* 11 (December 1969): 301.

16.   See Nassib G. Ziadé, "ICSID Conciliation," *News from ICSID* 13 (Summer 1996): 3–8 for a detailed discussion of the ICSID conciliation procedures.

17. Paul C. Szasz, "A Practical Guide to the Convention on Settlement of Investment Disputes," *Cornell International Law Journal* 1 (1968): 23.

18. Luther C. West, "Award Enforcement Provisions of the World Bank Convention," *Arbitration Journal* 23 (1968): 40.

19. John J. Baer, "Staying Out of Court," *International Business* 10 (July/August 1997): 10.

20. Ibid.

21. Chong Su Yun, "The Convention on the Settlement of Investment Disputes," pp. 311–12.

22. International Centre for Settlement of Investment Disputes, *Annual Report* (Washington, D.C.: International Centre for Settlement of Investment Disputes, 1987), pp. 4–5.

23. Josef P. Sirefman, "The World Bank Plan for Investment Dispute Arbitration," *Arbitration Journal* 20 (1965): 176–77.

24. C. F. Amerasinghe, "The International Centre for Settlement of Investment Disputes and Development through the Multinational Corporation," *Vanderbilt Journal of Transnational Law* 9 (Fall 1976): 813.

25. For a good argument supporting the ICSID annulment procedure, see Aron Broches, "On the Finality of Awards: A Reply to Michael Reisman," *ICSID Review — Foreign Investment Law Journal* 8 (1993): 92–103.

26. Michael Reisman, "Repairing ICSID's Control System: Some Comments on Aron Broches' 'Observations on the Finality of ICSID Awards,'" *ICSID Review — Foreign Investment Law Journal* 7 (1992): 196–211.

27. Broches, "On the Finality of Awards," p. 97.

28. Ibrahim F. I. Shihata, *Report of the Secretary-General to the ICSID Administrative Council Annual Meeting* (Washington, D.C.: International Centre for Settlement of Investment Disputes, 1988), p. 3.

29. Nassib G. Ziadé, "ICSID Clauses in the Subrogation Context," *News from ICSID* 7 (Summer 1990): 4.

30. Ibrahim F. I. Shihata, "ICSID and Paths to Institutional Cooperation," *News from ICSID* 9 (Winter 1992): 7.

31. Ryans and Baker, "The International Centre for Settlement of Investment Disputes (ICSID)," pp. 66–67.

32. See mimeographed "Model Clauses Recording Consent to the Jurisdiction of the International Centre for Settlement of Investment Disputes, ICSID/5" (Washington, D.C.: International Centre for Settlement of Investment Disputes, no date).

33. Gregory W. MacKenzie, "ICSID Arbitration as a Strategy for Levelling the Playing Field Between International Non-Governmental Organizations and Host States," *Syracuse Journal of International Law and Commerce* 19 (1993): 220.

34. Szasz, "A Practical Guide to the Convention on Settlement of Investment Disputes," p. 13.

35. International Centre for Settlement of Investment Disputes, *ICSID Bibliography* (Washington, D.C.: International Centre for Settlement of Investment Disputes, 1997) or Doc. ICSID/13/Rev.4

36. International Centre for Settlement of Investment Disputes, *ICSID Fourth Annual Report 1969/1970* (Washington, D.C.: International Centre for Settlement of Investment Disputes, 1970), pp. 5–6.

37. International Centre for Settlement of Investment Disputes, *Annual Report* (Washington, D.C.: International Centre for Settlement of Investment Disputes, 1997), p. 11.

38. International Centre for Settlement of Investment Disputes, "New Foreign Investment Legislation Referring to ICSID," *News from ICSID* 6 (Summer 1989): 8.

39. International Centre for Settlement of Investment Disputes, "Investment Promotion Treaties," *ICSID Newsletter*, No. 83-1 (January 1983): 3–9; "Tunisia-U.S. Investment Treaty," *Middle East Executive Reports* 16 (February 1993): 7.

40. International Centre for Settlement of Investment Disputes, *Annual Report 1997*, p. 11.

41. Ibrahim F. I. Shihata, *Report of the Secretary-General to the ICSID Administrative Council* (Washington, D.C.: International Centre for Settlement of Investment Disputes, 1992), pp. 2–3.

42. International Centre for Settlement of Investment Disputes, *ICSID 1997 Annual Report* (Washington, D.C.: International Centre for Settlement of Investment Disputes, 1992), p. 12.

5

Selected ICSID Cases

HISTORY OF CASES FROM 1972 TO 1997

Since the inception of operations of the International Centre for Settlement of Investment Disputes (ICSID) in 1966 through July 30, 1997, 45 cases have been registered with the agency for dispute resolution.[1] The first case brought to ICSID concerned a dispute between foreign investors Holiday Inns S.A., Occidental Petroleum and the Government of Morocco (Case No. ARB/72/1) in 1972. The last case involved WRB Enterprises and Grenada Private Power Limited v. Grenada (Case No. ARB/97/5). Of these cases, 42 involved arbitration and 3 involved conciliation. Of these latter three cases, two proceedings were closed after agreement was reached between the parties. In four cases registered with ICSID, annulment proceedings were requested. In none of these four cases was a total annulment of the award finally granted. The following 10 cases are considered representative of ICSID's procedures and will be analyzed in the following sections.

In order for the ICSID process to work in these cases, three steps must precede the formation of an ICSID arbitration or conciliation tribunal. First, the host state government — host to the foreign investment — and the home state of the foreign investor must be signatories of the ICSID Convention. Second, the host state must have notified ICSID of the class or classes of disputes that its government deems to be arbitrable. Finally, both the foreign investor and the host state must consent to the jurisdiction of

ICSID.[2] The ICSID tribunal assigned to such cases only can make decisions about disputes arising from an investment.

HOLIDAY INNS S.A., OCCIDENTAL PETROLEUM v. GOVERNMENT OF MOROCCO

The first case submitted to ICSID involved a dispute between Holiday Inns S.A., Occidental Petroleum and the Government of Morocco (Case No. ARB/72/1).[3] As part of a joint venture with Holiday Inns, Occidental Petroleum would build a Gulf Oil gasoline station when a Holiday Inn hotel was constructed. The two companies agreed to build four hotels in Morocco at the government's request for the purpose of developing tourism. The contract contained an ICSID clause. In addition to this agreement, the two companies formed Moroccan subsidiaries to facilitate payment by the Moroccan Government because local law restricted the ability of the government to contract with foreign companies. The agreement between the subsidiaries and the Moroccan Government did not include the ICSID clauses.

The dispute arose when the Moroccan Government failed to pay the foreign investors for the construction of the hotels. As a result, Holiday Inns, Occidental Petroleum, and their Moroccan subsidiaries initiated arbitration proceedings with ICSID. The dispute was registered with ICSID in 1972 for arbitration, but the Government of Morocco obtained a local court order that ordered Holiday Inns to resume construction at the expense of Holiday Inns. An arbitration tribunal was constituted that consisted of Gunnar Lagergren of Sweden, Paul Reuter of France, and J. C. Schultsz of the Netherlands. The Moroccan subsidiaries were not permitted to be parties to the arbitration proceedings because they did not have an ICSID clause in their agreements.

Holiday Inns and Occidental Petroleum, the claimants, argued in the ICSID proceedings that the unilateral actions by the Government of Morocco were against the basic agreement between the parties as well as the exclusive character of the ICSID arbitration system. The Moroccan Government argued that local courts had exclusive jurisdiction and that such legal remedies would protect the interests of both parties. The ICSID tribunal treated the agreements between the subsidiaries and the Moroccan Government as secondary documents that merely supplemented the original agreement, and the parent companies were allowed to enforce these agreements.[4]

The ICSID arbitral tribunal stated that it had jurisdiction to recommend provisional measures according to the terms of Article 47 of the Convention on the Settlement of Investment Disputes between States and Nationals of Other States. The tribunal recommended that,the parties abstain from any action incompatible with the upholding of the contract to ensure that the action already taken would not jeopardize any future action under the contract. A second recommendation concerned the exchange of information by the parties that involved the completion of construction of those hotels and their management. The tribunal also recommended consultations "in order to maintain in the hotels the character of the enterprise, which is part of the international chain of Holiday Inns Hotels."[5]

The parties to the dispute later amicably agreed to settle the dispute, and the proceedings were discontinued at their request in 1978. The major recommendations of the tribunal were made before it ascertained jurisdiction to consider the merits of the case. This significant issue has faced other international tribunals and remains quite controversial. The Secretary-General screens all cases that are registered with ICSID and, thus, registration of the request constitutes *prima facie* evidence that such a dispute is not outside the jurisdiction of ICSID. According to the Convention, the tribunal is not bound by the decision of the Secretary-General. However, such a decision by the latter should make the presumption that the tribunal does have the power to rule on provisional measures of the case at an early stage of the proceedings.

Although the parties settled the dispute amicably, this case was important for several reasons. It was the first case in which registration with ICSID was agreed to by the parties in dispute. Also, it established the jurisdiction of the arbitral tribunal once the parties had agreed to the ICSID proceeding. Thus, it upheld the Convention that had been signed by the state governments of the parties in dispute. The terms, "jurisdiction" and "competence," of the tribunal found in Article 41(1) of the Convention were established significantly in this case.

A more important reason why this case is significant stems from what happened during the arbitral proceedings. During the final stage of the case, the arbitrator designated by the claimants, Holiday Inns-Occidental Petroleum Corporation, informed the tribunal president that he had become a director of the latter company. After consultations among the arbitral tribunal members and the Secretary-General of ICSID, it was decided that if a member of a tribunal were to become a director of one of the parties, the letter and spirit of the Convention would be compromised. The arbitrator submitted his resignation and the tribunal was reconstituted in 1976, nearly four years after the dispute had been registered with

ICSID. The chairman of the ICSID Administrative Council appointed the new member. Thus, policy about an event unforeseen at the time of the establishment of ICSID was formulated, and a procedure for handling such events in the future was designed.

ALCOA MINERALS OF JAMAICA, INC., KAISER BAUXITE COMPANY, AND REYNOLDS JAMAICA MINES LIMITED v. GOVERNMENT OF JAMAICA

Three aluminum producers, Alcoa Minerals of Jamaica, Inc., Kaiser Bauxite Company, and Reynolds Jamaica Mines Limited entered into a contract with the Government of Jamaica to construct an aluminum factory in exchange for a 25-year bauxite mining concession in that country. The agreement promised no increase in local taxes of the project for 25 years and access to ICSID arbitration.

The companies built the factory and began to mine bauxite. A dispute arose between the three aluminum producers and the host state government when Jamaica levied a tax on bauxite mining in 1974 and charged the companies $20 million. Jamaica registered a reservation with ICSID to exclude any dispute related to extraction of minerals. This dispute was registered, with the agreement of the parties, with ICSID in 1974. Actually, three separate cases were registered with ICSID, one by each of the foreign investors against the Government of Jamaica (Case Nos. ARB/74/2, ARB/74/3, and ARB/74/4).[6]

The tribunal made three important rulings. It held that consent to the ICSID jurisdiction was signed by the parties, consent existed at the time the case was registered with ICSID, and notification of the reservation filed by Jamaica did not affect the prior consent. Such reservation would only pertain to agreements submitted to ICSID after the reservation was filed. Although the parties to the dispute in these cases had agreed to accept the jurisdiction of ICSID, Jamaica later withdrew unilaterally from the proceedings, even though such an act was contrary to the Convention's requirements.

A series of decisions by the Jamaican Government, headed by President Michael Manley, effectively resulted in the withdrawal of the country from the ICSID arbitration proceedings.[7] On March 8, 1974, an official communiqué from Conakry, Guinea, announced the establishment of an International Bauxite Association, essentially a cartel, to be comprised of the governments of Australia, Guinea, Guyana, Jamaica, Sierra Leone, Surinam, and Yugoslavia. Headquarters was established in Kingston,

Jamaica. It was during this time that Jamaica unilaterally decreed a sixfold increase in royalty and tax payments from aluminum producers.

The Jamaican Government, a signatory of the ICSID Convention, had broken off negotiations with the aluminum producers prior to the royalty–tax increase announcement. This government then cited a technicality and rejected the facilities of ICSID. Thus, the ICSID proceedings technically were discontinued after the claimants agreed to a final settlement from the respondent.

The Jamaican decision elicited very little negative response from the global development finance community. The World Bank had advanced Jamaica $20 million in development credits during the previous year. The Inter-American Development Bank and the U.S. Agency for International Development had also made millions of dollars of loans and grants to Jamaica. None of these agencies openly criticized the actions taken by Jamaica.

The critical implication from this case was that the credibility of ICSID's procedures and facilities was diminished by the ability of a contracting host state government to withdraw from proceedings in this manner. Another case with a similar principle involved a government that declined to pay its full share of the expenses of a proceeding to which it had agreed to participate. This state, not publicly identified by ICSID, also did not comply with the tribunal's award.[8]

In the Jamaica case, the host state government probably lost more credibility in the international investment community than did the ICSID procedures and facilities. President Manley, before his actions concerning the aluminum producers, had stated that contractual obligations and treaty commitments were merely scraps of paper. Even after the government had signed the ICSID Convention, Manley had stated that "the thought of a sovereign government submitting to international arbitration is unrealistic."[9] S. J. Rundt & Associates, international business consultants, warned investors in its *Weekly Intelligence* publication to be very careful of any investment contemplated in Jamaica.[10] At that time, several less expensive sources of bauxite were available to aluminum producers. In addition, the technology existed to extract aluminum oxide, the major ingredient in aluminum, from aluminous materials other than bauxite. Most economic analysts at that time forecast that the Jamaica Government's actions in this area would be costly to that country's development. The international stigma attached to the withdrawal by a government from an internationally sanctioned procedure after accepting that procedure certainly had long-term ramifications for Jamaica.

AGIP S.p.A v. GOVERNMENT OF THE PEOPLE'S REPUBLIC OF THE CONGO

AGIP S.p.A. of Italy entered into a contract with the Government of the People's Republic of the Congo for an oil products distribution venture. A dispute arose in the agreement, and the parties submitted the case to ICSID for arbitration on November 4, 1977 (Case No. ARB/77/1). The tribunal was comprised of Jørgen Trolle of Denmark, René-Jean Dupuy of France, and Fuad Rouhani of Iran. The tribunal made an award on November 19, 1979.

The dispute began when AGIP breached its agreement with the Congo. The Congolese Government nationalized AGIP's subsidiary, which was established to facilitate the oil products distribution venture. AGIP filed for arbitration but the government argued that no dispute had arisen because it had compensated AGIP when the subsidiary was expropriated. The Italian company held that the dispute had arisen before the government takeover and that compensation was inadequate.

The ICSID tribunal found no definition of the term "legal dispute" in the Convention and relied on a statement made by a World Bank director at the time the Convention was submitted to World Bank members for their approval. This statement defined a legal dispute as a conflict over rights rather than interests and, thus, the tribunal held that such a legal dispute, if to be proven, had to relate to a legal right or obligation or to the nature and extent of compensation for the breach of such a right or obligation. The tribunal found no such defined dispute before the nationalization by the Congolese Government and limited its inquiry to a determination of the adequacy of the compensation made after the nationalization.[11]

SOCIÉTÉ BENVENUTI & BONFANT v. GOVERNMENT OF THE PEOPLE'S REPUBLIC OF THE CONGO

Société Benvenuti & Bonfant, a French company, entered into an agreement with the Government of the People's Republic of the Congo to manufacture plastic bottles for the domestic market. A dispute arose in the agreement, and the parties requested registration with ICSID (Case No. ARB/77/2). This case resulted in the only judicial decision that rendered an ICSID award. The dispute was registered December 15, 1977, and an arbitration tribunal was constituted in 1978 that was comprised of Jørgen Trolle of Denmark (who later resigned and was replaced by Alex Bonn of Luxembourg), Rudolf Bystricky of Czechoslovak Republic, and

Edilbert Razafindralambo of Malagasy. An award was rendered on August 8, 1980.

The claimant, Société Benvenuti & Bonfant, then sued in a French court for recognition of the ICSID award. The lower court granted recognition of the award against the Congolese Government with the qualification that the award creditors first seek the court's authorization if they wanted enforcement of the award against Congolese assets. On appeal, the Cour d'appel in Paris removed this qualification. The higher court held that the recognizing court is limited to ascertaining the authenticity of an ICSID award to the exclusion of any consideration of the sovereign immunity.[12] A key point with regard to the outcome of this case is that ICSID awards should be recognized quickly and without judicial interference. Recognition in this manner makes the ICSID procedure preferable to other procedures under domestic laws or international conventions for the recognition and enforcement of foreign judgments or awards.

AMCO ASIA CORPORATION, PAN AMERICAN DEVELOPMENT LIMITED AND P.T. AMCO INDONESIA v. REPUBLIC OF INDONESIA

Amco Asia Corporation (Amco), Pan American Development Limited (Pan American), and P.T. Amco Indonesia (PT Amco) filed a request with ICSID for arbitration of a dispute against the Republic of Indonesia (Case No. ARB/81/1) on January 15, 1981.[13] This case is significant because it is the first ICSID arbitration award for which an annulment proceeding was requested by the signatory host state and the first in which the arbitral tribunal's award actually was annulled.

The claimants contended that, for the purpose of tourism development, they had invested in the construction of a hotel complex, the Kartika Plaza Hotel in Djakarta, in 1968 with an agreement with the Republic of Indonesia to manage the complex for 30 years. In 1980, the owner of the property, an Indonesian organization, with assistance from the Indonesian Army and local police, seized the complex in an armed military action and asked the government to cancel the investment license. Local courts rendered several decisions that rescinded the lease and management agreement between the claimants and the Republic. The latter contended that the military action was directed at the right of an Indonesian national to control the hotel and was not a government takeover. The Republic also contended that the license cancellation was justified legally and that local courts had acted in a binding and lawful manner. The Republic counterclaimed that the cancellation of the investment license was justified because of violations of Indonesian and applicable international law by the claimants and, therefore, that PT Amco should return tax and other concessions granted by the Republic of Indonesia.

Among the local law violations alleged by the Indonesian Government was an article that appeared in a Hong Kong newspaper. This article included statements by the major shareholder about the nationalization, the handling of the case by the Djakarta courts, and the impending ICSID arbitration. The government held that these statements were damaging to the country.

An arbitration tribunal was organized with the facilitation of ICSID. The tribunal members consisted of Berthold Goldman of France, Isi Foighel of Denmark, and Edward W. Rubin of Canada.

The applicable law determined in the proceedings was Indonesian law, that is, the law of the state party to the dispute, and appropriate parts of international law deemed by the arbitration tribunal to be applicable. The tribunal's decision made a wider interpretation of the Convention in this case than it had made in the case of Holiday Inns et al. v. Republic of Morocco. The tribunal assumed that the parties had acted in good faith and concluded that foreign control of the project was implied because it had been obvious to the host state government that foreign investors dominated the project. This, according to the tribunal, was true even though such domination was not stated in the agreement containing the ICSID clause that triggered the case. The tribunal also held that the ICSID Convention and Rules do not preclude the parties from revealing their case and that, furthermore, local newspaper accounts contained more revealing statements than did the article in the Hong Kong newspaper. The tribunal found in favor of the claimants, and the award amounted to $3.2 million. Indonesia's counterclaim was rejected.

The Republic of Indonesia applied for an annulment of the award on March 18, 1985, under Article 52 of the Convention. An ad hoc committee consisting of Ignaz Seidl-Hohenveldern of Austria, Florentino P. Feliciano of the Philippines, and Andrea Giardina of Italy was appointed. The ad hoc committee ordered a stay of the execution of the award.

The dispute was resubmitted to a new tribunal registered by ICSID on May 21, 1987, and June 24, 1987. The new tribunal consisted of Rosalyn Higgins of Great Britain, Marc Lalonde of Canada, and Per Magid of Denmark. The ad hoc committee rendered an award on June 5, 1990, and a decision on supplemental decisions and rectification of the award was rendered on October 17, 1990. A second annulment proceeding was brought by Indonesia later that year and early in 1991. A new ad hoc committee was appointed whose members were Sompong Sucharitkul of

Thailand, Arghyrios A. Fatouros of Greece, and Dietrich Schindler of Switzerland. A decision was rendered on December 17, 1992, which rejected the application for annulment of the award.

One of the principles of law that Amco argued was that only those parts of the award specifically annulled by the tribunal were annulled. All other findings remained *res judicata* for purposes before the tribunal. The latter affirmed that matters expressly annulled might be relitigated. Indonesia identified two such items that the tribunal agreed fell within the category of items that could be relitigated: the restitution of the tax and import concessions granted to PT Amco and the quantity of the damages (if any) owed to PT Amco.

ATLANTIC TRITON COMPANY LTD. v. PEOPLE'S REVOLUTIONARY REPUBLIC OF GUINEA

In two cases, both of which had the same host state signatory nation as a party, one of the parties to an ICSID arbitration requested the assistance of domestic courts to order provisional measures. One is the case of Maritime International Nominees Establishment v. People's Revolutionary Republic of Guinea and will be discussed in the next section. The other is a case in which Atlantic Triton Company Limited entered into a management contract with the People's Revolutionary Republic of Guinea for the conversion, equipping, and operation of fishing vessels and the training of crews.

In the Atlantic Triton–Guinea case, a dispute arose and the parties submitted the case to ICSID for arbitration on January 19, 1984 (Case No. ARB/84/1). A tribunal was constituted later that year whose members were Pieter Sanders of the Netherlands, Jean-François Prat of France, and A. J. Van den Berg of the Netherlands. An award was made on April 21, 1986. During the ICSID arbitration of this dispute, the Atlantic Triton Company instituted attachment proceedings in a French court against property owned by Guinea in France.[14] Before the ICSID Tribunal rendered its award, the Court of Appeal of Rennes, France, made an unqualified application of the rule and vacated the attachments. In short, the French court confirmed the exclusive character of consent to ICSID arbitration and the rule (Article 26 of the ICSID Convention) according to which domestic courts in signatory states must abstain from any action that can interfere with the conduct of an ICSID arbitral proceeding.

MARITIME INTERNATIONAL NOMINEES ESTABLISHMENT v. GOVERNMENT OF THE REPUBLIC OF GUINEA

The finding by the French court in the Atlantic Triton v. Government of the Republic of Guinea case was reaffirmed in the case in which Maritime International Nominees Establishment (MINE), a Liechtenstein corporation wholly owned by a Swiss national, entered into a bauxite transportation joint venture with the Government of the Republic of Guinea in 1971. The primary objective of this joint venture company was to outfit and manage oceangoing ships, in the form of purchase, lease, or charter, under the conditions that conformed to the interests of the parties, namely to transport bauxite from Guinea mines.

A dispute arose and the parties submitted the case to ICSID for arbitration on September 18, 1984 (Case No. ARB/84/4).[15] A tribunal was constituted on June 17, 1985, which was comprised of Donald E. Zubrod, Jack Berg, and David K. Sharpe, all of the United States. An award was made on January 6, 1988. This case is a good example of the possible complexity of ICSID arbitrations. Before it was registered, an American Arbitration Association (AAA) arbitration award was made. A U.S. District Court then heard the case before it was formally registered with ICSID. After an ICSID award was made, one of the parties brought annulment proceedings before the case was finally discontinued at the request of both parties to the dispute.

In 1972, MINE accused the Government of Guinea of a violation of the original agreement when the latter signed a contract with another company. Guinea accused MINE of defaults in the contract and claimed such action was necessary to satisfy bauxite buyers. The parties litigated the case for several years and, in 1978, MINE submitted a request for arbitration to the AAA. The AAA made an award in favor of MINE in 1980, which the Republic of Guinea did not appeal.

This case demonstrated that ICSID arbitrations are unique and that they can be outside the reach of traditional judicial processes in that they affect the recognition and enforcement of foreign arbitral awards. The Republic of Guinea did not recognize the AAA award to MINE, and the case was heard in a U.S. District Court in Washington, D.C.[16] This court affirmed the AAA award. However, the Court of Appeals for the District of Columbia reversed that decision when it determined in 1982 that Guinea's agreement to arbitrate before ICSID constituted a waiver of immunity under the U.S. Foreign Sovereign Immunity Act — although no such waiver could be inferred from a consent to ICSID arbitration because U.S. courts were powerless to compel ICSID arbitration and a dispute that arises from such an agreement is within the jurisdiction of the U.S. District Court. The Court then granted MINE's petition to enforce the AAA award against the Republic of Guinea. Prior to the U.S. Court case finding in 1982, MINE had, according to the Republic of Guinea, unilaterally refused to submit the dispute to ICSID jurisdiction and had initiated the AAA arbitration.

The case was then referred to ICSID's jurisdiction in 1984. After ICSID assumed jurisdiction, MINE sought to attach assets of the Republic of Guinea located in Europe on the basis of the AAA award. Attachment orders were obtained from courts in Antwerp and Geneva. The Court of Geneva advised MINE to discontinue the claim and, in a 1985 recommendation, the ICSID tribunal recommended that MINE discontinue its litigation in national courts and seek no new remedy in a national court.

Guinea also applied to domestic courts at this time to have the property attachments vacated. In 1985 and 1986, the tribunals of Antwerp and of Geneva, respectively, rendered their decisions. The Federal Tribunal of Switzerland — the Swiss Supreme Court — acknowledged the exclusivity of ICSID proceedings according to Article 26 of the Convention.[17] After the 1985 award by the ICSID tribunal, the Republic of Guinea initiated an annulment proceeding. An ad hoc committee was formed and was comprised of Sompong Sucharitkul of Thailand, Aron Broches of the Netherlands, and Kéba Mbaye of Senegal. The ad hoc committee rendered a decision in 1989, which partially annulled the 1985 award. The dispute was resubmitted to ICSID with a request for the appointment of a new tribunal in 1990. Later that year, the parties agreed to a settlement, and the proceeding was discontinued at their request.

The MINE v. Guinea case demonstrated another problem that was not part of the primary grounds of the dispute. As mentioned earlier, MINE is a Liechtenstein-based subsidiary owned by a Swiss national. When MINE entered into the original agreement with the Republic of Guinea in 1971, they agreed on an ICSID arbitration clause in the contract stating that they would treat the company as a Swiss national even though it was a Liechtenstein company. Liechtenstein was not an ICSID signatory but Switzerland was. MINE argued during the U.S. court proceedings that the clause was invalid because it exceeded the scope of the Convention.[18] MINE held in that proceeding that the Convention should only apply to situations in which the company involved is incorporated in a host signatory nation.

The arbitral proceeding was decided on other grounds, and this issue was not resolved. Article 25(2)(b), the Convention rule that governs the nationality question for ICSID jurisdiction, focused on the case of entities incorporated in the host state but under foreign control. The definition of what constituted "foreign control" was discussed in the drafting of this part of the Convention. Because consent of the parties is the foundation of the Convention, each party agreeing to ICSID arbitration should have discretion in the determination of its own satisfaction whether it will treat a particular corporation as a national of another signatory state, regardless of where that firm is incorporated. Again the flexibility of the Convention and the ICSID arbitral procedure lends a unique character to this institution.

GHAITH R. PHARAON v. REPUBLIC OF TUNISIA

Ghaith R. Pharaon entered into a contract with the Republic of Tunisia for tourism and holiday resort projects. A dispute arose, and the parties submitted the case to ICSID on September 24, 1986, for arbitration (Case No. ARB/86/1). A tribunal was constituted on January 20, 1987, which was comprised of Claude Reymond of Switzerland, Giorgio Bernini of Italy, and Karl-Heinz Böckstiegel of Germany.

This case was unusual in that it was the first case in which the foreign investor was not a company but an individual. Mr. Pharaon was an entrepreneur from the Middle East. He was involved in several international business ventures including ownership of a state-chartered bank in Detroit. This case was discontinued at the request of the parties after they agreed to a settlement. The discontinuance was issued on November 21, 1988, according to Arbitration Rule 43 (1).[19]

Since this case, five subsequent cases were registered with ICSID involving individuals as claimants.[20] These were Philippe Gruslin v. Malaysia in 1992, Antoine Goetz et al. v. Burundi in 1995, Robert Azinian et al. v. Mexico in 1997, Emilio Maffezini v. Spain in 1997, and Joseph C. Lemire v. Ukraine in 1998. These cases were all registered for arbitration and the Lemire v. Ukraine case was also registered under the ICSID Additional Facility. They are listed in Appendix II.

MOBIL OIL CORPORATION, MOBIL PETROLEUM COMPANY, INC. AND MOBIL OIL NEW ZEALAND LIMITED v. NEW ZEALAND GOVERNMENT

The case of Mobil Oil Corporation, Mobil Petroleum Company, Inc. and Mobil Oil New Zealand Limited, a U.S.-based multinational company group, requested an ICSID arbitration of a dispute against the New Zealand Government pursuant to an arbitration clause in an agreement between them (Case No. ARB/87/2).[21] The case was registered in 1987 and a tribunal was constituted whose members were Graham Speight of New Zealand, Maureen Brunt of Australia, and Stephen Charles of Australia.

This case is somewhat similar to the Atlantic Triton v. Republic of Guinea and MINE v. Republic of Guinea cases, discussed previously, in that domestic courts were asked to intervene in an ICSID proceeding. In each of those cases, the private party to the dispute instituted judicial proceedings against the signatory host state party with respect to a dispute that the parties had agreed to submit to the jurisdiction of ICSID. However in this case, the host state government, New Zealand, sought an injunction from the New Zealand courts to restrain the claimants from proceeding with the ICSID case.

The dispute had arisen because of changes in the original 1982 agreement between the parties for a project for the conversion of natural gas into synthetic gasoline. In that agreement, the Mobil subsidiary in New Zealand acquired rights of purchase on preferential terms of synthetic gasoline resulting from the project. The New Zealand Government enacted the Commerce Act in 1986 to promote competition in markets within New Zealand. The type of purchase agreement entered into by the parties was alleged to lessen competition and was prohibited retroactively. Thus, the government rendered the original agreement null and void. An ICSID clause had been included in the contract and, thus, the Mobil Group sought arbitration of the dispute from ICSID. The New Zealand Government then sought an injunction against the ICSID proceeding from the local court. The court held against the government and reaffirmed ICSID's exclusive jurisdiction. It stayed its proceedings until the ICSID arbitral tribunal had determined its jurisdiction. In November 1990, a settlement was agreed by the parties in the ICSID arbitral proceeding and requested that the proceeding be discontinued.

ASIAN AGRICULTURAL PRODUCTS LIMITED v. DEMOCRATIC SOCIALIST REPUBLIC OF SRI LANKA

Asian Agricultural Products Limited (AAPL), a Hong Kong company, entered into an agreement with the Democratic Socialist Republic of Sri Lanka to form a joint venture to do shrimp farming. A dispute in the agreement arose, and the parties requested registration with ICSID (Case No. ARB/87/3).[22] The dispute was registered on July 20, 1987, and an arbitral tribunal was constituted in January 1988, which was comprised of

Dr. Ahmed Sadek El-Kosheri of Egypt, Dr. S.K.B. Asante of Ghana, and Professor Berthold Goldman of France.

The dispute arose from the destruction in Sri Lanka of the principal shrimp-producing farm of Serendib Seafoods Ltd. (Serendib), a Sri Lankan firm whose shares were owned by AAPL.[23] The farm was destroyed during a counter-insurgency operation by the governmental security forces against Tamil rebels in 1987. The parties failed to reach an amicable settlement and the dispute was registered with ICSID.

An award was rendered on June 27, 1990, but was not a unanimous decision. A dissenting opinion by Dr. Asante was attached to the award. This case represented the first ICSID arbitration initiated pursuant to provisions making available such arbitration in a bilateral investment treaty rather than in an agreement with the foreign investor or in the domestic law of the host signatory state. This bilateral treaty was an agreement in 1980 between the Government of the United Kingdom of Great Britain and Northern Ireland and the Government of the Republic of Sri Lanka for the promotion and protection of investments.[24]

This treaty contained a provision that established the unconditional consent of each contracting state to submit any investment disputes to conciliation or arbitration before ICSID upon the request of an investor who is a national of the other contracting state. In the AAPL v. Sri Lanka case, the majority award and the dissenting opinion reached conflicting conclusions with regard to the applicable law.[25] The majority held that the parties had had no opportunity to exercise the prior choice of law permitted by the Convention because the case was initiated on the basis of the bilateral investment treaty between the investor's state and the host state. The dissenting arbitrator did not concur with the majority's finding because AAPL was not a party to the United Kingdom–Sri Lanka treaty and that jurisdictional issues should be distinguished from issues concerning applicable law. Dr. Asante held that Sri Lankan law should be the principal source of law together with applicable rules of international law.

SUMMARY AND CONCLUSIONS

This chapter has contained a representative discussion of ten cases that have been registered for ICSID arbitration or conciliation of investment contract disputes. The first case involving Holiday Inns and Morocco set a precedent for the ICSID procedure even though the case was discontinued and the parties agreed to an amicable settlement. The case of three aluminum companies versus Jamaica was important because of the withdrawal of the host state after joining a bauxite cartel, despite the ICSID rule that parties must complete the process once they commit to the ICSID procedure. The first annulment proceeding after an ICSID award was covered in the Amco Asia et al. v. Indonesia case. The MINE v. Guinea case demonstrated that ICSID arbitrations are unique in the way by which they affect the recognition and enforcement of foreign arbitral awards. The first case in which the foreign investor was an individual rather than a company was covered in Ghaith R. Pharaon v. Tunisia.

The cases covered in this chapter demonstrate that the ICSID procedures are quite flexible. They permit annulment procedures but also have no way other than international stigma to require parties, especially host states, to remain parties to the ICSID procedure.

NOTES

1. International Centre for Settlement of Investment Disputes, *ICSID Cases* (Washington, D.C.: International Centre for Settlement of Investment Disputes, 1996), and updated document.

2. See Article 25 of the ICSID Convention.

3. Georges R. Delaume, "ICSID Tribunals and Provisional Measures — A Review of the Cases," *ICSID Review — Foreign Investment Law Journal* 1 (Fall 1986): 392–93.

4. Ray August, *International Business Law: Text, Cases, and Readings* (Englewood Cliffs, N.J.: Prentice-Hall, 1993), p. 104.

5. Ibid., p. 392.

6. For a detailed analysis of the principles raised by these cases, see John T. Schmidt, "Arbitration Under the Auspices of the International Centre for Settlement of Investment Disputes (ICSID): Implications of the Decision on Jurisdiction in Alcoa Minerals of Jamaica, Inc. v. Government of Jamaica," *Harvard International Law Journal* 17 (1976): 90–112.

7. Robert M. Bleiberg, "Ill Wind From Jamaica," *Barron's*, July 15, 1974, pp. 7, 12.

8. James C. Baker and Lois J. Yoder, "ICSID Arbitration and the U.S. Multinational Corporation," *Journal of International Arbitration* 5 (December 1988): 94.

9. Bleiberg, "Ill Wind From Jamaica," p. 7.

10. Ibid., p. 12.

11. August, *International Business Law*, p. 107.

12. Georges R. Delaume, "ICSID Arbitration in Practice," *International Tax and Business Lawyer* 2 (Winter 1984): 73–74.

13. For a detailed analysis of this case, see Per Magid, Rosalyn Higgins, and Marc Lalonde, "AMCO v. Republic of Indonesia: Resubmitted Case Decision on Jurisdiction," *ICSID Review — Foreign Investment Law Journal* 3 (Spring 1988): 166–90.

14.   Bertrand P. Marchais, "ICSID and the Courts," *News from ICSID* 3 (Summer 1986): 4.

15.   A detailed decision in this case can be found in "Decision of the Tribunal of Geneva," *ICSID Review — Foreign Investment Law Journal* 1 (Fall 1986): 383–91.

16.   Joy Cherian, "Foreign Investment Arbitration: The Role of the International Center for Settlement of Investment Disputes," in Third World Legal Studies, *Foreign Investment in the Light of the New International Economic Order* (Windsor, Ontario: Third World Legal Studies, 1983), pp. 189–90.

17.   A fuller discussion of this part of the Maritime International Nominees Establishment v. Government of the Republic of Guinea,can be found in Bertrand P. Marchais, "ICSID and the Courts," pp. 4–7.

18.   Delaume, "ICSID Arbitration in Practice," pp. 63–64.

19.   International Centre for Settlement of Investment Disputes, *ICSID Cases*, p. 28.

20.   International Centre for Settlement of Investment Disputes, "List of ICSID Current Cases," (as of February 1998).

21.   International Centre for Settlement of Investment Disputes, *ICSID Cases*, pp. 29–30.

22.   Ibid., p. 30.

23.   Nassib G. Ziadé, "Some Recent Decisions in ICSID Cases," *ICSID Review — Foreign Investment Law Journal* 6 (Fall 1991): 514.

24.   Ibid., p. 515.

25.   Ibid., pp. 515–16. For a detailed discussion and analysis of this case, see "Asian Agricultural Products Ltd. (AAPL) v. Republic of Sri Lanka, Case No. ARB/87/3" in *ICSID Review — Foreign Investment Law Journal* 6 (Fall 1991): 526–97.

6

ICSID's Problems

During its 31 years of operations, several problems with the International Centre for Settlement of Investment Disputes (ICSID) and its procedures have been identified. These problems are analyzed in this chapter. They include the limited jurisdiction of ICSID's arbitration and conciliation activities, its lack of adequate case history, lack of enforcement power over its awards, the apparent recognition of the Calvo Doctrine and its effect on delaying membership in ICSID of Latin American nations, awareness of ICSID's facilities by the international business community, ICSID's inadequate resources with relation to the demand for its services, the agency's general obscurity relative to other multilateral institutions, and the Western cultural orientation of ICSID arbitrators.

LIMITED JURISDICTION

The limited jurisdiction of ICSID's dispute resolution procedure presents a problem. ICSID facilitates arbitration or conciliation only of disputes that arise between foreign investors from a signatory nation and host state governments that have signed the ICSID Convention. Most international business disputes are between private foreign investors and private individuals or companies located in the host state government. As discussed earlier, these disputes are settled amicably between the parties, are adjudicated in the courts, or are handled by private arbitration agencies such as the American Arbitration Association, the International Chamber of Commerce, or those located in Korea, Japan, or other countries.

However, an increasing number of international investment contracts are consummated between foreign investors and host state governments. In some industries, such contracts are prevalent. Petroleum companies are required to operate with contracts with many host state governments. Such companies are quite familiar with ICSID.[1] Thus, it would appear that an agency such as ICSID, which offers arbitration and conciliation services for such contracts, would become increasingly useful in the future.

LACK OF CASE HISTORY

Since the inception of ICSID in 1966, only 45 cases have been brought to ICSID for resolution of a contract dispute between a foreign investor from a signatory nation and a host state signatory government. Of these, 42 have been for arbitration and three for conciliation. At the end of ICSID's FY1997, at least nine of these cases were pending at some stage of the process, either with or without constituting a tribunal.

Very few of these cases have had an award rendered by a tribunal that was accepted by the parties. Of the conciliation disputes, two proceedings were discontinued after the parties reached an agreement. Fourteen of the arbitration cases were settled in a similar manner before an award had been rendered. Arbitral awards were made in thirteen cases but, in four of these cases, one of the parties brought annulment proceedings under Article 52 of the ICSID Convention and, in three of these cases, one of the parties resubmitted the case under the same article of the Convention.

Some of the cases involved national court decisions that related to ICSID. The cases brought before ICSID also involved several different areas of investment including agriculture, banking, construction, energy, health, industrial, mining, and tourism sectors.

Because only nine cases have had awards that have not been annulled or resubmitted, case law evolving from the ICSID procedural system has been relatively light, and, thus, legal principles and foundations derived from ICSID's proceedings have been relatively light. Applicable law evolves from a large body of cases that have had such findings. Very few important legal concepts from the arbitration and conciliation cases under the ICSID Convention have evolved considering the more than three decades of ICSID proceedings.

LACK OF ENFORCEMENT POWER

One of the major problems inherent in any multilateral international organization is the inability to enforce its rules, regulations, and findings. Most such agencies have been established according to a convention that prescribes the rules under which the agency operates. In the case of ICSID, the Convention requires that the parties to an arbitration panel or conciliation committee proceeding must accept the jurisdiction of ICSID and the findings and awards of the panel or committee. International agencies do not have a police force to enforce these rules. They cannot send in troops, as some individual countries have done, except in those cases in which the United Nations works in concert with them to do so. The only real enforcement in such cases is generally the stigma that accrues to the violating nation and that will reduce their future relations with the international community.

Three international aluminum producers brought an investment contract dispute against the Government of Jamaica in 1974. These companies were Alcoa Minerals of Jamaica, Inc., Kaiser Bauxite Company, and Reynolds Metals Company. Each company, a national of the United States, filed a dispute with the Government of Jamaica. Both the United States and Jamaica were signatories to the ICSID Convention. Jamaica did not participate in the selection of an arbitration panel according to the ICSID rules and did not attend the early sessions in 1974 and 1975.

The companies and the Government of Jamaica had, by initiating the procedure, agreed to the ICSID jurisdiction. In 1977, the ICSID proceedings were discontinued at the request of the claimant companies. Jamaica unilaterally withdrew from the proceedings and announced plans to join an international bauxite cartel, as was discussed in the preceding chapter.[2] Technically speaking, the proceedings had been discontinued at the request of the foreign private investor claimants after the Government of Jamaica had made a final settlement. The withdrawal of one of the parties, however, reduced the credibility of the ICSID procedures and facilities in the resolution of investment disputes of this type.

In addition to possible cases in which one of the parties withdraws from the ICSID procedure, problems can also arise when a party to the arbitration or conciliation declines to pay its share of the expenses or to comply with the final award of an arbitration panel or conciliation committee. One signatory host state government did, in fact, fail to pay its share of the procedure expenses and, when an award was made against it, refused to fully honor the award.[3] Again, such a situation can reduce further the credibility of the ICSID procedure.

The stigma from the international community against a country that opted out of an accepted multilateral set of rules was more severe against the Government of Jamaica than any apparent damage suffered by ICSID. Such a result might not always be the case.

THE CALVO DOCTRINE

A major problem that has faced ICSID and other multilateral institutions involving issues that could have legal solutions pertains to the so-called Calvo Doctrine and the reluctance of Latin American nations to become signatories of institutions such as ICSID. The Calvo Doctrine is named for an Argentinian diplomat and jurist, Carlos Calvo. The doctrine evolved from a treatise written by Calvo in 1896, which addressed the cries for protection in Latin American countries as a result of the diplomatic and military intervention in these countries by foreign investors in the nineteenth century stemming from European colonialism.

The Calvo Doctrine, although it is not generally recognized by international law, contends that, if these countries acceded to the international legal concepts, they would be at the mercy of the powerful states and this would be injurious to the weaker nations.[4] Thus, an unjustifiable inequality between nationals and foreigners would be established. The Calvo Doctrine also asserted that recognition of the international standard permitting foreign intervention at that time would go against the fundamental concept of territorial sovereignty maintained by independent nations.

In other words, any form of intervention, whether by foreign courts, foreign government agencies, foreign diplomacy, or foreign governments themselves, in favor of a foreign investor from that country represents an impermissible interference in the internal affairs of the host state.[5] The ICSID Convention and its proceedings, according to this argument, are surrogates for intervention from outside the host state. This argument assumes that international law does not permit such diplomatic intervention. This assumption nullifies a principal attraction of the ICSID Convention that consent to arbitrate according to its rules relieves the host government of any diplomatic importunities by the investor's home state, according to Article 27(1) of the Convention.[6]

The obligation to refrain from protecting one's own nationals has not been denied as a general principle of international law. In fact, the Latin American states have not codified this concept, except among themselves, when advocating the Calvo Doctrine. Essentially, this doctrine contends that a citizen can protect himself against his own government through administrative and judicial remedies as well as by political processes of the home state. Foreign investors cannot do this openly and should not do so covertly, that is, through its home state protection to gain the parity to which they might be entitled in principle.

The Calvo Doctrine attacks diplomatic efforts on behalf of a foreign investor by his home country. The theoretical basis of the right of diplomatic intervention rests on the assumption that the individual has no status in international law. An offense against the individual investor is considered an offense against his nation, which acquires a right to protect him.

Another area attacked by the Calvo Doctrine is how ICSID is used in relation to a foreign investor. It asserts that the rule in international law that foreigners must be treated equally with citizens, as mentioned above, is offended by the use of ICSID. In actuality, ICSID creates a simple procedural device to vindicate the rights of an aggrieved foreign investor. The host state still can require that local administrative and legal remedies be exhausted before the ICSID procedure is initiated.

The Calvo Doctrine was placed in so-called Calvo clauses in contracts between foreign investors and citizens of Latin American states that hosted the foreign investment. The foreign investor, by agreeing to the inclusion of a Calvo clause in the contract, would agree to waive all rights to diplomatic protection afforded him by his own country under international law. Once the foreign investor had waived all foreign legal redress, the foreign investor was left with only legal remedies available in the host state.

Calvo clauses have created a great deal of debate in international circles. Courts have held that each case involving a Calvo clause must be decided on its own merit. A landmark case in 1926, decided by the United States-Mexican Claims Commission, upheld the validity of a Calvo clause contained in a contract between the Mexican Government and a U.S. corporation.[7] The Commission held that alternative international remedies remained available for the foreign investor.

The use of these Calvo clauses by Latin American nations in contracts with foreign investors created a problem for these nations in the ratification of the ICSID Convention. ICSID's major purpose was to furnish a neutral international dispute resolution tool for contracts involving foreign investors and host state governments. The ICSID procedure could not be an available remedy in Latin American nations utilizing Calvo clauses. ICSID, itself, ironically includes a type of Calvo clause in Article 27 of the ICSID Convention. This article reads as follows:

(1) No contracting State shall give diplomatic protection, or bring an international claim, in respect of a dispute which one of its nationals and another contracting State shall have consented to submit or shall have submitted to arbitration under this Convention, unless such other Contracting State shall have failed to abide by and comply with the award rendered in such dispute.

(2) Diplomatic protection, for purposes of paragraph (1), shall not include informal diplomatic exchanges for the sole purpose of facilitating a settlement of the dispute.[8]

The inclusion of these clauses in the ICSID Convention had the effect of restricting ICSID membership to countries that did not recognize Calvo clauses, even though the intention of the writers of these clauses was to strengthen the ICSID dispute resolution procedures.

As a result of the recognition and use of the Calvo Doctrine by Latin American nations, few of these nations became signatories of the ICSID Convention when ICSID was established. Thus, the governments of a large region of the world that needed foreign private investment did not take advantage of this dispute resolution mechanism. The Calvo Doctrine and Calvo clauses hindered the ICSID from gaining credibility as an institution designed to significantly encourage flows of foreign direct investment to less developed countries (LDCs).

Another Reason for Latin American Opposition

Latin American nations had another possible reason for their opposition to the Convention.[9] Countries in this region have long been suspicious of the arbitral, as opposed to the judicial, process. This opposition has not been found in intergovernmental arbitration proceedings but has manifested itself in arbitration between a government and a private person. Such opposition might have stemmed from the foreign intervention experienced by these nations in the past. In terms of private law, several countries in Latin America have expressed an ambivalent attitude toward commercial arbitration, even though in some countries with Spanish background, namely Spain, arbitration has been the accepted practice for a long time. Thus, even commercial arbitration has been used infrequently in Latin America.

One of the arguments that can be used to refute the opposition of Latin America to ICSID is the World Bank's philosophy and the Convention itself. The World Bank has always stressed the voluntary nature of ICSID and the Convention. World Bank members are free to sign the Convention and become members of ICSID or they can choose not to join. Once they have become signatories, they can decide either to use the ICSID facilities or they can decide not to.[10]

Finally, another refutation of the opposition to ICSID by Latin American nations can be found in the Investment Guaranties Agreements concluded between the United States and several Latin American governments.[11] These agreements state that, if the United States makes a payment to an investor under its guaranty, it can succeed to the rights of the investor and can take the claim to a single arbitrator if settlement by negotiation cannot be reached between the U.S. Government and the Latin American government. The single arbitrator can be selected by mutual agreement of the parties or by the International Court of Justice.

Conclusion

During the 1990s, Latin American nations began to recognize the benefits of ICSID. Several nations in Central and South America have ratified the ICSID Convention and a few others have signed the Convention but not yet fully ratified it.[12] Among the nations that have become full members of ICSID are Argentina, Bolivia, Chile, Paraguay, Peru, and Venezuela. Colombia and Uruguay have signed the Convention. It would appear that the Calvo Doctrine will not be a problem for ICSID in the future.

One other breakthrough by foreign investors against the use of the Calvo Doctrine and Calvo clauses in Latin America can be demonstrated by the North American Free Trade Agreement (NAFTA) signed on December 17, 1992, by the Prime Minister of Canada and the Presidents of Mexico and the United States.[13] The investment chapter of NAFTA includes references to ICSID in the section on "Settlement of Disputes Between a Party and an Investor of Another Party." NAFTA parties have agreed that an "investor of a Party" — Party refers to Canada, Mexico, or the United States — can submit to arbitration, under either the ICSID Convention or the Additional Facility Rules of ICSID, described in Chapter 4, or the United Nations Commission on International Trade Law Arbitration Rules, any claim that another state party has violated obligations under the Investment Chapter of NAFTA causing loss or damage to the investor or an enterprise owned or controlled by the investor. This is a small step toward eliminating the acceptance of the Calvo Doctrine and the use of Calvo clauses.

MULTINATIONAL CORPORATION
KNOWLEDGE OF ICSID

Financial versus Legal Issues Involved

Because of the peculiar operations of ICSID, certain officials of multinational corporations (MNCs) are not familiar with the agency and its facilities. ICSID facilitates arbitration or conciliation of disputes involving foreign investors and host state governments. The investor can be a company or an individual, but is more commonly a company making an investment in a foreign country. This is an investment decision, and finance executives in the company usually make such decisions. However, the ICSID procedure involves arbitration or conciliation fraught with arcane legal jargon and the necessity to know case law dealing with dispute resolution.

Thus, chief financial officers of many MNCs are not familiar with ICSID and its facilities.[14] They believe that ICSID is a legal tool and has little to do with international investment. In contrast, a similar study of top international legal counsel of MNCs showed that, despite the fact that dozens of articles have appeared in law reviews and journals about ICSID, they believed ICSID to be a finance tool and, thus, claimed to be unfamiliar with ICSID and its procedures.[15] Other observers of the history of ICSID and its operations have lent credibility to this attitude. One such observer characterized ICSID as an "important novel contribution in the field of international law, and thus one which all lawyers at least must surely welcome as a valuable and unique experiment."[16] Because the bulk of literature published about ICSID has been written by lawyers or has appeared in law journals, this perception that ICSID is primarily a legal institution rings true. At any rate, when research has shown that many top legal counsel of U.S. MNCs during the 1970s lacked familiarity with ICSID even though dozens of articles about the institution had appeared in law journals or law reviews in the 1960s and 1970s, one could infer that international lawyers were not reading their own journals at that time.

Insignificant Institution to the
Business Academic Community

As of the end of ICSID's FY1997, the institution seemed to be a relatively unknown international agency to the business community. In the latest edition of *ICSID Bibliography* published by ICSID in April 1997, the bulk of the citations are law review or journal articles or law books and publications of the agency itself. Of 375 article and book entries in the latest edition, only 25 were written for business academic or arbitration publications.[17] None was cited in political science, international affairs, or economic development journals even though the work of ICSID has implications for these fields.

INADEQUATE RESOURCES FOR THE DEMAND

ICSID was established in 1966 and did not register a proceeding during its first five years of operations. During its next 25 years of operations, ICSID registered 38 cases for arbitration or conciliation. These were fairly well spread out during each five-year period of operations. In only two such periods did the number of cases registered exceed an average of one per year. In those two periods, FY1982–86 and FY1992–96, the average was more than two per year. From FY1992 until the present, 19 cases have been registered with seven in FY1997 alone. The 1990s represent the busiest period in the ICSID's history, and FY1997 was the busiest year.

Because ICSID merely facilitates the appointment of arbitral tribunals or conciliation commissions and does not have an active role in the proceedings, the agency must render the logistical support needed for these proceedings (for example, scheduling, site selection, and panel member appointments). In addition, the other activities discussed earlier need care and attention. These include the model clause development, work on the various publications produced by ICSID, sponsorship and organization of conferences, workshops, and symposia, and a myriad other activities dealing with investment laws, treaties, and other legislative matters in signatory states that advance the objective of expanding flows of foreign direct investment into LDCs.

If FY1997 is any indication, many of the problems with which ICSID has had to deal, for example, paucity of a body of cases, solution of the Calvo Doctrine problem in Latin America, enforcement of awards, lack of awareness on the part of international business companies, and so forth, have been solved. Thus, its services will be in greater demand in the coming years, especially in the area of arbitration of disputes between foreign investors and host states, a growing area in the field of foreign investment contracts.

ICSID always has maintained a small staff and a small budget to carry out its responsibilities. Arbitrators and conciliators are not paid by the agency, and the latter charges out-of-pocket costs of proceedings to the parties. It, thus, subsidizes the process. Its staff generally has consisted of a small group of attorneys, legal secretaries, and a few regular secretaries.

The trend of arbitration registrations from one per year to seven or more per year can overwhelm the agency, especially if the objective of speedy resolutions is to be maintained. Some of the proceedings already have extended into several years to the point where the parties in some cases have settled the dispute themselves. A greater share of the expenses of the proceedings might have to be paid by the parties.

OTHER PROBLEMS

Although hundreds of publications about ICSID can be cited, the institution remains rather obscure. A small, four-page brochure can be obtained from ICSID, which is sufficiently informative about the agency's procedures. When one considers the ICSID semiannual journal, its semiannual newsletter, the minutes of its administrative council, and the dozens of articles found in law journals and business periodical publications, it is difficult to understand why the agency remains so obscure. The financial and legal nature of the cases submitted to ICSID remains one of the reasons why the obscurity continues. As mentioned above, legal counsel of MNCs seem to believe that these cases involve financial investment issues, whereas chief financial officers of many of these same MNCs believe that the cases involve primarily legal issues. Thus, the lack of cooperation between the legal and financial functions in these international companies, coupled with the narrow jurisdiction of ICSID, could cause the agency to be underestimated in its value.

Finally, another possible problem can be found in the culture within which ICSID tribunals operate. These tribunals usually have been Western-oriented with European or American members.[18] Investment agreements have been interpreted with this Western orientation, which affects the proceedings and awards. In the case of Société Benvenuti & Bonfant v. Government of the People's Republic of the Congo (Case No. ARB/77/2), the tribunal held that "the obligation . . . not to nationalize . . . without just compensation . . . [constitutes] one of the generally recognized principles of international law." The tribunal's award compensated the injured foreign investor for the "full fair market value" of its loss. This award was more sensitive to the foreign investor. It is possible that ICSID's enforcement of binding arbitration agreements is restricted by its inability to render awards that are more sensitive to LDCs.

SUMMARY AND CONCLUSIONS

Several problems encountered by ICSID were discussed in this chapter. These problems include jurisdiction limited to disputes between foreign investors from signatory nations and host state signatories, lack of case history, lack of enforcement power, the Calvo Doctrine as a hindrance to Latin American country memberships, lack of awareness or confusion about ICSID's role on the part of top officials of MNCs, and inadequate resources in comparison with the rising demand for services.

NOTES

1. James C. Baker and John K. Ryans, Jr., "A Little Known Solution to Investment Disputes in High Risk Countries," *Akron Business and Economic Review* 6 (Fall 1975): 8, 12.

2. "Termination of Two Proceedings in Bauxite Cases," *World Bank News Release*, March 17, 1977, p. 1.

3. "Annual Meeting of the Administrative Council of the International Centre for Settlement of Investment Disputes," *Proceedings of ICSID Administrative Council* 21 (1987): 3.

4. See James C. Baker and Lois J. Yoder, "ICSID and the Calvo Clause: A Hindrance to Foreign Direct Investment in LDCs," *Ohio State Journal on Dispute Resolution* 5 (1989): 93–112.

5. Paul C. Szasz, "The Investment Disputes Convention and Latin America," *Virginia Journal of International Law* 11 (1971): 260.

6. Ibid.

7. North American Dredging Co. of Texas v. United Mexican States 4 *International Arbitration Awards* 21, 26 (1926).

8. International Centre for Settlement of Investment Disputes, "Art. 27(1) and (2)," *ICSID Convention on the Settlement of Investment Disputes Between States and Nationals of Other States* (Washington, D.C.: International Centre for Settlement of Investment Disputes, 1966).

9. Szasz, "The Investment Disputes Convention and Latin America," pp. 262–63.

10. Ibid., pp. 259–60.

11. Ibid., p. 264.

12. International Centre for Settlement of Investment Disputes, *Annual Report* (Washington, D.C.: International Centre for Settlement of Investment Disputes, 1997), pp. 15–17.

13. Antonio R. Parra, "ICSID and New Trends in International Dispute Settlement," *News from ICSID* 10 (Winter 1993): 8.

14. See James C. Baker and John K. Ryans, Jr., "ICSID, A Little-Known Solution to Investment Disputes," pp. 8–12.

15.   See John K. Ryans, Jr. and James C. Baker, "The International Centre for Settlement of Investment Disputes (ICSID)," *Journal of World Trade Law* 10 (January/February 1976): 65–79.

16.   David M. Sassoon, "Convention on the Settlement of Investment Disputes," *Journal of Business Law* (London), October 1965, p. 339.

17.   International Centre for Settlement of Investment Disputes, *ICSID Bibliography* (Washington, D.C.: International Centre for Settlement of Investment Disputes, 1997).

18.   Ray August, *International Business Law: Text, Cases, and Readings* (Englewood Cliffs, N.J.: Prentice-Hall, 1993), p. 89.

III

MULTILATERAL INVESTMENT GUARANTEE AGENCY

7

The Evolution of MIGA

The Multilateral Investment Guarantee Agency (MIGA) is the only truly global multilateral investment insurance institution. The agency insures private investment by foreign investors of MIGA member countries when such investment is made in a MIGA member country considered to be a developing nation. The foreign investment is insured against political risks that can manifest themselves in the host country. These risks consist of acts of the host government that impede the convertibility of local currency into an external currency; result in interference or repudiation of a contract or agreement between the foreign investor and a local investor or the host state government; result in loss of assets because of expropriation or nationalization by the host government; or result in loss or damage to assets owned by the foreign investor in the host state from violence caused by civil war, insurrection, coup, or revolution.

REASONS FOR THE ESTABLISHMENT OF MIGA

The establishment of MIGA was the result of several incidents. These ranged from the Cuban Revolution and its takeover of foreign private property to the formation in the United States of the Overseas Private Investment Corporation (OPIC), the bilateral investment insurance agency, to the formation of a multilateral investment insurance agency in the Arab countries, to studies over a long period by the World Bank concerning the problem of political risk and foreign direct investment (FDI) in less developed countries (LDCs).

Effects of Foreign Investment Expropriation from 1950 to 1970

During the 1950s, the Cuban Revolution led to the Fidel Castro regime. This regime expropriated all foreign private property in Cuba. No investment insurance was available to the foreign investors that owned this property, except for individual policies held with private insurers for small amounts of coverage. The massive takeover of private property in Cuba, especially property held by Americans, led to action in the U.S. Congress to satisfy U.S. investors in some way.

Other nationalizations of foreign investment took place during this period. In the 1960s, the Tunisian Government passed legislation to expropriate French investments in that country and made the law retroactive. In 1970, the Chilean Government took over the foreign copper companies, mostly American, under the guise that they had not paid their fair share of income taxes to the government. These and other takeovers produced a demand for some type of foreign investment insurance agency.

The Debt Crisis of 1982

Another area of international finance incurred problems in the early 1980s, which exacerbated the problem of inadequate flows of private foreign investment to the LDCs. In 1982, Mexico announced that it could not meet the payments on a large loan made to the country by an international syndicate of banks. This happened at the time another jumbo loan was being prepared for that country. The result was the first of many near defaults of sovereign loans during the early 1980s that led to massive rescheduling of these loans by the international banking community. Interest rates were relatively high at that time, whether LIBOR in the Eurocurrency market or U.S. prime rates, and these high rates made loan repayment quite difficult for the LDCs, who already were burdened with high energy import costs.

From 1981 to 1984, the net flow of FDI to LDCs declined from $53.4 billion dollars in 1978–81, the immediate period preceding the debt crisis, to $39.7 billion in 1982–85, the immediate period following the debt crisis, or by 26 percent.[1]

The nationalizations of the 1959–70 period and the international debt crisis of the 1980s combined to cause this significant decline in the flow of FDI into LDCs. This decline in external private funds created further political problems in many LDCs, making the need for private foreign investment insurance even more necessary if necessary development projects in the LDCs were to be adequately funded.

FORERUNNERS OF MIGA

Two important investment insurance agencies were the most significant forerunners of MIGA and furnished the catalyst for the international community to establish MIGA. These were OPIC, a bilateral national agency, and the Inter-Arab Investment Guarantee Corporation, a multilateral agency whose investment insurance was available only for Arabs investing in the Arab World.

Overseas Private Investment Corporation

The first institution created in the United States to deal with the insurance of foreign investment was the OPIC, established by the Foreign Assistance Act of 1969.[2] Since 1971, it has conducted the national investment guarantee program for the United States. OPIC provides insurance, loans, and loan guarantees to promote investment in risky LDCs. The agency supports only projects that help the economic and social development of LDCs.

The United States was the first nation to have an investment guarantee program and, in 1948, the program was implemented under the Economic Cooperation Act of 1948 and initially guaranteed only currency convertibility. The authority for this program was increased and further broadened until the end of 1959 and was given authority under several U.S. foreign assistance programs.

During this period, the program suffered from several problems. The business community was never very familiar with the program. Most of the investment guarantees issued were for projects in Europe and very few focussed on investments in the LDCs. The amount of funds available for investment insurance was never very sufficient.

The Cuban Revolution under Fidel Castro in 1959 resulted in massive expropriation of foreign investments in Cuba. This event triggered a demand within the U.S. international business community for a better national program for foreign investment insurance. During the 1960s, a more comprehensive national program emerged, first under the Foreign Assistance Act of 1961 during the Kennedy Administration and, finally under OPIC, the program began to flourish in the 1970s, especially after the expropriation of U.S. copper companies in Chile in 1970.

OPIC provides three types of political risk insurance coverage: currency inconvertibility and transfer risk — the investor's legal ability to convert and take out profits from a foreign investment, service debt, or make other remittances from local currency; loss of assets from expropriation or creeping expropriation, nationalization, or confiscation by a foreign government; and loss of assets or income caused by war, revolution, insurrection or politically motivated civil strife, terrorism, or sabotage. If the losses from these actions are caused by deliberate acts of the host government, they are classified as political risks and can be covered by OPIC insurance. OPIC does not cover losses that stem from commercial risks.

OPIC has conducted the national investment guarantee program of the United States as an independent agency since 1971. It is a bilateral agency in that it guarantees only the foreign investments of U.S. citizens made in LDCs or other countries where political risk can be present.

To be eligible for OPIC coverage, several criteria are required.[3] The equity investments in and loans to foreign projects must be owned by U.S. citizens and U.S. companies or their foreign subsidiaries. The projects must be in one of the 145 countries that have signed bilateral protocols with the United States. The projects must show that they have social and economic value to the host country and will not harm the U.S. economy.

OPIC's coverage is divided into two classifications: the "current insured amount," the amount of coverage actually in effect at a given time, and the "standby insured amount," or the assurance that OPIC will provide future coverage, up to the maximum amount specified in each contract covered.[4] OPIC insurance can cover up to $200 million per project or up to 90 percent of equity investments and 100 percent of loans, whichever is less. The maximum term is 20 years for OPIC insurance. The investment must be an initial project although it can include modernization or expansion of existing facilities.

Since OPIC was formed, it has insured investments worth nearly $80 billion. In 1995, OPIC wrote $8.6 billion in political risk insurance, up from $6 billion in 1994, and $2.4 billion in 1993. Its authorized insurance capacity is $13.5 billion.[5] Rates on OPIC political risk policies range from 12.5 cents to 90 cents per $100 of insurance, depending on the project and coverage.[6]

In addition to its political risk insurance activities, OPIC performs other functions. The agency conducts investment missions to LDCs offering investment opportunities for U.S. business firms. OPIC also makes direct loans to LDC projects but only for investments by small U.S.

businesses or cooperatives, defined as having revenues or net worth less than that of the smallest firm on the *Fortune 1000* list. These loans generally range from $100,000 to $4 million. For example, a $1 million loan was made to Jamaica Broilers, Ltd., a subsidiary of a U.S. company, to construct and equip a fully integrated poultry breeder farm. The same project received a $750,000 loan the following year to further expand and upgrade the farm. This farm's facilities are now the largest and most efficient in the Caribbean area.[7]

As mentioned in Chapter 2, bilateral agencies have some disadvantages compared with multilateral institutions. Chief among these disadvantages is that bilateral agencies tend to have political agendas that favor the home country. OPIC has had other problems in addition to being a bilateral agency that caters only to U.S. investors. In the past, it has had financial problems when required to cut its spending to conform to U.S. budgetary considerations. In addition, its coverage of political risks has been limited to coverage of only expropriation, currency inconvertibility, and war damage. It generally has not covered contract repudiation or interference when such stems from a political risk. Its financial coverage generally is less than that of a global agency such as MIGA. In U.S. Senate Subcommittee hearings on multinational corporations (MNCs), testimony criticized the agency's insurance as a benefit to MNCs in that it lowered political risk, did not encourage MNCs to invest in the poorest LDCs, and furnished little aid to LDCs.[8] Finally, although OPIC's twin objectives are to protect the interests of the U.S. investor and assist LDCs in their economic development, these two objectives can often be in direct contradiction. OPIC-insured projects can foster confrontations between the United States and host governments in some cases.

The Inter-Arab Agency

The Inter-Arab Investment Guarantee Corporation was established in 1974 by the Convention on the Settlement of Investment Disputes between Host States of Arab Investments and Nationals of Other Arab States to offer investment guarantees to investments that flow among its Arab member countries. Thus, this remedy resulted in a regional organization and did not offer a global solution to the insurance of foreign investments against political risk. However, the formation of this institution and the 1982 international debt crisis started when the Mexican Government defaulted on a jumbo loan and created the catalyst for intensive study by the World Bank of a global solution to the problem. As will be seen later, this organization and its convention was one of the models on which MIGA was based.

EARLY STUDIES BY REGIONAL GROUPS AND THE WORLD BANK

Foreign investment insurance of noncommercial risks on a multinational basis became a serious topic of discussion based on the political acts discussed above and the advent and weaknesses of several national insurance programs. An early proposal for such a program was made by a working group of the Council of Europe's Consultative Assembly in 1957. The Economic Committee of the Council of Europe reconsidered this in 1959. However, the proposed program was limited to European investments in African countries. These discussions were coupled at the private level by bankers and industrialists in the 1960s and among these was one such proposal by Dutch banker E. H. Van Eeghen at the International Chamber of Commerce meetings in 1960–61.[9] In 1965, the Organisation for Economic Co-operation and Development in conjunction with the International Chamber of Commerce proposed the establishment of an International Investment Guarantee Corporation.

This and the other institutions failed for several reasons. The significant reason was not so much the objectives — which most claimed were worthy — but the complex organizational structure of an agency such as the International Investment Guarantee Corporation.[10] These proposed agencies had five specific conflicts, especially with the World Bank — an institution that had been studying the problem for several years.[11] These conflicts were the linkage between the agency and the World Bank, the distribution of voting rights between developing and developed countries, the nature of financial participation by developing countries, subrogation as a means of recovery by the agency, and arbitration as a means of dispute settlement.

A global agency to insure foreign investment against political risks was the topic of several studies conducted by the World Bank off and on from 1961 to 1981. During the 1981 World Bank annual meetings, Bank President A. W. Clausen discussed a MIGA proposal during an address to the Bank's Board of Governors. During the 1970s, bank loans had furnished a great deal of foreign private investment. During the 1980s, such funding became balance of payments financing rather than project finance. World Bank officials, thus, pushed for an agency that could insure FDI project financing. The culmination of the events of the 1959–82 period — the Cuban expropriations of foreign investments after the Castro Revolution, the Chilean expropriations of foreign copper companies in 1970, and the LDC debt crisis of the early 1980s — prompted the World Bank to accelerate the establishment of a global agency that could alleviate these problems with international investment insurance.

Finally in 1985, the World Bank drafted a Convention Establishing the Multilateral Investment Guarantee Agency (MIGA Convention). This draft was presented to member governments and Switzerland for their approval.[12] The broad objective of MIGA is found in Article 2 of the MIGA Convention and is "to encourage the flow of investments for productive purposes among member countries and in particular to developing member countries."[13] The preamble to the MIGA Convention further recognizes that "the flow of foreign investment to developing countries would be facilitated and further encouraged by alleviating concerns related to non-commercial risks."[14] The insurance of foreign investment in LDCs would alleviate such risks. A study was undertaken for the OPIC, which concluded that, in 25 percent of the cases examined, foreign investments would not have been made without a guarantee of some type. In 18 percent of the cases, foreign investments would have been made without a guarantee. Thus, investment guarantees did appear to be important in many cases of FDI.[15]

ADOPTION OF MIGA

During the next three years, World Bank member governments examined and approved the MIGA Convention. By April 1988, governments of five capital-exporting and 15 capital-importing countries had ratified the MIGA Convention and subscribed capital amounting to one-third of MIGA's total authorized capital. The new agency's operations were facilitated by the contribution of U.S. capital, amounting to 20 percent of MIGA's authorized capital. As a result, MIGA became operative as an affiliate of the World Bank. Its first full year of operations was accomplished in the agency's FY1989–90.

ITS BENEFITS

MIGA's benefits are derived from its principal concepts and operating characteristics. To reiterate, the convention that established MIGA stated that the agency's primary objective "shall be to encourage the flow of investments for productive purposes among member countries, and in particular to developing member countries." To implement this objective, MIGA provides investment guarantees (or insurance) against major political risks in its developing member countries to foreign private investors from any of its member countries and investment marketing services to assist its developing member countries in attracting FDI.[16]

MIGA was designed to encourage foreign private investment in LDCs by the incorporation of several principal concepts.[17] These are: flexibility in the design of its coverage; underwriting on the basis of project specifics rather than on host country assessments, combination of guarantee operations with technical activities to improve investment conditions, special attention to the promotion of investment among developing countries, host governments' control over MIGA's involvement in investments in their territories, legal financial independence from the World Bank and the International Finance Corporation (IFC), complementarity to existing investment guarantee and insurance programs, financial self-sufficiency, joint political oversight and financial responsibility of both developed and developing member countries, and voluntary membership.

MIGA was established to alleviate the weaknesses of the international investment insurance industry. Most insurance agencies were unable or unwilling to provide the types of coverage foreign investors needed. Most national insurance agencies applied restrictive eligibility criteria to foreign investment projects. In general, private insurers did not offer investment insurance coverage for risk of loss from currency transfer or war and violence damages.

MIGA's operations have several significant characteristics.[18] First,the agency's insurance coverage is more comprehensive, broad, and flexible than most national systems or private market insurers. It covers four of the five areas of political risk, that is, noncommercial risk — currency inconvertibility, war and civil disturbance, expropriation or nationalization, and breach, interference, or repudiation of contract. It covers equity-type investments as well as licensing and franchise agreements, turnkey contracts, and investments involving transfer of technology. MIGA can insure expansion, modernization, and privatization projects as well as new investments.

Second, MIGA is an autonomous organization with full juridical personality. Thus, it is legally and financially separate from the World Bank. Its membership is open to World Bank members and Switzerland but a country can join MIGA no matter what its position is with the World Bank.

Third, MIGA carries out several supporting and service functions. These include research, provision of information and policy advice, and activities designed to encourage private foreign investment in the LDCs.

The latter activity includes cooperative ventures with the Foreign Investment Advisory Service, a division of the IFC. IFC's operations were discussed earlier.

Fourth, MIGA is self-supporting. Its solvency is insured by members' share capital of which 10 percent is paid in cash with another 10 percent paid in non-negotiable, non–interest-bearing promissory notes. The remaining 80 percent is subject to call. Its guarantees cannot exceed 1.5 times the amount of subscribed capital plus reserves plus a portion of its reinsurance coverage.

Finally, MIGA fully recognizes the sovereign rights of its member governments and does not guarantee any investment without the approval of the host government. It does not interfere with the political affairs of its members. Once all World Bank members have joined MIGA, its voting structure will become based on equal voting power. This will be true whether the member country exports or imports capital.

ALTERNATIVE SOURCES OF INVESTMENT PROTECTION

In addition to OPIC and the Arab agency discussed above, alternative means of investment protection have been available at times for U.S. investors.[19] In general, these have been categorized in three areas: bilateral treaties that include provisions prohibiting expropriation without compensation, statutory sanctions against nations who expropriate U.S. investments, and insurance programs including OPIC and private insurers.

In the treaty area, some protection has been available for private investors in any country with which the United States has negotiated the Friendship, Commerce and Navigation treaty. These treaties contain mutual covenants, which either forbid expropriation or provide a standard of compensation when expropriation is necessary for public interest.

Hickenlooper Amendments have been used to provide protection for U.S. private foreign investments. These are statutory provisions that require suspension of U.S. foreign aid to host countries that expropriate U.S. investments without adequate compensation. These sanctions have not been very effective.

Private Insurers

Private market insurance is also available to cover loss from both commercial and political risks.[20] Several multinational insurers offer coverage for expropriation of both new and existing foreign investments. Such coverage also can be available against currency inconvertibility and the risks of arbitrary drawdowns of on-demand bank guarantees or bonds. Commercial risks of contract repudiation also can be covered. Private coverage generally is not available for losses from war damage.

The largest of these private insurers is the American International Group. In addition to the American International Group, coverage is also available from Lloyds of London — usually on a reinsurance basis, the Chubb Group of Insurance Companies, the Insurance Company of North America, and the Continental Corporation. These property-casualty insurers generally cover the least risky of the LDCs and their coverage is limited in other ways. Their coverage is relatively less than that of the national government agencies or the multilateral institutions because one major loss can wipe out 1-2 years' premiums. Thus, their portfolios are large and quite diversified. Their coverage also has relatively short periods to maturity. In addition, most political risk insurance companies tend to co-insure or reinsure some of the higher risk guarantees in their portfolios.

Banks as Insurers

In recent years, some large international banks have entered the political risk insurance business. For example, Bank of America and Citicorp have established political risk departments that conduct licensed insurance operations.

SUMMARY AND CONCLUSIONS

Developing countries need private investment in order to improve their economies. For many reasons, domestic capital is insufficient to accomplish this. Foreign investment is needed to fill the gap. The most efficient foreign investment is private investment flowing into the LDC as direct investment.

In Chapter 1 many reasons for why political risk has generally been too high in many LDCs to encourage the necessary flow of private FDI into these countries were analyzed and discussed. Some type of investment insurance program was needed, especially in light of events such as the Castro Revolution expropriations of foreign private property, the debt crisis of the 1980s in LDCs, Tunisia's arbitrary takeover of French assets, the Chilean Government's takeover of the foreign copper companies, and many other instances including violence from civil wars, coups, and terrorism in many of these countries.

During the 1960s, 1970s, and early 1980s, investment insurance was offered by national government systems such as OPIC and by private property-casualty insurance companies. These programs did not provide sufficient coverage or were too political. After several years of discussion and debate in regional government organizations and the World Bank, a multilateral program to furnish investment insurance was designed and presented to World Bank members for their approval and funding. It was modeled after a multilateral investment insurance agency that had been established in the Arab world to insure investments of Arab investors in other Arab countries.

This program became MIGA, to be headquartered in Washington, D.C., which would insure investments of investors from member countries against losses from political risks in LDC member countries. The agency became operative in 1988 when five capital-exporting countries and 15 capital-importing countries had ratified the Convention establishing the agency. Its first full year of operations was accomplished in FY1990.

MIGA has a major advantage over other insurers, public and private. Its political risk coverage is the broadest of any of the other insurers. It is able to insure against losses from four of the five major political risks. Neither MIGA nor any of the other insurers protects companies against losses from unfair regulations in the host country, often a major cause of losses in foreign projects in LDCs. However, such losses can be made part of arbitration proceedings under the jurisdiction of the International Centre for Settlement of Investment Disputes (ICSID), provided the foreign investor is from an ICSID signatory country and the host state government is also a signatory. An award under this arbitration procedure is possible in such cases.

MIGA's operations will be discussed in the next four chapters. Chapter 8 contains a discussion about how MIGA operates. The agency's operations of its several functions for the FY1990–97 period will be discussed in Chapter 9. Selected projects, which MIGA has guaranteed during this period, will be analyzed in Chapter 10. Chapter 11 contains a discussion of the problems that MIGA has confronted since its first year of operations.

NOTES

1. Jurgen Voss, "The Multilateral Investment Guarantee Agency: Status, Mandate, Concept, Features, Implications," *Journal of World Trade Law* 21 (August 1987): 8.

2.   See Alan C. Brennglass, *The Overseas Private Investment Corporation: A Study in Political Risk* (New York: Praeger, 1983) and Benjamin A. Javits, *Peace by Investment* (New York: Funk & Wagnalls, 1950) for detailed discussion of the evolution of OPIC.

3.   "Project Finance," *Institutional Investor* 29 (October 1995): 122.

4.   S. Linn Williams, "Political And Other Risk Insurance: Eximbank, OPIC and MIGA," *Middle East Executive Reports* 11 (February 1988): 15.

5.   See Mark A. Hofmann, "OPIC Loses Bid for Reauthorization," *Business Insurance* 30 (1996): 1, 77, 78; Ronan Lyons, "OPIC Makes Political Capital," *Project & Trade Finance* 146 (1995): 30–31; Overseas Private Investment Corporation, *Introduction to OPIC* (Washington, D.C.: Overseas Private Investment Corporation, 1996) found at http://www.ita.doc.gov/mena/opic.html.

6.   Josh Martin, "OPIC: Your Link To Global Investment," *Management Review* 79 (March 1990): 48.

7.   Delphos International, "Financing," *Business America* 112 (March 25, 1991): 21.

8.   Dan Haendel, *Foreign Investments and the Management of Political Risk* (Boulder, Colo.: Westview Press, 1979), pp. 46–47.

9.   Klaus Peter Berger, "The New Multilateral Investment Guarantee Agency: Globalizing the Investment Insurance Approach Towards Development," *Syracuse Journal of International Law and Commerce* 15 (1988): 22.

10.   Ibid., p. 23.

11.   Ibid., p. 24.

12.   For detailed coverage of the evolution of this Convention, see Ibrahim F. I. Shihata, "MIGA and the Standards Applicable to Foreign Investment," *ICSID Review — Foreign Investment Law Journal* 1 (1986): 327–39.

13.   Ibid., p. 329.

14.   Ibid., p. 330.

15.   Ibrahim F. I. Shihata, "Increasing Private Capital Flows to LDCs," *Finance & Development* 20 (December 1984): 7–8.

16.   Multilateral Investment Guarantee Agency, *MIGA Business Profile 1997* (Washington, D.C.: Multilateral Investment Guarantee Agency, 1997), p. 1.

17.   Voss, "The Multilateral Investment Guarantee Agency," p. 9.

18.   G. E. Lota, "The Multilateral Investment Guarantee Agency: History," *Credit & Financial Management* 88 (1986): 38.

19.   Patrick K. O'Hare, "The Convention on the Settlement of Investment Disputes," *Stanford Journal of International Studies* 6 (1971): 160–61.

20.   Williams, "Political and Other Risk Insurance," p. 24.

8

MIGA's Structure

This chapter is devoted to a discussion of the operations and structure of the Multilateral Investment Guarantee Agency (MIGA). These activities include its organization structure, investment insurance and eligibility, MIGA insurance coverage, availability of coverage, the guarantee application process, the agency's reinsurance activity, co-payment procedures, how guarantees are paid, how the agency is funded, and its non-guarantee services including seminars and conferences, reports, and its collaboration with the International Finance Corporation (IFC).

MIGA'S ORGANIZATIONAL STRUCTURE

MIGA is legally and financially independent, although it is considered an affiliate of the World Bank. Its membership is open to all World Bank member states and Switzerland. MIGA is governed by a Council of Governors, which consists of one representative from each member country. The Council of Governors elects a board of directors that is responsible for the day-to-day operations of MIGA and the election of a president. The president is responsible for the conduct of ordinary business by the agency. The president of the World Bank is *ex officio* chairman of the MIGA board of directors.[1] Thus, the influence of the World Bank is maintained and can be quite heavy at times.

The voting structure of the agency follows from the Bretton Woods model of weighted voting. This model gives each member country 177 membership votes plus one additional vote per share subscribed. The drafters of the MIGA Convention attempted to avoid a majority vote by capital-exporting countries. To insure such an objective, both capital-exporting and capital-importing countries were guaranteed a minimum of 40 percent of total voting power during the first three years of MIGA operations. This was enabled by the assignment of supplementary voting shares when necessary. During this initial period, all decisions required a special majority of two-thirds of total voting power, which had to represent at least 55 percent of total capital subscribed.

The MIGA Convention requires the agency to be financially self-sufficient.[2] It must pay claims and other liabilities from premium income and any other revenues such as returns on investment. Only 10 percent of the subscriptions are paid in cash. An additional 10 percent are paid in the form of non-negotiable, non–interest-bearing promissory notes, which will only be redeemed if MIGA needs the cash to pay financial obligations. The remaining 80 percent of the subscribed capital is subject to call by the agency.

All member nations must subscribe to shares in proportion to their relative economic strength as measured by their allocation of shares in the capital of the World Bank. Member developing nations can make up to 25 percent of the paid-in cash portion of their subscriptions in their own currencies. Developed member countries make their subscription payments in freely convertible currencies. At the end of MIGA's FY1997, the agency had 160 signatory members, 141 of which had completed all membership requirements. MIGA's total capital amounted to almost $213 million.[3]

INSURING FOREIGN DIRECT INVESTMENT WITH MIGA GUARANTEES

MIGA offers guarantees against losses incurred by foreign investors that arise from the four major political risks — currency inconvertibility, expropriation, war and civil disturbances, and breach of contract — in less developed countries (LDCs). As mentioned earlier, the foreign investor must be from a MIGA member country, and the host state government must be a signatory of the MIGA Convention.

To clarify the above-mentioned eligibility, a foreign investor corporation can obtain coverage from MIGA if it is incorporated and has its principal place of business in a member country or nationals of a member country own a majority of the corporation. If state-owned enterprises operate on a commercial basis, they are eligible for MIGA coverage.

MIGA's coverage generally is limited to new investments. However, acquisitions that involve privatization of state-owned enterprises and new capital investments dealing with the expansion, modernization, or financial restructuring of existing enterprises also can be insured by MIGA.

MIGA'S COVERAGE

MIGA offers coverage for more types of political risk than other insurers, whether they are multilateral or bilateral government agencies or private insurers. All four major types of political risks are covered. See Figure 8.1 for a discussion of these four major political risks. MIGA's insurance coverage of these four political risks is discussed in the following sections.[4]

FIGURE 8.1
Political Risk Covered by MIGA

Currency Transfer Restriction
    These are restrictions that prevent lenders from converting local currency into foreign exchange and/or transferring the proceeds abroad.

Expropriation
    This is the act of a host government, which reduces or eliminates ownership of, control over, or rights to the insured investment and can be either a direct or indirect act.

War and Civil Disturbance
    This is an act that results in damage to, or destruction or disappearance of, tangible assets or interference with the ability of the foreign enterprise to operate and can include politically motivated acts of sabotage or terrorism.

Breach of Contract
    This refers to an act of a host government involved in a contract with the foreign investor, provided the investor obtains an arbitration award or judicial sentence for damages and is unable to enforce the award after a specified period or is unable to obtain the award or sentence.

Source: Multilateral Investment Guarantee Agency, *MIGA Annual Report 1997* (Washington, D.C.: Multilateral Investment Guarantee Agency), p. 11.

Transfer Restriction

MIGA's coverage against this risk protects against losses that stem from a foreign investor's inability to convert local currency into foreign exchange for transfer to another country. Such local currency can be in the form of remitted capital, interest on loans, principal payments on loans, remitted profits, royalties from licensing agreements, and other remittances such as management fees to the parent company. The coverage insures not only inconvertibility but also against excessive delays in the acquisition of foreign exchange caused by host government action, by adverse changes in exchange control laws or regulations, or by deterioration in conditions that govern the conversion and transfer of local currency. MIGA does not guarantee against currency devaluation.

Expropriation

If acts of the host government reduce or eliminate ownership of, control over, or rights to the investment insured by MIGA, the loss is protected. Creeping expropriation is covered as well. This is a form of expropriation that occurs over time, after a series of government acts. MIGA will pay the net book value of the insured investment. If funds are expropriated, MIGA pays the insured portion of the blocked funds. MIGA also can insure the outstanding principal and any accrued and unpaid interest for loans or loan guaranties.

Breach of Contract

MIGA's coverage protects against losses that arise from the host government's breach or repudiation of a contract with the investor. In the event of such interference by the host state government of a contract with a foreign investor, the investor must be able to initiate a dispute resolution procedure such as arbitration of the underlying contract and obtain an award for damages. A mechanism such as the International Centre for Settlement of Investment Disputes (ICSID) arbitral procedure can be utilized to obtain such an award.

War and Civil Disturbance

MIGA insures against loss from damage to, or the destruction or disappearance of, tangible assets caused by politically motivated acts of war or civil disturbance in the host country. These acts include revolution, insurrection, *coups d'état*, sabotage, and terrorism. In terms of equity investments, MIGA will cover the investor's share of the least of the book value of the assets, of their replacement cost, or of the cost of repair of damaged assets. In terms of loans and loan guaranties, MIGA covers the insured portion of the principal and interest payments in default as a direct result of damage to the assets of the project caused by war or civil disturbance.

MIGA's insurance contracts are for a longer term than those of other insurers. The coverage on MIGA contracts is for 15 years with possible extensions up to 20 years. At the other extreme are private insurers whose coverage generally is limited to 1–3 years.[5] The MIGA investment insurance guarantee cannot be terminated by MIGA unless the insured party defaults on contractual obligations. The coverage can be reduced or canceled by the insured on any anniversary date of the contract after the third anniversary.

MIGA bases its premiums on the type of project and type of coverage, for example, manufacturing or currency transfer. The project-specific conditions are considered. In contrast, most national, bilateral investment, insurance systems set premiums on the basis of the political riskiness of the country in which the foreign investment is made.[6] Annual premiums for each type of coverage or type of project are set in the range of 0.50–1.25 percent of the amount insured. Most rates offered by other insurers are lower because the host government subsidizes them, whereas MIGA is a self-supporting institution. Base rates can be raised or lowered for any particular project if that project's risk profile changes. The premium structure established by MIGA is shown in Table 8.1.

The percentages shown in Table 8.1 measure the maximum amount of guarantee available in each of the four risk categories and for the insured investment project.[7] In other words, MIGA can cover up to 90 percent of the investment contribution by the foreign investor and up to an additional 180 percent for earnings attributable to the investment — in the case of equity — or an additional 90 percent for interest accruing to the insured principal — in the case of loans or loan guaranties. The current amount of guarantee corresponds to the amount of coverage in force for that portion of the investment at risk during any one contract year. The difference between these two magnitudes is the standby amount of guarantee, the reserve of insurance coverage that the investor can put into effect at any annual election of coverage to account for any changes in the value or amount of the investment at risk. See Figure 8.2 for examples of the standby amount of guarantee. MIGA does not insure against losses that stem

TABLE 8.1
MIGA's Premium Rates
(Annual Base Rates by Percentage)

Type of Guarantee	Current	Standby
Manufacturing and Services		
Transfer Restriction	0.50	0.25
Expropriation	0.60	0.30
Breach of Contract	0.80	0.40
War & Civil Disturbance	0.55	0.25
Natural Resources*		
Transfer Restriction	0.50	0.25
Expropriation	0.90	0.45
Breach of Contract	1.00	0.50
War & Civil Disturbance	0.55	0.25
Infrastructure/Oil & Gas		
Transfer Restriction	0.50	0.25
Expropriation	1.25	0.50
Breach of Contract	1.25	0.50
War & Civil Disturbance	0.70	0.30

*Includes agribusiness and forestry projects involving land ownership or concessions and other types of projects involving large landholdings.
Source: Multilateral Investment Guarantee Agency, *Investment Guarantee Guide* (Washington, D.C.: Multilateral Investment Guarantee Agency, 1997), p. 8.

from unfair regulatory application by the host state. These losses can become part of an arbitration procedure filed with ICSID. No other public or private insurer generally covers such political risk.

An Example of a Potential MIGA Guarantee

Recently, the *New York Times* covered a story about a U.S. investor who had obtained exclusive rights to a river in northern Russia from the local government and the Russian Government. The U.S. investor ran an exclusive fly-fishing camp that had attracted several prominent clients from the United States. The camp was run for a year until the local government unilaterally rescinded the contract and resold the river rights. The fishing camp was closed by a military operation. The potential loss to the U.S. investor amounted to $1 million.

FIGURE 8.2
The Standby Amount of Guarantee

Retained Earnings

The investor is given the opportunity before the contract is executed to obtain additional coverage (up to 180 percent of the investment amount) from MIGA to insure future profits that may be retained or reinvested into the project enterprise. Ordinarily, this additional amount would be carried on standby until the earnings are realized.

Phased-in Investments

An investor who makes investment contributions over several years would place on current the amount of the investment to be made during the first year of the contract, with the balance placed on standby. As additional investment amounts are contributed, corresponding amounts are converted from standby to current at each anniversary date.

Source: Multilateral Investment Guarantee Agency, *Premium Rates* (Washington, D.C.: Multilateral Investment Guarantee Agency, n.d.), p. 3.

The businessman averted this loss because of his foresight that a government still trying to improve its justice system might attempt what was essentially a nationalization of his investment. He had included an arbitration clause in his contract with the local government and began an arbitration proceeding in Sweden. Because the Russian Federation is now a member of MIGA, such an investment could have been insured with a MIGA guarantee. The act to rescind the contract was a governmental act, and MIGA coverage is available for contract repudiation.

AVAILABILITY OF COVERAGE

MIGA has the capability of covering a foreign investment project to a greater extent than any other multilateral or national institution or any private insurer.[8] In each of the four risk categories, MIGA is able to insure equity investments for up to 90 percent of the investment contribution as well as an additional 450 percent of the investment contribution to cover earnings stemming from the investment. In the case of project loans, MIGA is able to insure up to 90 percent of the loan principal as well as an additional 135 percent of the principal to cover accrued interest. MIGA can pay up to 90 percent of the total value of any payments due under an insured agreement for technical assistance. MIGA is able to insure up to $50 million of investment in a single project on its own account at the present time. MIGA can mobilize additional coverage by obtaining the cooperation of other political risk insurers.

THE GUARANTEE APPLICATION PROCESS

The MIGA guarantee application process consists of two major steps. First, the investor seeking coverage submits a preliminary application (PA) before any commitment of the investment. The PA provides the information that MIGA requires to determine the eligibility of the investor and the investment. An example of the MIGA PA is shown in Figure 8.3. When MIGA determines that the investor and investment qualify for MIGA coverage, the agency sends a Notice of Registration with a Definitive Application for Guarantee (DAG) to the investor. The second step consists of the investor submitting the DAG to MIGA. The DAG provides the information necessary for MIGA review and preparation of the Contract of Guarantee. The investor submits the DAG along with any relevant project documentation. Such documentation can include any joint venture contract, feasibility study, and environmental assessment made prior to the project proposal. In addition, the material submitted must include the amount and type of investment, types of coverage desired, developmental effects of the project, and substantiation of the project's financial and economic viability. See Figure 8.4 for a graphic display of the MIGA guarantee process. If MIGA decides to cover the risk, the agency will undertake a period of underwriting review covering two to four months.

The entire guarantee process may take years to complete.[9] The notice of the registration can take only a few days after the foreign investor has applied for the guarantee. The assessment period can take from a few months to several years. Once MIGA decides to cover the risk, MIGA will take two to four months to undertake an underwriting review, as mentioned above. The final decision whether to invest is sometimes made simultaneously by the investor when the purchase of MIGA insurance is made because some projects are sufficiently marginal to necessitate investment insurance coverage in order for the investor to proceed with the project.

MIGA charges specific fees for some parts of the guarantee process.[10] No charge is made for filing a PA. However, once the process reaches the DAG stage, an application fee is charged by MIGA. If the DAG is accepted and an investment guarantee contract is offered to the investor, the application fee will be credited toward the first year's premium.

FIGURE 8.3
MIGA Preliminary Application for Guarantee

Multilateral Investment Guarantee Agency
Preliminary Application for Guarantee

The undersigned hereby requests that MIGA register the proposed investment to assure that its eligibility for a MIGA guarantee will not be prejudiced if the investment is committed or made while the registration is in effect. Upon acceptance, a Notice of Registration will be issued which will remain in effect for the period specified therein. This Notice does not constitute a commitment either for MIGA to offer a guarantee or for the investor to accept such guarantee.

MIGA will treat all information contained in this application as confidential, and will not disclose it outside the Agency except with the applicant's consent.

A. INVESTOR:
1. Name: _____
   Address: _____
   Telephone: _____ Telex: _____ Telefax: _____
2. Investor's legal status:
   • Individual; nationality: _____
   • Corporation; incorporated in: _____
   • Principal place of business: _____
   • Majority of capital owned by nationals of: _____
3. Authorized representative appointed to deal with MIGA:
   Name: _____
   Address (if other than investor): _____
   Telephone: _____ Telex: _____ Telefax: _____

B. INVESTMENT:
1. Host country: _____
2. Name of project enterprise (if available): _____
3. Product(s) and/or service(s) to be produced: _____
   _____
4. Total cost of project (including debt and other investor's contributions, if any): _____
   _____
5. Please list other investors (local and foreign): _____
   _____
6. Types and estimated values of *investor's* contributions for which a guarantee is desired (in the currency in which MIGA guarantee will be requested):

(a) Equity: _____

(b) Loan or loan guarantee by equity investor: _____

Repayment period: _____

(c) Other form(s) of investment: _____

Type of investment: _____

_____

Total contribution by investor: _____

7. If the investment project involves acquiring an *existing* enterprise:

(a) describe changes and restructuring to be performed: _____

_____

_____

_____

(b) indicate proportion of investor's contributions allocated to:

acquisition _____%, financial restructuring _____%,

and expansion/modernization _____%, respectively.

8. Estimated date of irrevocable commitment to invest or date of first disbursement:

_____

C. TYPE OF GUARANTEE REQUESTED:

1. Risks to be covered by MIGA:

° Currency Transfer   ° Expropriation

° Breach of Contract   ° War/Civil Disturbance

2. Please list other insurers from which coverage for non-commercial risks has been (will be) requested: _____

D. APPLICATION MADE BY:

I hereby affirm that none of the investment for which coverage is sought has been irrevocably committed or made as of this date, and I am aware that an investment irrevocably committed or made prior to MIGA's acceptance will not be eligible for coverage.

Signature of Investor: _____

Name and Title: _____

Date: _____

Mail Address: 1818 H Street, N.W., Washington, D.C. 20433

Offices at: 900 19th Street, N.W., Washington, D.C.

Telephone (202)473-6168; Telex: ITT 440098; Telefax: (202)334-0265

Source: Reprinted with the permission of Multilateral Investment Guarantee Agency

FIGURE 8.4
The MIGA Guarantee Process

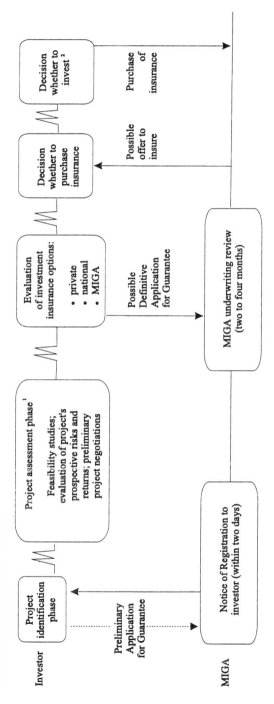

1 This phase can vary in duration from a few months to many years.

2 The decisions whether to invest in a project and to purchase investment insurance are often made simultaneously.

Source: Multilateral Investment Guarantee Agency, *MIGA Annual Report 1993* (Washington, D.C.: Multilateral Investment Guarantee Agency, 1993). p. 10. Reprinted with the permission of Multilateral Investment Guarantee Agency.

123

However, MIGA can, for certain reasons, decline to offer a guarantee contract at the DAG stage. If so, the application fee will be refunded. However, if MIGA offers a guarantee contract and the investor declines the offer, the application fee will not be refunded.

The application fee varies according to project sector and to the amount covered. For projects in the manufacturing and services sector, guarantees up to $25 million will be charged an application fee of $5,000. For guarantees in this sector for more than $25 million or for projects in the natural resources, oil/gas, and infrastructure sectors, the application fee is $10,000.

In addition to the application fee, MIGA charges a processing fee. This fee is for exceptional underwriting costs incurred in evaluating projects that can be environmentally sensitive or whose complex financial structures require advisors outside MIGA. This fee amounts to $25,000 but a higher amount can be charged in exceptional circumstances. If the expenses do not amount to $25,000, the unused balance will be refunded to the investor.

PAYMENT OF PREMIUMS

The foreign investor pays the first year's premium before the Contract for Guarantee is signed by MIGA. The premium payments thereafter are paid annually on or before the anniversary date. Shortly before the anniversary date, the foreign investor has the opportunity to modify its elections for the coming year. The renewal premium will reflect any changes made by the investor. See Table 8.2 for an example of the calculation of the estimated premium.

MIGA'S PROGRAMS TO SHARE THE RISK

MIGA has developed several programs during its short life designed to expand its coverage and at the same time reduce its own risk. These include reinsurance, co-insurance, cooperating underwriting, and the insurance brokers' program. These programs will be discussed in this section.

Reinsurance

Reinsurance has been the major reason for much of the growth of the private political risk industry. Reinsurance is insurance placed by an underwriter in another company to cut down the amount of the risk

TABLE 8.2
Calculation of the Estimated Premium

The following example illustrates how the base rates can be used to estimate the total premium cost for a MIGA guarantee:

Assumptions: Investment amounts —$5,000,000
                Guaranteed percentage — 90 percent
                Coverage — Currency Transfer/Expropriation
                Industry — Sugar refinery (Manufacturing)
                Maximum insured amount — Three times the original
                    investment [that is, 3 x $5,000,000 x 90% (or 270%)

1. Currency Transfer
    Maximum insured amount $13,500,000
    Current $ 500,000   x 0.0050 = $ 2,500
    Standby $13,000,000 x 0.0025 = $32,500
        Subtotal for Currency Transfer: $35,000

2. Expropriation
    Maximum Insured Amount $13,500,000
    Current $ 3,375,000 x 0.0060 = $20,250
    Standby $10,125,000 x 0.0030 = $30,375
        Subtotal for Expropriation: $50,625

        Total estimated premium for year 1: $85,625

Source: Multilateral Investment Guarantee Agency, Premium Rates (Washington, D.C.: Multilateral Investment Guarantee Agency, 1995), p. 5.

assumed under the original insurance. Private insurers must reinsure their portfolios to guard against major losses, which might wipe out much of their premium income. Lloyds of London provides the syndicates, which furnish much of the primary reinsurance market for political risk insurance.

Reinsurance can be accomplished by either treaty or project.[11] Project reinsurance is provided by a single reinsurer and includes a limited portfolio of investments. Thus, it is expensive and does not cover large risks. Treaty reinsurance is offered by a group of reinsurers and all investments that fit the requirements of the treaty are reinsured.

These same principles that are found in the private political risk, insurance market have been adopted by MIGA. Because MIGA is limited to its subscribed capital and premium and fee income for revenues to cover its guarantees, it has adopted the principles of a large and diversified portfolio of guarantees. In order to limit its own risk, the agency, thus, enters into co-insurance and reinsurance agreements with other insurers, both public and private.[12] The agency can guarantee or co-guarantee a project with a national insurance agency in a country where the national agency is too heavily exposed, co-guarantee large investments with national agencies, guarantee or co-guarantee with national agencies multinationally financed investments, and provide reinsurance of national investment guarantee agencies.

MIGA has reinsured portions of its investments with other leading insurers. These include Lloyds of London, national insurers such as the Export Credit Guarantee Department in the United Kingdom, and private insurers. In some cases, MIGA has had another insurer reinsure a portion of its initial coverage.

One of the most recent reinsurance developments in which MIGA was involved occurred in 1997. MIGA signed a quota share treaty, that is, entire portfolio, reinsurance agreement with ACE Insurance Company, Ltd., of Bermuda (ACE).[13] ACE is a wholly owned subsidiary of ACE Ltd., one of the world's largest excess liability insurers. This was the first such treaty between a private insurer and a multilateral agency and will provide 20-year coverage for projects in LDCs. This agreement will reduce MIGA's exposure to specific projects and will enable the agency to increase its capacity without increasing its liability. Before the ACE agreement, MIGA's underwriting limits were $225 million per country and $50 million per project, respectively. These limits now can be increased substantially.

Co-insurance

MIGA has entered into several co-insurance agreements with other investment insurers such as national government insurers from Australia, Canada, Italy, Japan, Norway, Spain, the United Kingdom, and the United States. Co-insurance is actually short for cooperative insurance in which more than one insurer will agree to share the covered risk. Such programs have increased the amount of political risk insurance available for foreign projects in LDCs. MIGA also has worked with private insurers such as the American International Group and Lloyd's of London.

Cooperative Underwriting

MIGA has collaborated with the private insurance market in another way to expand political risk coverage. The agency developed a cooperative underwriting program. This program is a type of co-insurance that encourages private insurers to cover projects in LDCs where they might not otherwise intend to insure. Under the cooperative underwriting program, MIGA is the insurer-of-record but spins off much of its coverage to private insurance underwriters. MIGA signed its first contract under this program in FY1997 with Enron Corporation, a U.S. company, for a power project in Indonesia.[14]

Insurance Brokers' Program

In addition to insuring investments directly with the foreign investor, MIGA also works indirectly through licensed insurance brokers.[15] These insurance brokers operate in many countries by providing services to business firms needing insurance. MIGA will pay a commission to brokers that bring projects to MIGA. During FY1992, MIGA used this program for the first time when it paid a broker's commission to the Export Credit Insurance Associates of San Francisco for a project undertaken in Poland. This program supplements the resources of MIGA and, essentially, expands the ability of its investment insurance program.

CO-PAYMENT PROCEDURES

Although MIGA can pay up to 90 percent of a project's equity investment, 90 percent of a project's loan principal, and 90 percent of the total value of payments due under a technical assistance contract, the investor must accept the risk for at least 10 percent of the loss stemming from any of the four political risks in a project insured by MIGA. The objective of this co-payment feature is to motivate the investor to monitor the project more carefully and, thus, reduce the moral hazard inherent in the project.

HOW MIGA GUARANTEES ARE PAID

By the end of FY1997, MIGA had yet to pay off a claim related to any of its political risk guarantees. MIGA guarantees are paid differently depending on which of the political risks are covered. For transfer restriction, MIGA will pay compensation in the currency of its contract of guarantee upon receipt of the blocked local currency from an insured investor.

For expropriation, MIGA will compensate the insured investor upon assignment to MIGA of the investor's interest in the expropriated investment, for example, equity shares or interest in a loan agreement. For breach of contract, MIGA will pay compensation if, after a specified period of time, the insured foreign investor has not received payment or if the dispute resolution procedure fails to function because of some action by the host government. For war and civil disturbance, MIGA will pay the book value of the total equity investment when the investment is considered a total loss as a result of the effective interruption caused by the war or civil disturbance. If a loan or loan guaranty is involved, MIGA will pay the insured portion of the principal and interest payments in default as a result of the business interruption.

A MIGA payoff of an investment guarantee contract can place moral pressure on MIGA member countries, especially those that are host states for the foreign investment project insured by MIGA. This pressure arises from the fact that, if MIGA is required to pay out an insurance award because of some political act by the host government, this award will be paid from the capital subscribed by all of MIGA's member governments. Thus, the irresponsible act of one member country places a burden on all MIGA members because the pay out can require a replenishment of MIGA's reserves from unpaid member country subscriptions. The MIGA procedure places pressure on all members to act responsibly in all phases of foreign investment projects. Such a feature makes MIGA distinct from national investment insurance schemes.[16]

HOW THE AGENCY IS FUNDED

MIGA is self-supporting, owned by its member countries, and operates on a sound financial and business basis with its solvency insured by its share capital. Its subscribed share capital, paid and unpaid, amounted to approximately $212.9 million at the end of FY1997. This does not include retained earnings. The share capital is comprised of a payment of 10 percent of a member state's subscription paid in cash with another 10 percent paid in non-negotiable, non–interest-bearing promissory notes. The remaining 80 percent is subject to call. The amount of MIGA's guarantees will never exceed 1.5 times the amount of subscribed capital plus reserves plus a portion of its reinsurance coverage.[17]

NON-GUARANTEE SERVICES

MIGA offers several non-guarantee services to member nations. These include seminars and conferences, reports and technical assistance, cooperative work with other international financial institutions, and dispute resolution activities.

Seminars and Conferences

MIGA established an in-house unit, Policy and Advisory Services (PAS), in its first full year of operations. PAS renders technical assistance to LDCs to reform their investment policies and institutions and assists countries in the promotion of their investment climate and opportunities. Among the activities supported by PAS is the organization and promotion of conferences dealing with foreign direct investment (FDI) issues in LDCs and transition economies.

One of MIGA's first conferences held under this program was for investment promotion. This conference was held in Ghana in 1990. A second conference in this series was the Hungary Investment Promotion Conference held in Budapest also in 1990. The latter conference highlighted specific investment opportunities in Hungary's agroprocessing, wineries, and electronics sectors. Representatives from 11 developed countries attended this conference. They and local investors committed $170 million to projects in LDCs. A MIGA/Botswana investment promotion conference was held in FY1993 under this program.

Africa

In Chapter 1, the foreign investment environment was analyzed. The most severe problems facing investment, particularly foreign investment, which are found in the developing world are prevalent in Africa. Thus, MIGA has formulated a policy to cope with these problems by targeting its investment promotion work more at Africa than at any other developing region.

For example, MIGA developed a series of workshops for African countries in FY1994 under the PAS program, which were held in Benin, Senegal, and the Ivory Coast. These workshops were designed for government officials who implement policy and were cosponsored with the Foreign Investment Advisory Service (FIAS), a unit of the IFC. FIAS will be discussed in a subsequent section. Topics discussed in these workshops included regulatory obstacles to foreign investment. The participants included top officials and private sector representatives from African countries.

In recent fiscal years, MIGA has conducted workshops, symposia, and conferences dealing with the mining sector in Africa.[18] In FY1997, for example, MIGA held its fourth annual African Mining Investment and Business Opportunities Conference in Denver, Colorado. The conference attendees included representatives from 28 sub-Saharan African countries and more than 500 mining companies from Asia, Europe, and North America.

Tourism

Another industry, that MIGA has singled out for emphasis in its investment promotion activities is the tourism sector in developing member countries. An example of a tourism conference was held in FY1997 when MIGA sponsored the Andean Region Investors Forum for Hotel and Tourism Development in Lima, Peru. This conference was attended by more than 200 participants from 12 countries, and 90 projects were discussed.

Reports and Technical Assistance

MIGA has furnished technical assistance to its member countries in a variety of ways. These include dissemination of information on investment opportunities, business operating conditions, and business partners in member countries; capacity building support to member country investment promotion agencies; and direct support of member countries' investment promotion activities.[19] From FY1992 to FY1997, MIGA carried out 117 of these technical assistance activities, which directly benefited 110 member countries. More than half of these activities were directed at Africa. One of the major programs in this area is the Investment Promotion Agency Network, a web-based electronic data base, which is discussed in more detail in Chapter 9.

MIGA has undertaken several research projects and drafted several reports as part of its technical assistance programs. Many of these projects were undertaken as a joint venture with the FIAS, mentioned earlier in this chapter. One of these studies concerned the competitive strengths and weaknesses of Central and Eastern European countries in attracting FDI in relation to LDCs competing for the same investments.

Much of what MIGA has done in this area in recent years is carried out by electronic means. The Investment Promotion Network program is a significant operation in information dissemination and is covered in Chapter 9. MIGA also has developed an investor tracking system. This investor tracking system is a specialized software package to assist investment promotion agencies in member countries to manage their investor information. MIGA trains system administrators and users at the Ghana Investment Promotion Center.[20]

Work with the International Finance Corporation

MIGA operates FIAS jointly with the World Bank. FIAS was established by IFC in 1986 to provide advice to member country governments that seek to develop policies and programs that encourage more and better FDI to flow into these countries. FIAS advises governments on the laws, policies, regulations, and procedures necessary to create a positive investment environment. FIAS advisory activities range from broad diagnostic evaluation of the investment environment to more specific advice on investment policies and/or institutions.

From its inception through FY1997, FIAS has completed 197 advisory projects in 93 countries. Nearly 40 percent of its work has been done in the lowest income LDCs. In addition to its advisory work, this unit has fulfilled its objectives by organizing multicountry conferences. In FY1996, IFC contributed about 25 percent of the funding needs for FIAS. Another 25 percent came from a general trust fund that had accrued contributions from 11 developed nations in recent years. The World Bank contributed about 15 percent to FIAS's budget and a group of multilateral agencies gave another 15 percent to the budget. Client countries contributed the remaining 20 percent.[21]

Several MIGA-FIAS activities can be cited, which include seminars on foreign investment and research projects. In FY1994, FIAS conducted a roundtable for Asian countries in Bangkok, which enabled high-level officials from these countries to discuss the policy environment necessary to attract FDI in infrastructure. Deregulation workshops for African countries were held in Benin, Ivory Coast, Ghana, and Senegal.

In addition to these activities, FIAS organized many seminars and workshops in FY1993.[22] For example, it held a seminar on investment promotion in China. This seminar introduced government officials to international experience with investment promotion tools and techniques. A workshop on foreign investment promotion techniques was held in Bolivia. The presentations highlighted cases of foreign investment in other countries including successes and failures. A workshop on foreign investment policy implementation in Tanzania, Uganda, and Zimbabwe was held as a joint effort by FIAS and MIGA.

FIAS also has worked with transition economies. It conducted diagnostic studies of the FDI environment in Bulgaria and Slovakia and recommended ways to remove FDI obstacles. A workshop was held in Washington, D.C., with Russian government officials to discuss Russia's foreign investment law. Diagnostic studies also have been carried out in Poland. FIAS also carried out a research project concerned with the competitive strengths and weaknesses of Central and Eastern Europe in attracting FDI.[23] In FY1993, FIAS held a roundtable for Asian countries in transition to a market economy, which provided a means for officials from six countries to discuss foreign investment policies in this transition.

Dispute Resolution Activities

The MIGA Convention gives MIGA the ability to deal with many different types of disputes in which the agency may become entangled. Such disputes include those between MIGA and member countries over the interpretation or application of the Convention, other disputes between MIGA and member countries and all disputes with a state that has ceased to be a member, and disputes between MIGA and its creditors.[24] The MIGA board of directors will settle the first type of dispute with appeals subject to its Council of Governors. Thus, an internal process is used rather than an independent judicial process, as in the case with the World Bank and other multilateral financial institutions. With regard to disputes between MIGA and its member countries with countries no longer members of MIGA, the Convention requires negotiation of the dispute, as well as the possibility of conciliation. If these methods do not result in settlement of the dispute, compulsory international arbitration must be used. With regard to disputes between MIGA and its creditors, the latter can sue MIGA before domestic courts that have jurisdiction under their respective national laws or by virtue of a prior agreement with MIGA. Such creditors, according to Article 44 of the Convention, cannot be MIGA members, guaranteed investors, or claimants that derive their claims from members.

Disputes that arise from a guarantee contract issued by MIGA are covered by Article 58 of the Convention. Such disputes are to be submitted to arbitration in accordance with the rules provided for in the contract. MIGA's operational regulations provide that such guarantee contracts will refer to ICSID arbitration rules.

SUMMARY AND CONCLUSIONS

This chapter has included a discussion of the various operations performed by MIGA. Its organization was covered. MIGA guarantees, its coverage, the availability of its coverage, the guarantee application process, and payments of premiums were all analyzed. The reinsurance, co-insurance, cooperative underwriting, and insurance brokers' program were discussed as were the co-payment procedures required by MIGA. The procedures utilized by MIGA to pay its guarantees were analyzed along with its funding process.

MIGA also performs several non-guarantee services. The objective of these services is to promote a better FDI environment in LDCs and include conferences, seminars, reports, and technical assistance to LDC member countries. MIGA has concentrated on the mining and tourism sectors in some of these conferences. Its operations in this area also include cooperative joint efforts with the FIAS, an IFC unit, and other multilateral and national agencies.

NOTES

1. For a detailed discussion of the MIGA organizational structure, see Klaus Peter Berger, "The New Multilateral Investment Guarantee Agency Globalizing the Investment Insurance Approach Towards Development," *Syracuse Journal of International Law and Commerce* 15 (1988): 24–25.

2. Jurgen Voss, "The Multilateral Investment Guarantee Agency: Status, Mandate, Concept, Features, Implications," *Journal of World Trade Law* 21 (August 1987): 18.

3. Multilateral Investment Guarantee Agency, *MIGA Annual Report 1997* (Washington, D.C.: Multilateral Investment Guarantee Agency, 1997), p. 53.

4. Multilateral Investment Guarantee Agency, *Investment Guarantee Guide* (Washington, D.C.: Multilateral Investment Guarantee Agency, 1997), pp. 4–5.

5. Laura Wallace, "MIGA: Up and Running," *Finance & Development* 29 (March 1992): 48–49.

6. James C. Baker, "Global Foreign Investment Insurance: The Case of MIGA with Comparisons to OPIC and Private Insurance," *Managerial Finance* 21 (1995): 28.

7. Multilateral Investment Guarantee Agency, *Investment Guarantee Guide*, p. 9.

8. Ibid., pp. 8–9.

9. Laura Wallace, "MIGA: Up and Running," pp. 48–49.

10. Multilateral Investment Guarantee Agency, *Investment Guarantee Guide*, pp. 10–11.

11. S. Linn Williams, "Political and Other Risk Insurance: Eximbank, OPIC and MIGA," *Middle East Executive Reports* 11 (June 1988): 24.

12. Voss, "The Multilateral Investment Guarantee Agency," pp. 17–18.

13. Multilateral Investment Guarantee Agency, *MIGA Annual Report 1997*, p. 16.

14. Ibid., p. 15.

15. Multilateral Investment Guarantee Agency, *MIGA Annual Report 1992* (Washington, D.C.: Multilateral Investment Guarantee Agency, 1992), p. 16.

16. Baker, "Global Foreign Investment Insurance," pp. 29–30.

17. Gerd-Peter E. Lota, "The Multilateral Investment Guarantee Agency: Benefits," *Credit & Financial Management* 88 (January 1986): 38.

18. Multilateral Investment Guarantee Agency, *MIGA Annual Report 1997*, pp. 46–47.

19. Multilateral Investment Guarantee Agency, *MIGA Business Profile 1997* (Washington, D.C.: Multilateral Investment Guarantee Agency, 1997), p. 17.

20. Multilateral Investment Guarantee Agency, *MIGA Annual Report 1997*, p. 49.

21. International Finance Corporation, *Annual Report 1996* (Washington, D.C.: International Finance Corporation, 1996), p. 115.

22. Multilateral Investment Guarantee Agency, *MIGA Annual Report 1993* (Washington, D.C.: Multilateral Investment Guarantee Agency, 1993), p. 23.

23. Multilateral Investment Guarantee Agency, *MIGA Annual Report 1994* (Washington, D.C.: Multilateral Investment Guarantee Agency, 1994), pp. 35–36.

24. Ibrahim F. I. Shihata, "MIGA And Dispute Settlements," *Middle East Executive Reports* 12 (April 1989): 23.

9

MIGA's Operations to Date

Multilateral Investment Guarantee Agency (MIGA) was established in 1988 but its first investment guarantee contracts were issued in FY1990. During its eight years of active operation, it has become one of the most successful multilateral institutions, and its services have been in tremendous demand. In this chapter, an analysis of its operations will be presented.[1]

COUNTRY MEMBERSHIP

MIGA's membership is limited to World Bank members and Switzerland. When the agency began operations, it started with 52 members while 21 others were in the process of completing membership applications. The organization has had a steady increase in membership each year of its existence. By the end of FY1997, MIGA had 141 full members with another 19 in the process of joining. Of the current members, 19 are industrialized nations and 122 are less developed countries (LDCs).

MIGA'S IMPACT ON DEVELOPMENT

In the mid-1980s, foreign direct investment (FDI) flows to LDCs reached a low point of about $9 billion annually. After MIGA was established and had initiated its investment guarantee program, FDI into LDCs increased significantly. A study completed by the International Finance Corporation (IFC) showed that FDI flows into LDCs amounted to $36 billion in 1992.[2] Although MIGA was not the sole contributor to this significant increase in FDI into the LDCs, it was one of several economic institutional changes that led to a more favorable private investment climate in the LDCs.

By the end of FY1997, MIGA had issued 293 investment guarantee contracts. These guarantees covered foreign investments in 52 LDCs and transition economies made by investors in 25 member countries. The estimated FDI generated by these projects insured by MIGA is nearly $20 billion, whereas the amount of the guarantees totaled $3.4 billion. See Table 9.1 for the operations of MIGA during FY1990–97.

MIGA'S GUARANTEE ACTIVITIES

In the first eight years of MIGA's operations, the number of investment guarantee contracts issued and the outstanding contingent liability that these contracts represent have increased.[3] Including reinsurance agreements, MIGA's outstanding maximum contingent liability has increased from $132 million at the end of FY1990 to almost $2.5 billion at the end of FY1997. This contingent liability is reinsured to $187.4 million by ACE Insurance Company, Ltd. (ACE) of Bermuda.

The ACE affiliation is an example of the ability of MIGA to obtain outside insurers to reinsure portions of its guarantees, and thus reduce its risk. ACE provides quota-share reinsurance on risks in countries where MIGA provides coverage for political risk. ACE is a group that, through its Bermuda-based subsidiaries, provides excess liability insurance, directors' and officers' liability insurance, and property catastrophe reinsurance, as well as satellite, aviation, excess property, and financial lines coverage.[4] The ACE coverage permits MIGA to increase its capacity to $75 million per project and $325 million per country. The ACE reinsurance will have maturities of up to 20 years and will cover political risks for more than double the policy terms usually available in the commercial political risk insurance market.[5]

MIGA also collaborates with national and private insurers in the projects it guarantees by entering into facultative reinsurance and co-insurance arrangements. These collaborations amounted to $92.5 million at the end of FY1997. In addition, MIGA also entered into a $15 million cooperative underwriting program with a private insurer involving Enron Corporation and a power project in Indonesia. MIGA's outstanding contingent liability on an annual basis is shown in Table 9.1.

TABLE 9.1
MIGA Operations

(FY1990–97)

Fiscal Year	1990	1991	1992	1993	1994	1995	1996	1997	Total
Guarantees	4	11	21	27	38	54	68	70	293
Amount of guarantees issued ($millions)	132	59	313	374	372	672	862	614	3,398
Accrued contingent liability outstanding ($millions)	132	191	421	745	1,048	1,622	2,276	2,499	
Estimated foreign direct investment facilitated ($billions)	1.0	0.9	1.0	1.9	1.3	2.5	6.6	4.7	19.9
Estimated number of jobs created	2,700	3,680	2,920	1,720	7,800	8,800	7,200	4,000	38,820

Source: Multilateral Investment Guarantee Agency, *MIGA Business Profile 1997* (Washington, D.C.: Multilateral Investment Guarantee Agency, 1997), p. 4.

MIGA'S PREMIUM INCOME

The large increase in MIGA's investment guarantee activities has resulted in a large increase in the agency's income from premiums and commitment fees during its eight years of operations. Premium and fee income rose from under $500,000 in FY1990 to $26.2 million in FY1997. Its earnings net of reinsurance income sharing amounted to $24.6 million in FY1997.

MIGA'S PORTFOLIO

MIGA's portfolio of investment guarantee contracts, as measured by maximum contingent liability, is quite diversified by industrial sector and by host region. This is also true when the portfolio is measured by the number of contracts issued by host region.

The sector in which MIGA's guarantees, by maximum contingent liability, have increased the most rapidly has been infrastructure. From FY1992 to FY1997, the infrastructure sector share of MIGA's guarantees has increased from 1 percent to 17 percent. More than one-third of MIGA's current active applications are for infrastructure projects. This sector will remain a large recipient of MIGA guarantees in the future. The change in sector share of MIGA's portfolio from FY1992 to FY1997, measured by contingent liability, is shown in Table 9.2.

TABLE 9.2
MIGA's Portfolio by Sector: Maximum Contingent Liability
(in percent)

Sector	FY1992	FY1997
Financial	38	36
Mining	30	15
Agribusiness	14	2
Manufacturing	12	25
Services	4	—
Tourism	1	2
Infrastructure	1	17
Oil and Gas	—	3

Source: Multilateral Investment Guarantee Agency, *MIGA Business Profile 1997* (Washington, D.C.: Multilateral Investment Guarantee Agency, 1997), p. 7.

When the portfolio is measured by contracts issued by host region according to contingent liability, MIGA's guarantees have been made on a global basis. However, the emphasis during the 1990s has been on guarantees for investments in Latin America and the Caribbean. Investment guarantee contracts issued by MIGA for investments in these countries totaled more than $1 billion by the end of FY1997. Latin America and the Caribbean also are the most important host regions when measured by the number of contracts issued by MIGA. See Table 9.3 for a breakdown of the portfolio by host region, measured by contingent liability. The number of contracts issued by host region is shown in Table 9.4.

MIGA has issued more than half of its investment guarantees to the middle half of LDCs. The World Bank has identified the LDCs that have

TABLE 9.3
MIGA Portfolio by Host Region: Maximum Contingent Liability
(in percent)

Region	FY1992	FY1997
Latin America & the Caribbean	36	44
Asia	35	23
Europe & Central Asia	28	23
Africa	1	7
Middle East	—	3

Source: Multilateral Investment Guarantee Agency, *MIGA Business Profile 1997* (Washington, D.C.: Multilateral Investment Guarantee Agency, 1997), p. 8.

TABLE 9.4
MIGA Portfolio by Host Region: Number of Contracts Issued
(in percent)

Region	FY1992	FY1997
Latin America & the Caribbean	32	38
Asia	32	26
Europe & Central Asia	26	20
Africa	9	13
Middle East	—	3

Source: Multilateral Investment Guarantee Agency, *MIGA Business Profile 1997* (Washington, D.C.: Multilateral Investment Guarantee Agency, 1997), p. 9.

received the largest share of FDI flowing to developing countries. The top 10 countries that receive FDI have received only 25.3 percent of MIGA's guarantees. In contrast, MIGA has directed 23.1 percent of its portfolio of guarantees toward 17 International Development Association (IDA)–eligible countries. IDA, as described earlier, limits its economic assistance to the lowest-income World Bank member countries. Data on the top 10 FDI-recipient countries and MIGA guarantees are shown in Table 9.5 and MIGA guarantee activity in 17 IDA-eligible countries is shown in Table 9.6.

MIGA's portfolio can be measured in another way. When one analyzes the agency's current portfolio by maximum contingent liability from contracts issued according to the investors' country of origin, the portfolio is found to be spread across several industrialized and developing countries. The five developing nations from which MIGA-guarantee investors come are, of course, among the highest income developing countries. This trend differs greatly from MIGA's portfolio five years ago when the agency had

TABLE 9.5

MIGA Guarantee Activity in Top 10 Countries Receiving Foreign Direct Investment

Ranking in 1996[b]	Country	MIGA Guarantees Outstanding[a] (as of June 30, 1997)	
		Millions of Dollars	Percentage of Portfolio
1	China	98.8	4.0
2	Mexico	0.0	0.0
3	Malaysia	0.0	0.0
4	Indonesia	80.4	3.2
5	Brazil	201.0	8.0
6	Poland	44.8	1.8
7	Thailand	0.0	0.0
8	Chile	0.0	0.0
9	Argentina	169.2	6.8
10	Hungary	37.6	1.5
Total		631.8	25.3

[a]Source: World Bank, *Global Development Finance* (Washington, D.C.: World Bank, 1997).

[b]Multilateral Investment Guarantee Agency, *Annual Report 1997* (Washington, D.C.: Multilateral Investment Guarantee Agency), p. 21.

Source: Multilateral Investment Guarantee Agency, *MIGA Business Profile 1997* (Washington, D.C.: Multilateral Investment Guarantee Agency, 1997), p. 10.

TABLE 9.6
MIGA Guarantees in 17 International
Development Association–Eligible Countries

Country	MIGA Guarantees Outstanding (as of June 30, 1997)	
	Millions of Dollars	Percentage of Portfolio
Pakistan	158.1	6.3
China	98.8	4.0
Kyrgyz Republic	63.8	2.6
Bangladesh	61.8	2.5
Mali	50.0	2.0
Nepal	32.8	1.3
Guyana	30.6	1.2
Honduras	29.5	1.2
Azerbaijan	16.5	0.7
Guinea	8.3	0.3
Uganda	7.6	0.3
Sri Lanka	5.4	0.2
Georgia	3.4	0.1
Egypt	2.2	0.1
Vietnam	1.9	0.1
Madagascar	1.7	0.1
Tanzania	0.4	0.1
Total	572.8	23.1

Source: Multilateral Investment Guarantee Agency, *MIGA Business Profile 1997* (Washington, D.C.: Multilateral Investment Guarantee Agency, 1997), p. 11.

insured investors from only industrialized countries. The trend toward insuring investments flowing from developing countries is within the agency's goal of encouraging private investment flows from developing to developing member countries. A comparison of this trend from FY1992 to FY1997 can be seen in Table 9.7.

ACTIVE APPLICATIONS BY HOST REGION

One of the bright spots in the current operations of MIGA is its backlog of active preliminary applications for coverage of prospective investments. By the end of FY1997, the agency had processed approximately

TABLE 9.7
MIGA Portfolio by Investor Country
(by percentage of maximum contingent liability)

Country	1992	1997
United States	57	33
Canada	13	6
France, Luxembourg, Cayman Islands, Germany	10.5	8
Switzerland	8	4
Japan	5	3
Norway, Spain, Italy, Greece, Sweden, Belgium	3	5
Singapore	3	0
Netherlands	1	24
United Kingdom	0	11
Turkey	0	4
South Africa, Uruguay, Argentina, Korea	0	2

Source: Multilateral Investment Guarantee Agency, *MIGA Business Profile 1997* (Washington, D.C.: Multilateral Investment Guarantee Agency, 1997), p. 12.

3,900 applications for investment guarantee contracts to cover political risks of FDI. More than 1,000 of these applications have become active preliminary applications that can be approved for MIGA guarantees. These projects are located in 112 developing countries or transition economies. The applications are spread fairly evenly among the four major geographic regions with more than 150 applications for projects in Africa and the Middle East to nearly 280 for projects in Asia and the Pacific Area.

INCOME, ADMINISTRATIVE COSTS, AND AGENCY PROFICIENCY

MIGA's net income has shown steady improvement during its eight years of operations. The improvement in profits stems primarily from increased premium income although administrative costs, after peaking in FY1992, have shown a steady decline on an annual basis since then. Investment income has remained fairly steady over this period. MIGA has not suffered a claims loss during its eight years of operations.

MIGA's small staff of less than 90 people has been quite productive during the 1990s. This small staff has issued $614 million in coverage in FY1997, which facilitated $4.7 billion in FDI. This represents a ratio of more than 7 to 1. In addition, MIGA's total administrative costs in FY1997 amounted to $11 million. Most multilateral development institutions have budgets far more than the spending reported by MIGA. The net income per MIGA staff member has increased substantially during each of the last five fiscal years. During this period, administrative expenses per staff member have either remained steady or have declined.

The return on assets (ROA) for MIGA's operations shows marked improvement during the past five fiscal years. ROA, although a commonly used measure to assess business performance, is not an appropriate measure to analyze MIGA's operations because 80 percent of its initial assets were not paid in and 10 percent of its assets were in the form of promissory notes that do not accrue interest. A more proper measure is ROA employed. Either one of these measures shows that MIGA's operations have had improved efficiency and profitability during the fiscal years since 1992.[6] MIGA's ROA has increased from slightly more than 2 percent in FY1990 to about 8 percent in FY1997. Its ROA employed has increased from 4 percent in FY1990 to 12 percent in FY1997.

COOPERATIVE ACTIVITIES

MIGA actively conducts cooperative affiliations with member countries in the development of programs that are designed to increase the flow of FDI into these countries. For example, in 1991, MIGA cooperated with the Government of Tanzania to establish an investment promotion center and advised the government in passing the National Investment Protection Policy Act. This law is expected to assist in the generation of extensive foreign investment for the first time in Tanzania.[7]

MIGA/Palestine Liberation Organization
Agreement on Investment Guarantees

In 1997, MIGA signed an agreement with the Palestine Liberation Organization to create a special insurance fund designed to be "a small MIGA." The Palestine Liberation Organization is not recognized as a sovereign state and, therefore, cannot be a member of MIGA. The special fund of $30 million will be used to guarantee political risk insurance in the Palestinian territories. MIGA will administer the fund for a small commission. Contributions to the fund will be solicited from other industrialized countries. The fund will furnish about $2 million in coverage per project.[8]

This agreement covers the regular political risks that MIGA guarantees including nationalization, war and civil disturbance, currency transfer restrictions, and breach of contract. In this case, the term "war and civil disturbance" includes border closings. These have been a major concern to investors in this area. The first guarantee to be covered by this agreement deals with a new water treatment plant.[9]

Cooperative Agreement between MIGA and the Compagnie Française d'Assurance pour le Commerce Extérieur

In 1994, MIGA signed a cooperative agreement with the French export credit guarantee agency, Compagnie Française d'Assurance pour le Commerce Extérieur. This relationship increased the level of coverage to French companies to protect their investments from the risk of loss from political risks.[10]

TECHNICAL ASSISTANCE ACTIVITIES

MIGA operates a very active program of technical assistance. This assistance includes three categories: dissemination of information on investment opportunities, business operating conditions, and business partners in member countries; capacity building support to member country investment promotion agencies; and direct support of member countries' investment promotion activities. Since FY1992, MIGA has implemented 117 such technical assistance activities, which have directly benefited 110 member countries. More than half of these activities have been set in Africa.

These technical assistance programs include many development activities. Among these are the introduction of new methodologies and technologies in management, marketing, and communication. These methodologies have enhanced the institutional capacity of developing member countries in which they have been implemented and have assisted such nations to effectively plan, execute, and follow-up investment promotion programs and activities. The agency attempts to recover the cost of these activities. The following sections include a discussion of some of these technical assistance activities in addition to conferences, missions, and seminars on investment that are conducted by MIGA's staff.

Policy and Advisory Services

One of the first investment advisory activities implemented by MIGA is the Policy and Advisory Services (PAS) whose principal function is to advise, promote, and direct research efforts in order to enhance the flow of FDI to LDCs in keeping with the primary objective of MIGA. Advisory functions of PAS are carried out by the Foreign Investment Advisory Service (FIAS), a joint venture of MIGA's PAS and the IFC.[11]

FIAS has been quite active in the 1990s. The program initiated 17 advisory projects in FY1990 which included: the establishment of a responsive Board of Investments in Bangladesh to facilitate private investment, a project in Hungary to analyze investment incentives and the legal framework in the privatization of state-owned enterprises, and a review of the foreign investment policy issues in several African countries. Another 21 advisory projects were carried out in FY1991 including advice on investment promotion strategies for the governments of Kenya, Lesotho, Morocco, the Philippines, Uruguay, and Venezuela. In FY1992, FIAS began to assist Namibia with the drafting of new investment legislation aimed at improving the flow of FDI into that country.

In FY1993, the advisory and promotional functions of MIGA were reorganized. FIAS became a jointly managed venture of MIGA, IFC, and the World Bank responsible for policy advisory services. The primary focus of PAS was changed to promotional activities. FIAS facilitated a MIGA-organized investment promotion conference in Pakistan in 1992 and completed 28 advisory projects in 25 countries in FY1994. Nineteen of these countries were MIGA members. Among these projects were diagnostic studies in Bulgaria, Cameroon, Slovakia, and Swaziland, among others, which provided analysis and recommendations on areas of FDI including national legal frameworks, privatization, foreign exchange and trade regimes, corporate taxation, and promotion strategies.

Investment Promotion Activities

MIGA has implemented an active investment promotion program during the 1990s, which includes promotional conferences and executive training programs. For example, MIGA provided such services to the mining and tourism industries in FY1995. The agency conducted the second investment promotion conference for the mining sector in African countries. This conference was held in Toronto, Canada, in May 1995 and was attended by more than 400 mining executives from North America, Asia, and Europe who examined mining investment opportunities in 27 African countries. The World Bank and IFC, as well as corporations, gave their support to this conference. MIGA conducted follow-up visits to mining sites in West African countries later in the year and collaborated with the Organisation for Economic Co-operation and Development (OECD) in a training program for mining sector representatives from Central Asia and the Balkans in June 1995.

In March 1995, MIGA organized the first Conference and Exhibition on Investment Opportunities for Hotels and Tourism in the Arab World. This conference was held in conjunction with the Inter-Arab Union of Hotels and Tourism, the French-Arab Chamber of Commerce, the Inter-Arab Investment Guarantee Corporation — the multilateral forerunner of MIGA — and the Lebanese business magazine, *Al-Iktissad Wal-Aamal*. Private investors from Europe, North America, and Japan were among the more than 400 conference participants for the three-day conference. Government and private sector representatives from most Arab countries of the Middle East also attended. Follow-up investor site visits to Jordan, Lebanon, and Syria were arranged after the conference.

In FY1995, MIGA implemented several technical assistance and investment promotion projects. Among these was the establishment of the Investment Promotion Agency Network (IPAnet), discussed in the following section. MIGA also convened another major conference on opportunities in African mining. This conference was held in Montreal, Canada, in May 1996 with more than 30 African countries participating and more than 400 mining executive and financial institution representatives from Africa, Asia, Europe, and North America. In addition, MIGA held its first Symposium on Mining Investment and Business Opportunities in Central Asia and the Balkan and Caucasus Countries in Montreal in May 1996. Ten countries in these regions participated in the symposium. In addition to MIGA's continuing emphasis on the tourism industry, MIGA also strengthened its efforts at improving the flow of FDI from developing to developing member countries. It held a symposium, Asian Outbound Investment, Trade, and Financing Strategies, in Kuala Lumpur, Malaysia, in March 1996. Investment promotion agency and business representatives from 25 countries attended this symposium, designed to promote the flow of FDI between Asia and Africa, Latin America, the Middle East, and East Europe.

During FY1997, MIGA continued to focus on the mining and tourism industries. The agency held its fourth annual African Mining Investment and Business Opportunities Conference, in Denver, Colorado, in June 1997. This conference has now been recognized as the most important international conference dealing with mining in Africa. MIGA also held a workshop for mining sector officials from the Middle East and North Africa on How to Do Business with Foreign Companies, as well as three similar workshops held in Istanbul, Turkey, for public sector mining officials. These three workshops were held in cooperation with the OECD and the Turkish International Cooperation Agency.

The emphasis on African mining sector foreign investments is a recognition by MIGA that, although political unrest and uncertainty about the future of Africa is a prevalent perception held by foreign investors, the non-commercial loss guarantees provided by MIGA have been a buffer against this uncertainty.[12] Mining could prove to be a strong export market for African countries if sufficient capital investment can be found. The capital investment most relevant to these projects is FDI.

These conferences, seminars, symposiums, and workshops are representative of the many technical assistance and investment promotion activities carried out by MIGA in the 1990s. The agency has collaborated with IFC, through its joint venture with FIAS, with the World Bank, OECD, and national investment agencies to fulfill its mission of promoting the flow of FDI to LDCs. The following section is devoted to a discussion in detail of the electronic internet association of investment promotion agencies, IPAnet, formed by MIGA in 1994.

INVESTMENT PROMOTION AGENCY NETWORK

Finally, one of the most recently developed activities implemented by MIGA is IPAnet. This program, initiated in 1994, is a global, internet-based investment marketplace designed to promote investment in emerging markets. IPAnet is essentially an internet association of investment promotion agencies based in LDCs, or Category II countries as MIGA classifies them. The home page for this world wide web-based program is: http://www.ipanet.net. The web site furnishes investors with investment opportunities, sources of finance, laws and regulations governing investments, and lists of the institutions that play key roles in international investment. IPAnet contains investment data bases, searchable directories, business news, market intelligence, and other highlights that are hyper-linked to other web sites. MIGA cooperates in this program with other multilateral institutions such as United Nations Industrial Development Organization, United Nations Conference on Trade and Development, and G-77 countries' chambers of commerce networks. At the end of FY1997, companies and individuals from more than 150 countries had used IPAnet for investment information. IPAnet provides a package of management information software as well as training to assist investment promotion agency administrations.

IPAnet has been quite successful in its first two years of operations. According to the *MIGA Annual Report 1997*, the electronic network has 4,000 registrants from more than 150 countries. The web site offers access to nearly 10,000 documents covering more than 100 countries.

LEGAL TECHNICAL ASSISTANCE

MIGA has devoted most of its non-guarantee advisory services to technical assistance and investment promotion during its eight years of operations. However, the agency has devoted more resources to legal assistance in recent years. The agency first worked directly or with the cooperation of FIAS to advise member countries on the liberalization of their foreign investment laws and regulations. These activities branched into evaluation of the investment climate and relevant investment regulations as well as assistance in drafting new investment laws in such countries as Bangladesh, Fiji, Mauritania, Pakistan, Sri Lanka, and Zambia. The agency also developed a special training program for government officials on the role and significance of bilateral and multilateral treaties designed to attract FDI.[13] MIGA also has assisted member countries in the negotiation of bilateral treaties on the promotion and protection of investments by convening training seminars. In FY1996, MIGA also assisted four member countries to delimit their common maritime boundaries with the precision demanded by international oil firms that prospect for oil. In FY1997, MIGA negotiated agreements to establish two investment guarantee trust funds to stimulate investment in regions with special needs. One of these funds is aimed at Bosnia and Herzegovina to encourage small and medium-sized investors to participate in the reconstruction of Bosnia. A second fund is aimed at West Bank and Gaza and will enhance the ability of MIGA to cover investments in municipalities under Palestinian authority.[14]

However, in recent years, MIGA's activities in the legal advisory sector have begun to focus on mediation of investment disputes not insured by MIGA. This activity was initiated in FY1994 when MIGA assisted in such mediation between investors and host state governments of several countries in Africa and East Europe. Several other investment disputes were resolved with MIGA's assistance in FY1996. The findings of these settlements are not disclosed because of their legal nature. However, it appears that three such settlements have been negotiated, including a hotel project in Africa and a telecommunications project in Asia.

SUMMARY AND CONCLUSIONS

The operations of MIGA for its first nine years were analyzed in this chapter. Its membership has nearly tripled during its first nine years of operations. During this period, FDI flows into LDCs have increased significantly, concomitant with the increase of MIGA's outstanding contingent liability from $132 million to $2.5 billion. An analysis of its portfolio shows that its coverage is fairly well diversified, as are its active applications by region.

MIGA's financial statements have shown steady improvement during its nine years of operations. Its efficiency, as measured by various means, has increased steadily.

The chapter also contained a discussion of MIGA's cooperative activities with other public forums and institutions as well as its technical assistance activities. These latter functions are directed at LDCs to promote better investment climates and include conferences, seminars, and other investment promotion activities including IPAnet, MIGA's internet investment information site.

NOTES

1. Much of the information in this chapter has been drawn from Multilateral Investment Guarantee Agency, *MIGA Business Profile 1997* (Washington, D.C.: Multilateral Investment Guarantee Agency, 1997).

2. Multilateral Investment Guarantee Agency, *MIGA: The First Five Years and Future Challenges* (Washington, D.C.: Multilateral Investment Guarantee Agency, 1994), p. 11.

3. Ibid., p. 5.

4. Ronald Gift Mullins, "World Bank Unit in Deal with Private Reinsurer," *Journal of Commerce*, April 25, 1997, p. 1A.

5. Gavin Souter, "ACE Assumes More Political Risk," *Business Insurance* 31 (May 5, 1997): 2.

6. Multilateral Investment Guarantee Agency, *MIGA Business Profile 1997*, p. 16.

7. Douglas Corkran, "Tanzania Opens Its Doors to U.S. Business," *Business America* 112 (July 1, 1991): 11.

8. Maria Kielmas, "Political Risk Coverages Come to the West Bank," *Business Insurance* 31 (May 5, 1997): 29.

9. Abid Aslam, "Middle East: PLO, MIGA Sign Political Risk Insurance Accord," *Inter Press Service*, March 4, 1997, p. 2.

10. "Finance: COFACE in Cooperative Agreement with MIGA," *Les Echos*, December 13, 1994, p. n.a.

11. James C. Baker, *International Business Expansion into Less-Developed*

Countries: The International Finance Corporation and Its Operations (New York: International Business Press, 1993), pp. 236–37.

12. "Political Risk has Receded," *The Mining Journal*, June 24, 1994, p. 466.

13. Multilateral Investment Guarantee Agency, *MIGA Annual Report 1993* (Washington, D.C.: Multilateral Investment Guarantee Agency, 1993), p. 22.

14. Multilateral Investment Guarantee Agency, *MIGA Annual Report 1997* (Washington, D.C.: Multilateral Investment Guarantee Agency, 1997), p. 50.

10

Selected MIGA Cases

From its first full year of operations in FY1990 through FY1997, the Multilateral Investment Guarantee Agency (MIGA) has been increasingly active in fulfilling its primary objective, the guarantee of foreign investment in less developed countries. During this period, MIGA has issued 293 guarantee contracts for investments that meet the agency's criteria.[1] These investment guarantee contracts have been issued for investment projects in 52 developing countries and transition economies by investors from 25 member countries. The total estimated foreign direct investment facilitated by MIGA's guarantee contracts amounts to $19.9 billion. The amount of the guarantees issued amounted to $3.398 billion. Seventeen cases were selected from the eight-year period of MIGA's operations. They were selected for a variety of reasons and will be discussed in the following sections of this chapter.

FREEPORT MCMORAN COPPER CO., INDONESIA

One of the first investments insured by MIGA was a $50 million guarantee for the $500 million expansion of a copper, gold, and silver mining project in Irian Jaya, Indonesia, by the U.S. company, Freeport McMoran Copper Company.[2] This investment enabled Freeport McMoran to assist the Indonesian economy through increased earnings, employment, and local procurement. The political risks covered losses from breach of contract and war for a 14-year period.

This expansion project was a very complex investment. The original investment had been constructed in the early 1970s and involved building a road through the jungle, tunneling through two mountains, erecting an aerial tramway from the mine to the mine site, and constructing a slurry pipeline to the coast, a length of 115 kilometers. The expansion boosted ore production by nearly 150 percent, an additional 1,100 jobs were created, and the Indonesian Government earned $90 million in foreign exchange revenues.

MIGA's involvement was the catalyst in putting the final financing package together. The U.S.-German owners wanted to raise 75 percent of the capital by non-recourse loans from commercial banks. Such funding relies on the cash flows from the project and is not backed by non-project assets. Thus, the risks must be divided among the lenders, suppliers, buyers, and owners. MIGA's presence by providing the $50 million of coverage was the key part of the financing and encouraged the other parties to join the project. The Overseas Private Investment Corporation (OPIC) also participated in this project by extending $100 million in coverage after insuring the original project. At this point, private insurers covered the remainder of the project with short-term renewable coverage.[3]

GENERAL ELECTRIC COMPANY, HUNGARY

During its first year of operations, MIGA entered into a reinsurance agreement with OPIC to assist General Electric Company's (GE) $150 million acquisition of a part interest in the Tungsram Company Ltd., of Hungary.[4] Tungsram produces light bulbs and other lighting products. GE's foreign investment was one of the largest since the implementation of economic reforms in East Europe.

The project was designed to modernize and expand Tungsram's manufacturing and distribution operations as part of a joint venture between GE and the Hungarian Credit Bank to acquire, modernize, and expand Tungsram. The MIGA reinsurance guarantee covered the political risks of currency transfer and expropriation.

MIGA's coverage was a $30 million reinsurance contract for a portion of the political risk coverage.[5] OPIC previously had approved $130 million in investment insurance guarantees for this project. The World Bank assumed $30 million of the OPIC risk.

MCDONALD'S CORPORATION, CHILE

During FY1991, MIGA issued 11 investment guarantee contracts. One of these was issued to McDonald's Corporation of the United States for $5 million of the investment by McDonald's in four joint-venture restaurants in Chile to be opened over a five-year period.[6] Additional restaurants could be added. The initial investment created 600 jobs and increased local procurement substantially. The project included management training for Chilean managers and employees of the restaurants. The political risks covered were for losses from currency transfer and war and civil disturbance.

RIO ALGOM LIMITED, CHILE

Another project to which foreign investment was partially guaranteed by MIGA in Chile was a $5 million guarantee to Rio Algom Limited, a Canadian company, to assist Rio Algom's Cerro Colorado copper mine in Chile.[7] The total project cost was $280 million, of which 35 percent was financed by Rio Algom equity. The project was estimated to generate more than $1.5 billion in export earnings for Chile and to employ 500 people. MIGA enlisted the support of OPIC and the Ministry of International Trade and Industry of Japan for this project. The political risks covered losses from currency transfer, expropriation, and war and civil disturbance.

CITIBANK, N.A., PAKISTAN

MIGA began to guarantee foreign bank investments in FY1992. One of the first of these investment guarantee contracts for financial institutions was the issuance of three loan and equity guarantees totaling $49.8 million for Citibank of New York to expand its branch banking operations in Pakistan.[8] The benefits from these projects were increased lending authorizations and the diversification of financial services and resources for productive investment in Pakistan. This expansion generated $11.6 million in tax revenues for the national government and created 100 additional jobs during the 1992–97 period. The political risks covered by these guarantees were for losses from currency transfer and expropriation.

BANK OF BOSTON, ARGENTINA

Another guarantee of branch banking operations of a foreign bank was made by MIGA to Bank of Boston of the United States.[9] This $50 million guarantee enabled Bank of Boston to expand its branch banking operations in Argentina. The expansion added six new branches to the 34 offices Bank of Boston already operated in Argentina. The project created 40 new jobs and generated $1.9 million in annual tax revenues for the Argentinian Government. The political risks covered by MIGA were for losses from currency transfer and expropriation.

MULTISERV RUSSIA, S.A., RUSSIA

MIGA guaranteed a foreign investment in Russia for the first time in FY1993. The agency insured $9.9 million of investment to Multiserv Russia, S.A., a Belgian company for machinery and equipment for a steel slag processing operation in Magnitogorsk, Russia.[10] This project was part of the world's largest steel mill in the world, Magnitogorsk Metall Kombinat. It introduced modern metal recovery systems in Russia to process environmentally hazardous slag stockpiles. Political risks covered by this guarantee contract were for losses from war and civil disturbance, and the coverage was for 15 years. This guarantee by MIGA was instrumental in the financing of this project.

BARCLAYS METALS LTD. AND SEREM, UGANDA

In FY1993, MIGA issued a guarantee contract for $10 million to Barclays Metals Ltd. of the United Kingdom and SEREM of France for a joint venture to extract cobalt in Uganda.[11] The total cost of the project was estimated to be $49 million, making it the largest project in Uganda since its independence in 1962. The project is expected to generate annual exports of $160 million and annual revenues for the Ugandan Government of $53 million. The Western part of Uganda will be aided by the project by becoming the second largest export earner for the country. Some 260 jobs were created by the project. The local community was benefited by the provision of potable water, medical care, and education by the foreign companies. The political risks covered by the investment guarantee were for losses from expropriation and war and civil disturbance.

ARCADIAN PARTNERS, L.P., TRINIDAD
AND TOBAGO

During FY1994, MIGA issued four investment guarantee contracts to Arcadian Partners, L.P., for investments in the fertilizer facilities of Arcadian Trinidad Urea Ltd. and Arcadian Trinidad Ammonia Ltd., the first companies to be privatized in Trinidad and Tobago.[12] The insurance coverage totaled $50 million of a project whose cost totaled $175 million and represented the first MIGA guarantee in Trinidad and Tobago. Export revenues and employment were increased by these projects, which made significant contributions to the government's privatization objectives.

MOTOROLA INTERNATIONAL DEVELOPMENT CORPORATION, PAKISTAN

MIGA once again turned to a foreign investment in Pakistan when it issued an investment guarantee contract in FY1994 for $24.3 million to Motorola International Development Corporation, a subsidiary of Motorola Inc. of the United States and SAIF Telecom (Pvt.), a privately-held Pakistani company, against losses from the political risks of expropriation, currency transfer, and war and civil disturbance.[13] This joint venture created Pakistan Mobile Communications Incorporated, a company that is installing and operating a nationwide cellular telephone network. At the end of the fifth year of operations, this project will service a significant share of Pakistan's cellular telephone consumers. Cellular telephone service was made available in remote, previously inaccessible areas by this project. The project created more than 340 jobs and provides training for employees in electronics, computer operations, and modern business practices.

BRITISH GAS PLC., TUNISIA

During FY1995, MIGA issued a foreign investment loan guarantee contract totaling $64.8 million to British Gas Plc. to develop a gas field in Tunisia.[14] The guarantee included $14.9 million in reinsurance by the Export Credits Guarantee Department, the U.K. export-import bank. This guarantee was MIGA's first for a project in Tunisia and its first reinsurance agreement with the Export Credits Guarantee Department. British Gas will build and operate offshore platforms at the Miskar gas field, as well as a suboceanic gas pipeline and an onshore natural gas processing plant. This gas field is estimated to furnish 90 percent of domestic gas production. British Gas formed a wholly owned subsidiary, British Gas Tunisia Ltd., which will employ more than 250 workers and provide operational, safety, environmental, and security training. The political risks covered by the guarantee are for losses from currency transfer, expropriation, and war and civil disturbance.

INTERNATIONALE NEDERLANDEN BANK, N.V., SLOVAK REPUBLIC

Also in FY1995, MIGA issued its first investment guarantee contract for a project in the Slovak Republic. It was made to Internationale Nederlanden Bank, N.V. of the Netherlands for an investment of $55.5 million to expand its existing branch in Bratislava.[15] This branch will concentrate on lending to infrastructure projects in the energy and telecommunications sectors. The guarantee covers losses from the political risks of currency transfer and expropriation.

CAPITAL INDONESIA POWER I C.V., INDONESIA

During FY1996, MIGA issued an investment guarantee contract to an Indonesian affiliate of General Electric Capital Corporation of the United States. This unit, Capital Indonesia Power I C.V., received a $50 million guarantee for its $61.2 million equity investment in a project to construct and operate two 615-megawatt coal-fired electricity-generating plants in Indonesia.[16] The plants, located at the Paiton Power Generating Complex, will sell power output to the government-owned electricity corporation. More than 260 jobs will be created by this project, and 2,500 construction workers will build the facility. Existing roads and telephone service will be improved by the project. The electricity generated by the project will add to the capacity, which at present is so insufficient that frequent blackouts occur and, thus, impede economic development in Indonesia. The guarantee covers loss from risks of currency transfer and war and civil disturbance.

UNION CARBIDE CORPORATION, KUWAIT

During FY1996, MIGA issued its first investment contract for a project in Kuwait to Union Carbide Corporation, a U.S. company, for part of its equity investment in the construction and operation of a petrochemical facility in the Shuaiba Industrial Complex on the eastern coast of Kuwait.[17] Union Carbide Corporation entered into a joint venture with Petrochemicals Industries Company of Kuwait to form Equate Petroleum Company KSC, the first hydrocarbon joint venture of this type in Kuwait. The facility will produce ethylene for use in the production of polyethylene and ethylene glycol for domestic sale and export. In addition to the additional export revenues of $500 million annually by 1997 generated by the project, more than 100 permanent jobs will be created. These workers will receive training in plant operation and management as well as health, safety, and environmental issues. The guarantee covers risk of loss from war.

COMPAÑIA ESPAÑOLA DE PETROLEOS, S.A., ALGERIA

MIGA reinsured Compañia Española de Seguros de Crédito a la Exportacion for $10 million of the $240 million investment by Compañia Española de Petroleos, S.A. of Spain in an oil and gas project.[18] The political risks covered are for losses from expropriation and war and civil disturbance. The project is a joint venture with Sonatrach, an Algerian company, and will generate $65 million in annual foreign exchange for Algeria, and will employ 50 workers who will receive language and technical training. Local businesses will provide rental equipment, transportation, food, fuel, and construction services.

PHILIPS ELECTRONICS, N.V., BRAZIL

In FY1997, MIGA issued an investment guarantee contract for $27 million to Philips Electronics, N.V., of the Netherlands for its $30 million loan to Philips do Brasil, Ltda, its Brazilian subsidiary.[19] Part of this guarantee was reinsured. Philips do Brasil will use the loan proceeds to improve production technologies and to expand output at its plant in Sao José dos Campos. This plant is the only manufacturer of color TV picture tubes in Brazil. The plant's annual production will be increased by 20 percent, thus enabling the plant to meet the increased demand for color television sets in Latin America. The plant will add 300 workers to its current workforce. The political risks covered by the guarantee insure against losses from expropriation and currency transfer restrictions.

LUXEMBOURGER, SWISS, AND FRENCH INVESTORS IN GUINEA

During FY1997, MIGA issued guarantees totaling $8.3 million to cover equity and loan investments for a project in Guinea.[20] The project enterprise, Société des Grands Moulins de Guinée, S.A., 21 percent-owned by local interests, will construct and operate a mill with the capacity to produce 170 tons of wheat flour and bran per day. Bran will furnish export revenues immediately, whereas the wheat flour will be sold only locally in the beginning. After wheat flour output is expanded, it will also be exported. The wheat flour will be higher quality than is available now and will be less expensive than exported flour, benefiting local users. The project will generate $1.4 million in foreign exchange annually. The importation of modern technology and quality control techniques will benefit the country. A total of 70 new jobs will be created by the project. These new employees will receive administrative and technical training, and the project will sponsor university training programs for the community.

MIGA's coverage was issued to protect the foreign investors against the risks of expropriation and war and civil disturbance. Equity and loan investments were covered by the guarantees for Société de Promotion Financière et d'Investissement, S.A., of Luxembourg, Agro-Industrial Investment and Development, S.A., of Switzerland, and Promofin Outremeer, S.A., of Luxembourg, whereas loans made by Faisal Finance, S.A., of Switzerland, Banque Belgolaise, S.A., of Belgium, and Crédit Lyonnais Belgium, S.A., of Belgium were covered by the MIGA guarantees.

CONCLUSIONS

The cases discussed in this chapter are representative of the 293 investment guarantee contracts issued by MIGA during its first eight years of operations. All major political risks have been covered. The guarantees have been issued for periods exceeding 10 years, longer than other investment insurers. Some projects have included reinsurance by MIGA, and MIGA itself has had some of its guarantees reinsured by other institutions. Almost all of the projects guaranteed by MIGA have increased employment. Some have resulted in increased foreign exchange earnings and tax revenues. Many have resulted in training of domestic workers in a variety of skills. All of the projects have benefited the host state in some form.

NOTES

1. Multilateral Investment Guarantee Agency, *MIGA Business Profile 1997* (Washington, D.C.: Multilateral Investment Guarantee Agency, 1997), p. 4.

2. Multilateral Investment Guarantee Agency, *MIGA Annual Report 1990* (Washington, D.C.: Multilateral Investment Guarantee Agency, 1990), p. 12.

3. Laura Wallace, "MIGA: Up and Running," *Finance & Development* 29 (March 1992): 49.

4. Ibid.

5. "World Bank Agency Reinsures GE Project," *The Wall Street Journal*, June 6, 1990, p. A18.

6. Multilateral Investment Guarantee Agency, *MIGA Annual Report 1991* (Washington, D.C.: Multilateral Investment Guarantee Agency, 1991), p. 15.

7. Ibid., pp. 15–16.

8. Multilateral Investment Guarantee Agency, *MIGA Annual Report 1992* (Washington, D.C.: Multilateral Investment Guarantee Agency, 1992), p. 13.

9. Ibid., p. 16.

10. Multilateral Investment Guarantee Agency, *MIGA Annual Report 1993*, (Washington, D.C.: Multilateral Investment Guarantee Agency, 1993), p. 13.

11. Ibid., p. 12.

12. Multilateral Investment Guarantee Agency, *MIGA Annual Report 1994* (Washington, D.C.: Multilateral Investment Guarantee Agency, 1994), p. 22.

13. Ibid., p. 24.

14. Multilateral Investment Guarantee Agency, *MIGA Annual Report 1995* (Washington, D.C.: Multilateral Investment Guarantee Agency, 1995), p. 16.

15. Ibid., p. 22.

16. Multilateral Investment Guarantee Agency, *MIGA Annual Report 1996* (Washington, D.C.: Multilateral Investment Guarantee Agency, 1996), pp. 25–26.

17. Ibid., p. 39.

18. Multilateral Investment Guarantee Agency, *MIGA Annual Report 1997* (Washington, D.C.: Multilateral Investment Guarantee Agency, 1997), p. 24.

19. Ibid., p. 34.

20. Ibid., pp. 22–23.

11

MIGA's Problems

The Multilateral Investment Guarantee Agency's (MIGA's) operations in its first decade have been an unqualified success when measured by several methods. The agency has filled a gap long needed in the guarantee of private foreign investment projects in less developed countries (LDCs) against loss from major political risks on a multilateral basis. However, MIGA has been faced with a few problems. These problems are discussed in this chapter. An evaluation of the present nature of these problems as well as a look at the future will be covered in Chapters 13 and 14.

The work of this agency was needed in the late 1950s when the Castro Revolution in Cuba resulted in the expropriation of massive amounts of foreign investment and later when the Chilean Government expropriated the foreign copper companies and, in Tunisia, when French assets were arbitrarily expropriated. After the Cuban Revolution, another 25 years passed before the concept was approved by the World Bank and even more years elapsed until sufficient state governments had ratified the MIGA Convention.

As described in Chapter 9, MIGA's membership has increased in every year of its operations from 52 in FY1990 to 141 in FY1997. The agency issued 293 foreign investment project guarantees during these eight years. These agreements amounted to nearly $3.4 billion of risk insurance for an estimated $19.9 billion of foreign direct investment (FDI) facilitated. Nearly 40,000 jobs have been created by these projects. More than 1,000 applications with intent to register for foreign investment guarantees had been filed with MIGA by the end of FY1997.[1] Premium and commitment fees collected by MIGA have grown in every year of its operations. Its portfolio is well diversified by industrial sector and by host region of the projects, and the portfolio is becoming spread among more and more host countries. The goal of encouraging FDI flows from developed to developing countries has been achieved. The efficiency and profitability of MIGA have increased since FY1993 as measured by return on assets employed or by insurance coverage or FDI facilitated per staff employee.

In contrast, problems stemming from MIGA operations can be identified. MIGA could have insufficient resources to maintain operations in the many areas discussed in Chapter 9 at the increasing rate of the first eight years of operations. The demand for MIGA's services, given the political and economic crises that occur around the world from time to time, could soon overwhelm MIGA's resources. The Calvo Doctrine, a problem faced by the International Centre for Settlement of Investment Disputes (ICSID), and other legal problems also have created obtacles for MIGA.

INSUFFICIENT RESOURCES

MIGA has two types of resources available to fulfill its objectives. These are its staff and its financial resources. MIGA has a staff of less than 90 people. This staff is highly qualified for what the agency does. In FY1997, the staff issued $614 million of political risk insurance coverage and facilitated $4.7 billion of FDI. The ratio of FDI to insurance coverage was 7:1. The insurance coverage issued amounted to about $6.8 million per staff member and the FDI facilitated amounted to about $52.2 million per staff member.

MIGA's growth was hindered from its inception by the size of its staff. When the agency began operations in 1989, its staff numbered less than a dozen employees and some of these were on loan from the World Bank. It, therefore, began operations with several challenges, including finding a means to increase membership, recruit permanent staff, develop necessary marketing materials, procedures, and systems needed to attract and process investor applications, and the design of a technical assistance program.

The larger problem was that the FDI decision-making process used by most companies requires months or years to produce. MIGA could not implement its program very quickly so that, when firms were made aware of its investment guarantees, MIGA was able to insure only new investments.

Therefore, during its first four years, for example, it issued fewer guarantees than were issued in FY1997 alone.

In addition to the political risk insurance coverage issued by MIGA, the agency also is involved in several other activities designed to provide technical assistance to member countries, to promote investment flows into these countries, or legal advice to change investment policies practiced by the governments of these countries. These services have included the organization of international and national conferences, seminars, symposia, and workshops about various aspects of foreign investment. Training of public officials in methods that are designed to encourage FDI flows into LDCs often has been included as a follow-up to these conferences, seminars, symposia, and workshops. The agency has furnished legal assistance in the drafting of bilateral and multilateral treaties designed to enhance foreign investment environments in member states.

The technical assistance to member countries has included the dissemination of information on investment opportunities and direct support for investment promotion activities of member countries. The latter has included the advent of Investment Promotion Agency Network in 1994, an electronic association of investment promotion agencies of member countries, which has a web site on the internet and which is hyperlinked to web sites of listed organizations furnishing investment opportunity data, directories, and other information concerning FDI into LDCs. This internet program has generated nearly 4,000 registrants from more than 150 countries and enabled access to 10,000 documents about investment opportunities in 100 countries.

MIGA has collaborated with other agencies to supplement its small staff in the fulfillment of its objectives. The agency has a joint venture with the Foreign Investment Advisory Service of the International Finance Corporation and cosponsors many programs with the Foreign Investment Advisory Service. MIGA has collaborated with the Organisation for Economic Co-operation and Development, the United Nations Industrial Development Organization, United Nations Conference on Trade and Development, the G-77 chambers of commerce—a group representing the LDCs of the world, and other multilateral organizations.

The International Finance Corporation and MIGA have a combined large and diversified staff with a lot of hands-on experience. These agencies have staff that include financial officers with project appraisal skills, insurance officers with skills in political risk measurement, attorneys who can structure agreements between local and foreign investors and between investors and governments, economists who can assess a nation's international comparative advantage in a given sector, and engineers who specialize in the technical appraisal of projects.[2] However, if MIGA's operations continue to grow at the rate witnessed in the first eight years, the agency's staff could become stretched too thin to fulfill its primary objectives in the same highly efficient manner of the 1990s.

Another problem related to MIGA's resources was incurred in the first five years of the agency's operations. Slow growth in country membership in its earliest years hindered capital growth and investment income of the agency and constrained staff growth. In addition, MIGA's investment income during this period suffered from low yields. This problem was exacerbated when MIGA's objective of being financially self-sustaining was recognized. MIGA's management had a conflict between needing to expand its guarantee business and maintaining self-sufficiency.[3]

TOO MUCH DEMAND FOR INVESTMENT INSURANCE

MIGA relies on its own resources to provide political risk insurance coverage and reinsurance for the FDI projects that it approves, as well as the resources of other public and private insurers in the reinsurance of some of its guarantees. At the end of FY1997, the total amount of capital subscribed by its 141 member countries amounted to $1,067.2 million. Of this amount, only $212.7 million had been paid in to the agency. Of the amount paid in, $100.2 million, or about 47 percent, is in the form of non-negotiable, non–interest-bearing promissory notes.

The maximum amount of contingent liability of MIGA under guarantees issued and outstanding at the end of FY1997 totaled $2,499 million. The maximum amount of contingent liability is MIGA's maximum exposure to insurance claims, which includes "standby" coverage for which MIGA is committed but not currently at risk. The MIGA Convention mandates a 3.5:1 ratio of risk to assets. At the end of FY1997, MIGA's estimate of its actual exposure to insurance claims exclusive of standby coverage was $1,634.7 million. About 69 percent of the contingent liability represented guarantees issued, which will expire in or after FY2007.

As mentioned earlier, MIGA had more than 1,000 applications with intent to register from investors. These applications total nearly $200 billion in exposure, with the 100 best of these totaling $1.6 billion insurance guarantee exposure. This added to the nearly $2.5 billion in exposure at the end of FY1997 creates exposure totaling $4.1 billion. Exposure of this magnitude would place MIGA near its maximum mandated exposure limit.

MIGA has not had to pay off on any risk guarantee during its first eight years of operations. However, such a record probably cannot continue in light of the economic consequences of the Yugoslavia situation, the Kuwaiti/Iraq war, and the Asian currency crisis. Although its reserves, especially those unpaid at the present, are much larger than the maximum contingent liability, the demand for its guarantee services, as measured by its application backlog of more than 1,000 active applications, could cause these reserves to be insufficient in the long run to fulfill its objectives at the current rate.

THE CALVO DOCTRINE

The Calvo Doctrine, which was for many years a problem for ICSID, has never been a serious obstacle for MIGA. At least five Latin American nations had signed the MIGA Convention by FY1990, MIGA's first full year of operations. At the end of FY1997, Mexico was the only major Latin American country that had not become a MIGA member.

In the early period shortly after MIGA's establishment, some in Latin America had argued that any type restriction on national sovereignty was unacceptable. MIGA was considered such a restriction. These Latin American advocates believed they could attract FDI without MIGA guarantees.[4]

During the 1990s, the popularity of the Calvo Doctrine began to wane. All nations except Brazil and Mexico have become signatories of the ICSID Convention and only Mexico remains a non-member of MIGA. Reasons for Mexico's reluctance to join MIGA will be discussed in the next chapter. This problem does not appear to be a serious obstacle to either agency at the present time.

MISCELLANEOUS PROBLEMS

In addition to the major problems just discussed above, MIGA has been criticized for other concerns. Some companies are not committed to the use of MIGA products. For example, one major electric power company believes that MIGA's annual premium rate of 4 percent precluded the use of its facilities for the Indian power market where its insurance might have been attractive. Another criticism is that MIGA does not have the capacity to deal with the electric power market's requirements, particularly on large cost investment projects.[5] MIGA has responded to the latter criticism by stating that its project and country ceilings preclude sole MIGA coverage of large projects. The agency added that its co-insurance and reinsurance facilities give it the ability to leverage substantial coverage. With regard to the 4 percent premium criticism, the agency's *Investment Guarantee Guide* shows annual premium base rates no higher than 1.75 percent on a combined current and standby basis, regardless of industry sector or political risk covered.

Others have argued that MIGA's business portfolio would remain relatively small in its first few years of operations as well as too risky because of its process of adverse selection in the approval of coverage for FDI projects. It, thus, was believed that MIGA would have too few projects over which to spread its risk, even if it reinsures or co-insures the projects.[6] Thus, the potential risk of loss would be too high and, if MIGA were to remain self-supporting, premiums would have to be higher. Of course, this argument has been refuted by the number of projects covered during its first eight years of operations and the number of co-insurance and reinsurance contracts it has approved. It has been limited so far primarily by the relatively small size of its staff.

Other concerns in its formative years were the issues of what MIGA considered an expropriatory act by a member government host to a foreign investment and what, in cases of expropriation of foreign investment, would constitute fair and adequate compensation.[7] Because it has not yet paid off on a claim dealing with expropriation, these issues have not been faced and, therefore, not fully resolved.

SUMMARY AND CONCLUSIONS

MIGA has not encountered the variety of serious problems faced by ICSID during its history. The one relatively common problem concerning the Calvo Doctrine impeding Latin American nations from becoming a signatory of ICSID in the past was never a serious problem for MIGA. Mexico appears to be the only Latin American nation not yet a signatory of the MIGA Convention.

MIGA's most serious challenge appears to be the large demand for its guarantee services. During its eight years of full operations, the agency has insured nearly 300 projects and has a backlog of more than 1,000 active applications. Given its investment promotion activities and the burgeoning demand for its guarantees, MIGA's small staff might not be able to cope with such demand in the future.

Finally, the increasing contingent liability fostered by MIGA's growth in investment guarantee issuance could become a serious problem in the future. So far, the agency has not had to pay an investor's claim. This could change as MIGA becomes more involved in the most risky nations where

FDI is needed the most, that is, Africa. Thus far, MIGA has placed a significant amount of interest on the African mining sector in its investment promotion function.

NOTES

1. During this period, nearly 3,900 preliminary applications were made to MIGA. These have been reduced to approximately 1,000 with intent to register. Because of the length of time required to organize an FDI project, some companies later cancelled plans or obtained coverage in some other manner.

2. Foreign Investment Advisory Service, *Foreign Investment Advisory Service* (Washington, D.C.: Foreign Investment Advisory Service, 1990), p. 7.

3. Multilateral Investment Guarantee Agency, *MIGA: The First Five Years and Future Challenges* (Washington, D.C.: Multilateral Investment Guarantee Agency, 1994), p. 9.

4. "New Guarantees for International Investment" (an interview with Yoshio Terasawa, MIGA Executive Vice President), *Tokyo Business Today*, February, 1989, p. 64.

5. "MIGA Leverages up Insurance Capacity, Writes Record Cover," *International Trade Finance*, August 11, 1995, p. 11.

6. S. Linn Williams, "Political And Other Risk Insurance: Eximbank, OPIC and MIGA," *Middle East Executive Reports* 11 (March 1988): 25.

7. Ibid.

12

Theories of the Evolution of ICSID and MIGA

In Chapters 3–11, the International Centre for Settlement of Investment Disputes (ICSID) and the Multilateral Investment Guarantee Agency (MIGA) were introduced and their evolution, operations, selected cases, and problems were discussed and analyzed. Both ICSID and MIGA evolved after several years of discussion of the conceptual foundations for their existence. Both had precursors, which were limited in their scope but which became catalysts for the founding fathers of these agencies.

At this point, how ICSID and MIGA evolved and how their evolution relates to the theories of international organization building can elicit tendencies, which can be generalized to those multilateral organizations needed in the future. For example, in light of the Asian currency crisis of 1997–98, some development experts have advocated the establishment of a global institution capable of going beyond the functions of the International Monetary Fund (IMF). Such an agency could insure the debt of developing countries and act as a global central bank with a lender of last resort function. The formulation and establishment of such institutions can be facilitated if past agency building can be explained by tested theories of international organization.

Several theories have been formulated to explain international relations, specifically the way by which international organizations are established. Some of these are conventional theories, which explain organizational development by the underlying distribution of political or economic power.[1] These theories will be discussed in this chapter and their relevance to the evolution of ICSID and MIGA, the focal points of this treatise, will be analyzed as explanations for the way in which these institutions were formulated and established.[2]

From these organization theories has emerged a set of intraorganizational dynamics driven by states whose objective is to use their power to shape outcomes in their favor.[3] As shown below and earlier in Chapters 3 and 7 on the evolution of ICSID and MIGA, states whose foreign investors had encountered disputes with host state governments or had encountered risk of loss from political risks were able to use their hegemonic power to eventually move the World Bank to establish ICSID and MIGA.

MULTILATERALISM

The theory of multilateralism attempts to explain institutional organizations that coordinate national relations among groups of three or more states on the basis of selected principles. These principles, which provide for ordering of relations among these states, specify appropriate conduct for a class of actions without regard to the particular interests of any of the parties.[4] Multilateral has been defined as an adjective that modifies the noun institution. Specifically, institutions have been defined as "persistent and connected sets of rules, formal and informal, that prescribe behavioral roles, constrain activity, and shape expectations."[5] This definition can be used to describe the character of the Conventions or Articles of Agreement that established ICSID and MIGA. They are, essentially, a set of connected rules, formal and informal, which created these institutions.

A generic form of multilateralism is found in institutional arrangements that define and stabilize the international property rights of states, manage coordination problems, and resolve collaboration problems. The issue becomes not so much the number of parties, however, but the kind of relations that are instituted among them.[6] An arrangement stemming from multilateralism is expected by the members of the grouping to yield some equivalence of benefits on an aggregate basis and over time.[7] These are the expectations political scientists refer to as "diffuse reciprocity."

The formal international organizations explained by multilateralism have their separate and unique identities. Such entities have their own headquarters, letterheads, voting procedures, pension plans, and other institutional perquisites. Their major roles, as mentioned above, are to define and stabilize international property rights and resolve collaboration problems.

For example, the governance of the oceans was solved by a multilateral organization. The International Telegraph Union was established in 1865 to solve the coordination problem stemming from the transmission of diplomatic messages from one government to another. The Concert of Europe, a cooperative movement among the five leading powers in Europe, maintained peace between the Napoleonic and Crimean wars from 1815 to 1854 and is a major example of a multilateral organization that resolved a collaboration problem.

However, prior to the 20th century, multilateralism spawned very few formal organizations. Even during the early part of this century, the League of Nations failed as an attempt at multilateralism. After the end of World War II, a global move to institutions, especially more formal organizations, broke the trend of the previous 150 years. Beginning with the World Bank and IMF, many multilateral institutions across broad areas of interest have been created, including ICSID and MIGA.

In the twentieth century, the multipurpose universal membership organization was added to the variety of institutions formed under multilateralism. Such organizations have broad agendas, all member states — large or small — have a constitutionally mandated vote, and are capable of handling collective projects in an *ex ante* coordinated manner.[8] Furthermore, the theory of hegemonic stability can be incorporated in multilateralism to explain institution building.[9]

The United States, as a principal hegemony, has been responsible for advocating and supporting the proposals for several international organizations. The formation of the World Bank and IMF are major examples of organizations that would have had trouble were it not for U.S. support. Many multilateral organizations receive 25 percent or more of their subscribed capital from the United States. Without this sizable share of the capital, many of these organizations could not survive as they were intended. The International Labour Organization is an example of a UN agency that has had financial problems since U.S. support was terminated.

Most major international problems involve many countries simultaneously. These include pollution, energy, airline traffic, and rules for international trade and investment.[10] Multilateralism, thus, facilitates the solution of these problems and appeals to the less formal, less codified habits, practices, ideas, and norms of international society. Multilateral organizations provide platforms on which the players learn to alter perceptions of interests and beliefs. The establishment of the World Bank is an illustration of an institution that promoted the interests of the major nations in the new United Nations, especially the United States.

Three theoretical paths to understanding comprise the concept of multilateralism: the individualist paradigm — in which states enter into contractual relations with other states in a rational, self-interested way; the social-communicative approach — whose focus is on the identities and powers of individual states including communication, persuasion, deliberation, and self-reflection; and, finally, an institutional approach — whereby several competing conceptions are evoked about what institutions are and what their role is.

GAME THEORY AND HEGEMONY

Game theory has been used to explain the behavior of nations in their desire to build multilateral institutions. Martin assumes that state governments are self-interested and will apply multilateralism only when it serves their interests.[11] For example, collaboration problems have been solved using a form of the prisoners' dilemma.[12] Symmetrical interests among the parties are present in cooperation, coordination, or collaboration problems. The interests of major nations were expressed in the establishment of ICSID and MIGA. Foreign investors from the major industrialized countries either had disputes arise in their agreements with host state governments or had suffered losses from political risks encountered in the host state government.

However, it took several years to form a multilateral institution that offered arbitration or solutions to contract disputes. The Montivideo Treaty of International Procedural Law of 1888 included a statement that gave "the same force to judgements or decisions by arbitration in the territory of others that they have in the issuing country."[13] As mentioned in Chapter 3, only four countries ratified this treaty. The Geneva Protocol on Arbitration Clauses of 1923 and the Geneva Convention on the Execution of Foreign Awards of 1927 also were attempts to remedy this problem. After other attempts, 69 countries finally ratified the New York Convention of 1958, which required that disputes be submitted to arbitration rather than to the courts. The World Bank then initiated a study in 1962 to determine the feasibility of forming a multilateral institution, culminating in the Convention on the Settlement of Investment Disputes between States and Nationals of Other States, whose approval established ICSID in 1966. The problems faced by investors from the hegemonic states such as the United States finally forced the issue to be resolved with the formation of a multilateral institution designed to resolve such investment disputes.

The formation of MIGA was the answer to another problem facing hegemonic interests. The Castro revolution in Cuba resulted in the expropriation of all foreign investment. U.S. investors lost a large amount of property. Very little if any was insured. Shortly afterwards in 1969, the Overseas Private Investment Corporation (OPIC) was established by the United States as a bilateral quasi-governmental agency designed to furnish investment insurance, but only for U.S. investors in less developed countries (LDCs). OPIC's coverage, therefore, is limited to foreign direct investment in LDCs placed by U.S. investors. Its guarantees are limited by government funding and not all political risks are covered. Other major states wanted more protection for their investors in foreign projects. For example, French investors had suffered arbitrary expropriations of their property in Tunisia without adequate if any compensation. Thus, the interests of these foreign investors from major industrialized countries played a major role in the formation of MIGA.

After 1945, the decolonization movement led to a principle associated with multilateralism, that is, the sovereign equality of states. Bilateral agencies such as OPIC did little to help investment projects in the smaller LDCs. Private insurers do not have the resources to commit investment guarantees to long-term periods and their coverage is limited to a small part of the investment and only one or two political risks. In 1974, the Inter-Arab Investment Guarantee Corporation was formed. Although it is a multilateral institution, its investment guarantees are limited to investment flows among its Arab member countries, as discussed in Chapter 3.[14]

A hegemony is a preponderant influence or authority, that is, in leadership or dominance. The theory of hegemonic stability holds that hegemonic powers are similar in their desire to organize the international system. The fact that the United States emerged after World War II as the world's leading hegemony resulted in a much different world as we see it today than if Nazi Germany, the Soviet Union, or even Great Britain had become the world's leading power.[15]

The United States as a major hegemon played a major role in the formation of multilateral institutions after World War II, particularly for the two discussed in this book. Hegemonic interests, as pointed out by Ruggie, emphasize the benefits of multilateral institutions.[16] These benefits include lower transaction costs, the deflection of challenges to the institution by its weaker members, and increased stability under conditions of changes in relative power.

The creation of ICSID and MIGA demonstrated some of these benefits. An investor that faces a dispute with a host government can seek a remedy from local courts or government agencies. However, such a remedy depends on the willingness of the host government to submit to the court's jurisdiction. Many such countries do not or will not; thus the foreign investor has little guarantee of court access.[17] The ICSID, although restricted by its own limitations, offers the foreign investor a possible solution to this dilemma.

A MIGA-like concept was the subject of several World Bank studies between 1961 and 1981. At the 1981 Annual Meeting of the World Bank, MIGA was proposed. Its Arab precursor was used as a model. A Convention Establishing the Multilateral Investment Guarantee Agency was presented to World Bank members in 1985 for their approval. The requirements for establishment were completed in 1988 and MIGA's first year of operations was completed in 1989–90.

CONCLUSIONS

Both the sovereign equality of nations and the hegemonic interests of the large industrialized nations were responsible for the establishment of these two agencies. Just as the small nations were important in the formation of the World Bank and IMF and the success of such multilateral institutions as the Uruguay Round of the General Agreement on Tariffs and Trade negotiations, the Law of the Sea Conference, and the Vienna Convention on Protection of the Ozone Layer, they were instrumental in keeping the ideas of ICSID and MIGA alive until the major nations recognized the value of these multilateral institutions to their self-interests.[18]

Certain theories of international organizations, including multilateralism, hegemony, and game theory, can explain why some institutions, such as ICSID and MIGA, have such a tortuous route to establishment but, when they are finally formed, result in performing functions that are in the best interests of the global community. They demonstrate the extent to which powerful states will give up control over international decision-making in exchange for stability. The degree to which they do so depends on whether such a state will value future international interactions as highly as it values them at the present.[19]

NOTES

1. John Gerard Ruggie, "Multilateralism: the Anatomy of an Institution," *International Organization* 46 (1992): 564.

2. James C. Baker and Susan M. Edwards, "Selected Multilateral Financial Institutions: Their Role in the Private Sector and Theories of Their Evolution," in Robert D. Goddard, III (ed.), *Proceedings of the 1997 Annual Meeting of the*

Association for Global Business (Boone, N.C.: Association for Global Business, 1997).

3. John Echeverri-Gent, "Between Autonomy and Capture: Embedding Government Agencies in Their Societal Environment," *Policy Studies Journal* 20 (1992): 348.

4. Ruggie, "Multilateralism," pp. 570–71.

5. Ibid., p. 565.

6. William Diebold, Jr. (ed.), *Bilateralism, Multilateralism and Canada in U.S. Trade Policy* (Cambridge, Mass.: Ballinger, 1988), p. 1.

7. Robert O. Keohane, "Reciprocity in International Relations," *International Organization* 40 (Winter 1986): 1–27.

8. Volker Rittberger, "Global Conference Diplomacy and International Policy-Making," *European Journal of Political Research* 11 (1983): 167–82.

9. Ruggie, "Multilateralism," p. 564.

10. James A. Caporaso, "International Relations Theory and Multilateralism: The Search for Foundations," *International Organization* 46 (1992): 1.

11. Lisa Martin, "Interests, Power, and Multilateralism," *International Organization* 46 (August 1992): 767.

12. Duncan Snidal, "Coordination Versus Prisoners' Dilemma: Implications for International Cooperation and Regimes," *American Political Science Review* 79 (December 1985): 923–42.

13. Ibid., p. 83.

14. James C. Baker, "Global Foreign Investment Insurance: The Case of MIGA with Comparisons to OPIC and Private Insurance," *Managerial Finance* 21 (1995): 25–26.

15. Ruggie, "Multilateralism," p. 585.

16. Ibid., p. 586.

17. James C. Baker and Lois J. Yoder, "ICSID Arbitration and the U.S. Multinational Corporation: An Alternative Dispute Resolution Method in International Business," *Journal of International Arbitration* 5 (1988): 82.

18. Miles Kahler, "Multilateralism with Small and Large Numbers," *International Organization* 46 (1992): 681–708.

19. Martin, "Interests, Power, and Multilateralism," p. 791.

IV

CONCLUSIONS

13

An Evaluation of ICSID and MIGA

EVALUATION OF ICSID AND ITS OPERATIONS

Introduction

One measure of the influence of the International Centre for Settlement of Investment Disputes (ICSID) on international commercial transactions is the cash flow expectations of the companies involved in foreign investment projects, especially those that involve agreements with host state governments. The magnitude and timing of these expectations can be included as inputs into a present value analysis of the foreign investment projects in which the firms are involved. However, one of the missing ingredients for such an analysis is a significant body of casework dealing with dispute settlement experience according to the ICSID system.

The ICSID Arbitration Procedures

ICSID arbitration provides many assurances to both the foreign investor and to the host state government.[1] These assurances have been written into the ICSID Convention (Convention) and a host state's ratification of this treaty is tantamount to its acceptance by that government. First, the ICSID arbitration procedures cannot be affected by the nonparticipation of the host government and any award is enforceable in the courts of any signatory state, according to the Convention. Thus, the foreign investor should be encouraged to invest in developing states that are ICSID signatories, knowing that these safeguards exist.

Second, the host state government is assured by several Convention requirements. A host government is not required to enter into an arbitration procedure to which it has not consented. In addition, the investor's home state government will not be able to intervene in the process as long as the host state adheres to the ICSID procedures. The host government is protected from frivolous claims because the ICSID Secretary-General screens the request to insure that the claim is based on a proper investment agreement over which ICSID has jurisdiction. If the investment project involved is a politically or economically sensitive activity, the host state government can exempt it from the Convention's procedures by prior declaration. Finally, Article 71 of the Convention gives the host state government the ability to renounce the Convention's jurisdiction if the host state government believes it has been applied in an arbitrary manner.

Cost of Arbitration Procedures

Although the cost of the ICSID arbitration procedure is relatively less than arbitration by other institutions, it can be expensive.[2] Total costs of an ICSID arbitration proceeding generally exceed $100,000, excluding fees of the legal counsel for the parties. This amount can run much higher, especially if annulment proceedings are registered after the award.

As a result of these costs, the ICSID Administrative Council approved a new procedure in 1984, which includes a pre-hearing conference. This pre-hearing conference was designed to expedite arbitration proceedings and, thus, result in significant savings.

ICSID conciliation has been relatively inexpensive. Only three such proceedings have been registered by the agency. In one of these, the proceeding was discontinued and, in another, the proceeding involved only one conciliator whose recommendations were accepted by both parties at a total cost of less than $11,000.

The Recent Buildup in ICSID Cases

ICSID, at the time of this writing, is in its 32nd year of operations. During its first five years, no cases were registered. During the next 25 years, the agency registered an average of one case in three five-year periods and two cases per year in the other two five-year periods. During FY1997, a record seven cases were registered. Thus, the number of cases registered has increased significantly during the 1990s. More awards have been made, and the procedures have quickened somewhat. The agency is gaining more recognition as it considers more cases and adds to its body of findings.

During its history, ICSID has restated and modified its policies with regard to its arbitration and conciliation procedures and rules. In FY1984 for example, the Secretary-General of ICSID proposed changes to its rules and regulations for arbitration or conciliation proceedings. These changes were made to clarify some rules and to permit more flexibility in the implementation of the proceedings. With the ability to make such changes, ICSID has remained one of the most flexible arbitration institutions.

Membership Problems

Many of the problems discussed in Chapter 6 have been alleviated or eliminated. In addition to more cases being registered and more awards being made, the problems with Latin American countries and the Calvo Doctrine apparently have been resolved. Only Brazil and Mexico have balked at signing the Convention. Mexico might not desire ICSID membership because the North American Free Trade Agreement (NAFTA) includes a procedure for dispute resolution between member nations. For reasons discussed earlier, Canada remains the only major developed country that has yet to sign the Convention. Many East European and former U.S.S.R. countries as well as China, all primarily communist at the time of ICSID's establishment, have joined ICSID or are in the process of doing so.

Indications of ICSID's value are found in many of the Latin American countries, which formerly espoused the Calvo Doctrine as a reason for not signing the ICSID Convention. For example, because of several problems, foreign investment in Peru had been almost nonexistent prior to 1990. However, investment in Peru has become more appealing for foreign investors because the government there ratified the Convention. The clear process for dispute resolution provided by ICSID is seen as a favorable step in that country.[3]

ICSID Model Clauses

Many more companies are including ICSID model clauses in their agreements with host states. These clauses permit the triggering of ICSID arbitration procedures when a dispute arises that cannot be solved amicably.

Treaty and Investment Law Work

ICSID's work in compiling the treaties and investment laws of signatory nations has been extraordinary. Since the inception of ICSID, nearly 1,200 investment treaties have been formulated. Of these, about 75 percent provide for ICSID arbitration of the settlement of disputes that arise from such treaties.

Many investment laws have been legislated in member countries and these contain similar references to ICSID arbitration. Some of these laws and many of the most recent treaties provide for submission of these disputes to arbitration under the ICSID Additional Facility Rules. Others provide for arbitration under the rules of the United Nations Commission on International Trade Law.

Meetings and Publications

ICSID's support of conferences, workshops, symposia, and colloquia to discuss international investment and dispute resolution has increased over the years. It has continued to produce many publications designed to promote foreign investment law, including its semiannual journal, newsletter, administrative council minutes, *ICSID Cases*, *ICSID Bibliography*, news releases, and other works.

Opinions of ICSID by Multinational Corporate Executives

In the past, top international legal counsel and chief financial officers of leading multinational corporations (MNCs) were asked for their opinions about several operational aspects of ICSID. Many were critical of certain procedures and practices. At the present time, many of these perceptions are still held by officials of these same MNCs. In contrast, some of the reservations are no longer relevant because of the body of cases developed during the past few decades. The concerns discussed in this section are included for illustrative purposes and will be analyzed for their current relevance.

Adequate Safeguards for MNCs

Several problems with ICSID arbitration have been cited with reference to whether it represents adequate safeguards for major MNCs investing in less developed countries (LDCs). For example, some are concerned with ICSID's lack of power to enforce its panels' awards. This, of course, assumes lack of understanding of the treaty-like status of the Convention and the fact that ICSID awards are enforceable in the courts of all signatory states. Some fear creeping expropriation and the apparent lack of obligation of a revolutionary government to respect the agreements of its predecessors. Although consent under the Convention cannot unilaterally be withdrawn by either foreign investor or host state, it can still happen — as it did in the case of the aluminum companies and Jamaica. Others, however, believe that ICSID's connection with the World Bank should help its enforcement of awards against a host country that needs international credit.

Which Party the Convention Favors

Most executives of MNCs believed that the Convention favored the host signatory state in an arbitral proceeding. One executive stated that, even though the execution of arbitral awards are governed by the laws concerning the execution of judgments in force in the state where execution is sought, that state can avoid execution by passing a law insuring immunity from execution. Thus, a national of another contracting state that is involved in the dispute is at a serious disadvantage.

Another stated that the Convention permits a contracting state to limit the scope of its submission to the jurisdiction of ICSID in addition to requiring exhaustion of local remedies and application of its own laws. Thus, as a practical matter, the investor can often be forced to accept these restrictive conditions imposed by a host state, while at the same time being required by Article 27 of the Convention to waive any right to seek diplomatic protection, except in cases where the contracting state fails to comply with the Convention or abide by an award.

Another believed the host state is favored because it has available the doctrine of state sovereignty when a case is being presented or considered. However, this executive did not believe the Convention was at fault because a sovereign state always has a wider basis for technical justification of its acts than a non-sovereign entity, by definition. Another executive added to this opinion that the Convention acknowledges the state's greater position of power and autonomy relative to the investor.

Another executive believed that the Convention favors the host state because the list of panel members is top heavy with member nations' administrative functionaries. The Convention does not require a panel of arbitration or conciliation members to be from signatory states but, because most states have become signatory nations and because each contracting state can designate up to four persons to each panel and the administrative council can designate up to 10 persons for each panel, it seems reasonable that, given the qualifications necessary for panel members, they will be top heavy with administrative functionaries. This should not give the host state any more favoritism than a foreign investor because the investor is also from a contracting state.

Utilization of ICSID

Executives were asked whether their firm had used or plans to use the facilities of ICSID. The answers to this query may have changed in the time since this survey was undertaken because of the wider use of ICSID in general. Only one of seven executives who answered this query stated that his firm has used the ICSID facilities. This firm had used the agency's facilities in Africa in two mining investments.

The reasons given by the other company officials were quite diverse. One firm attempts to work out its problems with the sovereign host state. Another had not used or contemplated using ICSID but had included an ICSID clause in its agreement with a host country. Another had not had a dispute with sovereign partners but might contemplate using ICSID if a problem were to arise. Another company official believed that ICSID does not remove the investor's obligation to work with the host government and attempts to resolve difficulties privately. The presence of ICSID, in other words, cannot improve an already bad relationship. Another firm enters into projects in which it uses the rules of, or the services of, such organizations as the American Arbitration Association or the Japan Commercial Arbitration Association. Another firm uses its lawyers to proceed through the courts to settle disputes.

Further Steps Needed

Executives were asked what further steps they believed were needed to insure the fair settlement of disputes that are between a company of one country and a different host government and involve the failure of either party to fulfill contractual obligations. One executive believed the arbitration and conciliation panels should have more members from private industry, that ICSID should have some punitive powers to enforce awards, and that insurance coverage of some kind should be available in contracts between foreign investors and host signatory states. This latter suggestion may have been covered by the advent of the Multilateral Investment Guarantee Agency (MIGA).

Another executive believed that an international commercial court should be available to develop an international commercial law, rather than having to involve national law in a domestic court. This suggestion might not be possible because international law does not cover private enterprise projects because of the problem of the conflict of laws among sovereign states. Another believed the time required for an arbitration proceeding and subsequent enforcement of an award should be shortened. Some of the arbitral proceedings have taken several years.

One suggestion concerned the seemingly never-ending problem of educating the private investment community about the ICSID procedure. This executive believed that it was not enough to merely ratify the Convention but that host countries should learn what acceptance of the Convention means and what the responsibilities are that go with it. He stated that a company is generally a continuing entity as is a country. The problem is that governments change.

Another executive suggested that a multilateral investment code should be developed, which details the rights and obligations of the host state, the foreign investor, and the state of which the investor is a national. A code, which embodied these principles, was proposed at a Workshop on Foreign Direct Investment held in Wellington, New Zealand, April 6–7, 1995. This proposal included a draft convention on the protection of private property, a declaration on international investment and multinational enterprises, codes of liberalization of capital movements, and current invisible operations, all to be developed under the auspices of an organization such as the Organisation of Economic Co-operation and Development.[4]

Finally, one executive believed that a serious question exists regarding the enforcement of an ICSID award, particularly when the host signatory state in question has a new or hostile government. Again the Convention states that an ICSID award is enforceable in the courts of any contracting state.

Recognition of ICSID by Major Regional Groupings

ICSID and its facilities and benefits are being recognized by major regional groupings in the formulation of their rules and regulations. For example, one of the prominent features of NAFTA is its procedure for dispute resolution between member nations. This agreement builds on several methods previously established in Canada and the United States but it also relies on the ICSID procedures as a model, especially with regard to time constraints in the dispute resolution process, procedures to guarantee the impartiality of the panelists, binding decisions, and in the arbitration panel selection methodology.[5]

Summary and Conclusions

After 32 years of operations, it seems that most of ICSID's problems have been alleviated or eliminated. The two most serious problems, inadequate case body of results and lack of Latin American country memberships, seem to have been resolved. During the 1990s, the number of cases registered with ICSID has increased significantly and, in FY1997, a sharp increase in registered cases shows that ICSID has been discovered by MNCs that contract with host state governments in their foreign direct investment (FDI) projects. With regard to the initial snubbing of ICSID membership by Latin American nations — a result of the Calvo Doctrine — since 1983, almost all of these nations became signatories of the Convention. Only Brazil and Mexico remain non-signatory countries.

As the problems related to these two issues have subsided, many more MNCs have become aware of the services of ICSID. Most of the concerns expressed by MNC officials, as stated in the preceding section, have been alleviated. At the 25th anniversary of ICSID, its Secretary-General applauded the increasing acceptance of ICSID as measured by the number of member countries and by the increasing inclusion of ICSID model clauses in their contracts with foreign investors.[6] In addition, member countries have shown greater interest in ICSID by incorporating references to the agency in their national investment legislation and in bilateral investment treaties.

EVALUATION OF MIGA AND ITS OPERATIONS

Introduction

ICSID and MIGA both have underlying major objectives that are similar in nature. The major services of both institutions are designed to improve the FDI climate in LDC members. However, MIGA has not incurred the number and variety of problems that have plagued ICSID, mainly because MIGA's operations are not restricted in its jurisdiction to the extent that ICSID's are and, therefore, MIGA's service has a much broader audience than that of ICSID.

The concept of investment insurance can have much broader implications than the more narrow focus of the arbitration of a dispute in a contract between a foreign investor and a host state government. A MIGA investment guarantee can run as high as $50 million or more whereas an ICSID arbitral proceeding can be concerned with a dispute that amounts to a few million dollars at most.

MIGA filled a niche in the global market for investment insurance in many ways. The agency augmented the capacity of other insurers with its co-insurance or reinsurance. It is able to insure investment in countries that are restricted or excluded by the policies of other insurers. MIGA serves investors that do not have access to other official insurers. It provides coverage to investors of different nationalities in a multinational syndicate and, therefore, offers convenience in insurance contracting and claims settlement. Finally, it provides coverage of forms of investment not offered by other insurers and on terms designed to be more effective in the encouragement of investment.[7]

MIGA has, however, incurred a few problems during its first decade of operations. These problems have been overcome by the growth in the demand for its services. Concomitant with this growth in its investment guarantee business is the growth in FDI flows into LDCs. MIGA has been a significant catalyst in this result. The comments about MIGA by the business community have confirmed that MIGA's operations have had a positive impact on the FDI environment in LDCs.

Foreign Direct Investment Increase after MIGA's Beginning

A major objective of the MIGA's investment insurance program is to encourage increased flows of FDI into LDCs. In the mid-1980s, FDI flows to these countries reached a low point of about $9 billion annually. After MIGA was established and had initiated its investment guarantee program, FDI into LDCs increased significantly. A study completed by International Finance Corporation showed that FDI flows into LDCs amounted to $36 billion in 1992.[8] This study showed that during the 1989–94 period, FDI flows to 118 LDCs grew at an annual rate of 23 percent, reaching 37 percent in 1991 and 33 percent in 1992. More than 80 percent of the recorded FDI flows during this period were directed at the more dynamic economies in Latin America and East Asia.

The advent of MIGA was not the sole reason for this growth of FDI into LDCs. However, the beginning of global investment insurance was one of the many positive changes in the environment of the LDCs, which created strong positive responses by MNCs and banks in the industrialized nations toward the improved investment climates in the developing world. In the past few years, the significant increase in the demand for MIGA guarantees shows that the development of this concept has been a strong catalyst toward a favorable private investment climate in the LDCs.

Growth of Demand for MIGA Guarantees

A survey of all of the investors insured by MIGA was made in 1994 by an independent consultant.[9] This study found that 32 of the 34 contract holders who responded to the survey stated that they would use MIGA again if they needed investment insurance. These same investors said they would recommend MIGA's services to other investors.

In this same study, the investors were asked to rate the importance of MIGA guarantees to their decisions to make the covered investments.[10] Of the 34 respondents, 19 rated the insurance "absolutely critical" or near that end of the rating scale. The remaining 15 investors rated MIGA coverage "useful" or better.

Inadequate Financial Resources Problem

Earlier analysis showed that MIGA's insurance exposure can approach or exceed its mandated maximum exposure limit if the best of the current applications are approved. MIGA's formula for capital subscription makes it difficult for the agency to acquire new capital. However, other sources of investment insurance, either by MIGA or with MIGA's cooperation, are possible. The ACE Insurance Company, Ltd. of Bermuda treaty project, discussed earlier, can furnish additional coverage. The regional development banks, including the Islamic Development Bank, are in the process of forming units that offer regional MIGA-like services. It has been estimated that $1 billion of additional resources could be mobilized from the World Bank and other financial institutions. MIGA coverage of private bank loans can produce a synergistic effect on FDI from these sources, thus replicating Overseas Private Investment Corporation (OPIC) and Citibank coverage. Such international banks as ABN Amro and Internationale Nederlanden Bank, N.V. are interested in offering this coverage. More national government insurers like OPIC are being established. Austria is an example of a nation forming a new bilateral agency.

Expert Opinions of MIGA's Establishment

Several leaders of the insurance industry expressed strong opinions about the value of a multilateral investment insurance agency during 1987, the formative year of MIGA's inception.[11] For example, Drury Davis, then vice president and director of political risk insurance for the March & McLennan Company, pointed out that the political risk market had a large demand for insurance capacity. He projected the cost of construction of a bridge in Turkey to be $780 million for which the insurance capacity to cover the risk was unavailable. Frank Boylan, then senior vice president of trade services for Alexander & Alexander, believed MIGA could promote multicountry ventures, whereas private insurers did not have the financial resources to offer insurance for these projects. He thought MIGA could cover much larger projects than OPIC could cover. Robert Shanks, then general counsel for OPIC, agreed with Mr. Boylan. John Salinger, then president of the political risk division of the American International Group, said that MIGA's guarantees were needed because its operations would be more flexible than OPIC's insurance. He believed that MIGA also could offer longer term coverage than could be obtained in the private sector.

Evaluation of MIGA Cases

Three cases in which MIGA guarantees were made for foreign investment can be cited as examples of the success MIGA has had in the foreign investment insurance field and in the enhancement of the private sector in LDC member countries. These cases involve a 1991–92 Karnaphuli Fertilizer Company Ltd. (KAFCO) ammonia and granular urea processing plant investment in Bangladesh, a 1992 Bank of Boston branch expansion project in Argentina, and a 1993 investment by Greenwood Mills, a U.S. company, in the construction and operation of a fully integrated garment production facility in Pakistan.

Karnaphuli Fertilizer Company Limited of Bangladesh

During FY1991 and FY1992, MIGA issued four investment guarantees for part of a $516 million project by Marubeni and Chiyoda Company of Japan in KAFCO in Bangladesh. This project was for construction and operation of a large ammonia and granular urea processing plant. This was the largest private investment ever made in Bangladesh, and the investment was put together by MIGA, four other investment insurers, eight export credit agencies, two development assistance agencies, and a consortium of private equity and debt investors.[12]

MIGA reviewed this project in September 1996. The project has had a very large impact on the country. Bangladesh uses this investment as a model foreign investment. KAFCO has served as an example for advanced technology, product quality, human resources management, and investment in social infrastructure. MIGA found the following as positive development results of this project:[13]

an aggressive training program, which is a demonstration of a strong commitment to human capital development with 1,000 participants;

creation of more than 600 permanent jobs for local nationals and another 300 jobs through contractors, with only five foreign expatriates;

utilization of modern fertilizer technology that permits Bangladeshi ammonia to be introduced as an export product;

provision of a complete social infrastructure for project employees, including housing, transportation, medical services, a school, a mosque, and recreation facilities;

stimulation of several local business firms with backward linkages of $32 million in local inputs;

strong forward linkages with the creation and/or expansion of many businesses;

the economic impact of $90.8 million in annual export earnings and $3.56 million in annual duties and taxes; and

improved environmental impact management.

Bank of Boston in Argentina

MIGA issued a guarantee to cover a $50 million loan by the Bank of Boston in FY1992. This loan was made to enable its Argentine branch to expand operations by initiating a financing program for residential mortgages. The presumption underlying this bank branch expansion was the forecast of a pent-up demand for long-term, low interest rate mortgages in Argentina. An expansion of the Bank of Boston branch there would give the bank the top position to address this demand.

The project was reviewed by MIGA in April 1997 and was found to have been very successful.[14] Mortgages with five-year maturities and 24 percent interest rates had been replaced by mortgages with 13- and 20-year maturities with interest rates of 12–15 percent. Residential mortgages made up 50 percent of the branch's retail business, and the bank had plans for further expansion in Argentina. This project increased the ability of Argentine citizens to own their own homes. Private housing had become an important part of the national construction business, and the multiplier effects on the brick, cement, wood, steel, and home furnishing industries were considerable. This project boosted the construction industry as a major sector in Argentina. Other banks had followed the lead of Bank of Boston so that competition in the banking industry had increased as well as employment. The project also increased jobs in the mortgage sector with 200 new employees working directly and many more in support jobs. New infrastructure was developed by the project in the form of roads and schools connected to the new residential areas. Finally, the project generated additional government tax revenues totaling $2 million annually.

Greenwood Mills in Pakistan

In FY1993, Greenwood Mills, a U.S. company located in South Carolina, made an investment totaling $9.85 million for the construction and operation of a fully integrated garment production facility in Pakistan. MIGA issued a guarantee for $8.4 million against the risks of currency transfer, expropriation, and war and civil disturbance.

This project was the largest foreign investment in the textile industry in Pakistan and is a joint venture consisting of Greenwood Mills, locally owned Crescent Textile Mills, and the general Pakistani public. The project was designed to supply 70 percent of Pakistan's annual jean production output and about 8 percent of its total cotton garment exports.[15]

Some changes were made in the project after it was initiated.[16] Some additional investment from other investors failed to materialize and, thus, Greenwood Mills increased its investment in the project to $13.8 million. MIGA later agreed in FY1995 to cover a total of $12 million in its guarantee. When the project was initiated, the joint venture company, Crescent Greenwood, Ltd., was 42.1 percent owned by Crescent Textile Mills, 40.5 percent by Greenwood Mills, 10 percent by the International Finance Corporation, and 7.4 percent by the Asian Finance and Investment Corporation, Ltd.

A MIGA evaluation in late 1997 found the project had generated several beneficial development effects.[17] These included:

employment of 2,750 people, of whom 355 were women, with good working conditions, benefits, and training programs;

strong backward linkages with $20 million spent in the project's first full year of operations for local inputs, primarily cotton, but also locally-sourced equipment and spare parts;

forward linkages in the form of expenditures for transportation and employment services and food supplies;

technological benefits in the form of state-of-the-art equipment;

export earnings amounting to $19.2 million in 1996 and $3.2 million in duties and taxes paid to the government;

extensive provision of a complete social infrastructure for the project's employees in the form of housing, schooling for dependents, transportation, medical services, and recreation facilities; and

improved environmental practices and worker safety.

Membership Problems

The Calvo Doctrine problem, which hindered ICSID, has not had much of an impact on MIGA. Mexico is the only major country in Latin America that has not become a MIGA-signatory nation. This could be the result of the inclusion in NAFTA of similar protection and, thus, Mexico would not wish to duplicate this coverage. OPIC cannot cover projects in Mexico but private insurers do guarantee investments in that country. However, these insurers generally run out of coverage fairly quickly.

Australia was the major capital-exporting country that delayed its membership in MIGA. However, Australia has signed the Convention and should become a member shortly.

SUMMARY AND CONCLUSIONS

ICSID and MIGA are institutions that were established to fill gaps in the FDI environment in LDCs. Their facilities have improved this environment and, although the results cannot be quantified, have increased the flow of FDI into these countries.

Both agencies have overcome a variety of problems and, in essence, are still coping with some of these obstacles. Both have faced, in varying degrees, the Calvo Doctrine problem, which has restricted Latin American nations from becoming members of multilateral financial institutions. Both have been hindered by small staffs in the face of recent burgeoning increases in the demand for their services. However, their collaboration with other international agencies has expanded their ability to fulfill the objectives of the Conventions that established them.

Specifically, ICSID was designed to facilitate the arbitration or conciliation of contract disputes between foreign investors from signatory states and host state governments. Such jurisdiction is quite narrow and covers a field of disputes that no other public or private arbitration institution can handle. It had expanded its services to include the compilation and publication of investment laws and treaties of member nations as a service for the global public at large. In addition, it promotes its dispute resolution procedures through conferences, seminars, publications, and model clauses for inclusion in investment contracts, national legislation, and investment treaties.

MIGA was designed to mitigate political risks and provide financial compensation to foreign investors for losses caused by covered risks resulting from host government actions during the term of an FDI. It also has an expanded agenda to offer advisory services to member LDCs and transitional economies aimed at improving the investment environment in these countries for foreign investors so that FDI flows into such countries will be increased.

During the last three years of MIGA operations, FY1995–97, the agency has expanded its investment insurance coverage significantly. Insurance contracts and commitments on portions of foreign investors' exposures in new projects have averaged more than $700 million during this period. Thus, MIGA can now be ranked among the five largest investment risk insurers in the world. The FDI facilitated in these projects will total nearly $20 billion when they are completed. MIGA, after a very slow start, has become a major player in the insuring of foreign investment against political risk.

Finally, when the contributions to development in its member countries are evaluated, MIGA can be classified as one of the most beneficial multilateral institutions thus far created. The projects insured by MIGA will create nearly 40,000 new jobs in the host countries with substantially larger indirect employment benefits stemming from training and other technology flows. These projects will contribute to the host countries' foreign exchange earnings and savings. Better production technologies have been introduced into these countries along with better management techniques. Domestic economies are stimulated by the payment of salaries and purchase of goods and services by the new employees during the life of the projects. Thus, the total economic impact of these projects insured by MIGA against loss from political risk could exceed the impact from a much larger loan financing of such projects.

This chapter has included an evaluation of ICSID and MIGA. Although both agencies have encountered problems, which, at times, have hindered their operations, most of these issues have been resolved. These agencies have contributed quite successfully to the improvement of the foreign investment climate in their member LDCs.

NOTES

1. Thomas Kuchenberg, "The World Bank: Arbiter Extraordinaire," *The Journal of Law and Economic Development* 2 (1968): 277.

2. International Centre for Settlement of Investment Disputes, *ICSID 1986 Annual Report* (Washington, D.C.: International Centre for Settlement of Investment Disputes, 1986), p. 4.

3. Miguel Grau, "Peru: Privatization Programs," *Latin Finance* 49 (July 1993): 106.

4. William H. Witherell, "Towards an International Set of Rules for Investment: The OECD Initiative," *News from ICSID* 12 (Winter 1995): 3–6.

5. Gary Horlick, "Dispute Resolution under NAFTA," *Journal of World Trade* 27 (February 1993): 21–41.

6. Ibrahim F. I. Shihata, *ICSID 1990 Annual Report* (Washington, D.C.: International Centre for Settlement of Investment Disputes, 1990), p. 5.

7. Multilateral Investment Guarantee Agency, "MIGA: The Mission and the Mandate," found on the internet at http://www.miga.org/mandate.htm, (May 9, 1997, p. 1).

8. Multilateral Investment Guarantee Agency, *MIGA: The First Five Years and Future Challenges* (Washington, D.C.: Multilateral Investment Guarantee Agency, 1994), p. 11.

9. Ibid., p. 7.

10. Ibid., p. 9.

11. Steven Brostoff, "World Bank OKs Political Risk Unit," *National Underwriter* 91 (April 13, 1987): 6, 115.

12. Multilateral Investment Guarantee Agency, *MIGA Annual Report 1997* (Washington, D.C.: Multilateral Investment Guarantee Agency, 1997), p. 19.

13. Ibid.; Multilateral Investment Guarantee Agency, *Kafco Bangladesh Project Monitoring Report* (Washington, D.C.: Multilateral Investment Guarantee Agency, 1997), pp. 1–2.

14. Multilateral Investment Guarantee Agency, *Banco de Boston Argentina Project Evaluation Report* (Washington, D.C.: Multilateral Investment Guarantee Agency, 1997), pp. 1–2.

15. Multilateral Investment Guarantee Agency, *MIGA Annual Report 1994* (Washington, D.C.: Multilateral Investment Guarantee Agency, 1994), pp. 23–24.

16. Multilateral Investment Guarantee Agency, *Crescent Greenwood, Ltd. Pakistan Project Evaluation Report* (Washington, D.C.: Multilateral Investment Guarantee Agency, 1997), p. 3.

17. Ibid., p. 2.

14

Conclusions

The primary objective of this book was to present in one place a discussion of the evolution, operations, and results of two rather obscure multilateral agencies that were formed to improve the developing country environment for foreign investors. These agencies, which are both affiliates of the World Bank and were spawned by World Bank studies and promotion, are the International Centre for Settlement of Investment Disputes (ICSID), created in 1966, and the Multilateral Investment Guarantee Agency (MIGA), created in 1988.

Any conclusions about these agencies drawn from the discussion and evaluation found in the preceding chapters must consider the global economic environment faced by investors today. Currency markets have been very volatile — for example, the Mexican peso crisis of the early 1990s, the Asian currency crisis of 1997, and the trillion-dollar volume days on the foreign exchange markets that have become the normal trend. Global stock markets also have been very volatile in recent years, and the sharp declines in October of 1987 and 1997 have shown that prices on these markets can, at times, be highly correlated. Banks have collapsed in the industrialized world — savings and loans in the United States in the late 1980s and Japanese banks in 1997, and systemic risk has worried international bank regulators because of its contagious effect on banks, national economies, and international capital markets.

Cronyism and political corruption are rampant in many countries and have been blamed for a major part of the 1997 Asian currency crisis and for capital market manipulation in many regions of the world. Bureaucratic political systems are entrenched in many less developed countries (LDCs) and protective marketing systems control the distribution process in many countries, including economic powers such as Japan. More and more foreign direct investment (FDI) projects are based on agreements between foreign investors and host state governments or their agencies.

Because of all of these reasons, the flow of FDI into the developing countries has been greatly restricted. The environment for FDI flows into LDCs must be enhanced so that these countries' economic systems will produce sufficiently for per capita income to increase. ICSID and MIGA are two agencies designed to alleviate the problems just mentioned and to enhance the flow of FDI into LDCs.

As discussed in Chapter 1, the operations of ICSID and MIGA, particularly in recent years, have contributed to the enhanced investment environments of many LDCs. Even in Africa, particularly sub-Saharan Africa, FDI has increased in some countries. MIGA has focussed attention on the mining industry in Africa with the organization of several conferences and seminars, which have brought investors from the industrialized world to examine the possibilities in this area. Still, a great deal of work is necessary before African nations can resemble the Asian countries and their economic successes of recent years.

THE FUTURE OF ICSID

Calvo Problem Slowly Disappearing

Much of the operations of ICSID in Latin America were restricted during its first two decades because of the Calvo Doctrine (see Chapter 6 for details). According to the Calvo Doctrine, contract disputes between foreign investors from member countries and host state governments that had signed the ICSID Convention should be settled by the local legal system (including its courts) rather than the ICSID. Many of the very countries where foreign project agreements might be candidates for ICSID jurisdiction rejected membership in the agency. Thus, ICSID's world was constricted by this so-called legal doctrine. "Calvo clauses," based on the doctrine, were placed in foreign investment project contracts. These clauses triggered resolution of any contract disputes by the local court system and the avoidance of the remedies of any foreign legal system or international agency.

However, since 1983 when the first Latin American state signed the Convention, this legal philosophy practiced in Latin American countries has softened. Slowly, Latin American governments began to see the benefits of ICSID's conflict resolution procedures. Among the Latin American nations that have ratified or are in the process of ratifying the ICSID Convention are Argentina, Bolivia, Chile, Colombia, Ecuador, Paraguay, Peru, Uruguay, and Venezuela. In recent years, contract dispute resolution cases have been registered for ICSID facilitation in Argentina and Venezuela. Several Central American countries have also joined ICSID and disputes in Costa Rica and Mexico are currently under ICSID jurisdiction for resolution. Thus, the Calvo Doctrine problem seems to be waning and could be alleviated completely during the fourth decade of ICSID's operations.

More Publicity to Encourage Use by Multinational Corporations

Nearly 400 books and articles with ICSID as their major subject have been published in the legal literature. ICSID has published many different pamphlets, annual reports, minutes, newsletters, and other documents that discuss its operations and procedures. One of these documents, a short informational brochure of four pages, actually includes all of the information a novice to the agency needs to become well-informed about its operations. ICSID could make available brochures such as this one to top management of the leading multinational corporations on a global basis. ICSID officials could also make appearances at major world trade conferences to tout the facilities of the agency.

One solution to the awareness problem might be to adopt a very successful program that is used by the Inter-American Development Bank. This agency sends officials to trade conferences around the world to inform local businesses of trade and investment opportunities in Latin America. These officials discuss the role of the bank and promote projects that are feasible but have not been financed by it. ICSID could make presentations to these conferences about its arbitration/conciliation facilities and the benefits of its model clauses. ICSID publishes and promotes a great deal about the agency but much of its promotion is within the legal community or the World Bank community.

More Business Literature, Fewer Law Review Studies

The key to more awareness of ICSID and its benefits is wider publicity of the services offered by the agency. The agency is involved in dispute resolution in LDCs where foreign investors are involved. Thus, one would expect ICSID's operations to be included in the legal and arbitration literature. However, FDI is a form of international business and is directed at projects that enhance economic development in LDCs. Thus, the agency should be addressed in the business, international business, finance, economic development, and political science literature. When coverage of the agency becomes more widespread in areas other than law and arbitration literature, global awareness, especially in relevant areas, will grow.

Case Body is Growing: Six More Cases in 1997

As FDI flows to LDCs continue to increase at the rate of the past few years and as private sector investment begins to crowd out public sector investment, thus making the investment climate more positive in these countries, more project contracts between foreign investors and host state governments will be executed. As more of these contracts are made there probably will be more disputes between the parties, and, therefore, a greater demand for the arbitration and conciliation services of ICSID.

Based on the increased activity of the past few years and particularly FY1997, this forecast seems imminent. Six new arbitration cases were registered by ICSID in FY1997. The host member states in these cases are located in Latin America, Africa, and East Europe. Three of them are Latin American nations where, just 15 years ago, the Calvo Doctrine restricted countries in that region from signing the ICSID Convention. Two of the host states are located on the continent with the most difficult environment for FDI. One is a transition economy moving from a communist regime to a free market, private enterprise environment.

As ICSID's case body and experience with the arbitration procedures unique to dispute resolution between a private investor and a host state government expand, its potential should be realized in the years to come.

Conclusions

Shortly after the establishment of ICSID, several questions were raised about the institution.[1] Some wondered whether it would become popular as an institution. Would it reduce the number of certain types of legal disputes? Would the agency show that most disputes between investors and host state governments are no more important than ordinary business disputes? Would they also show that these disputes would have no consequences on the relations between the parties other than a judicial settlement, that is, would violent confrontations between the parties be replaced by settlement in the judicial system?

After more than three decades of operations, ICSID seems to have provided positive answers to these questions. In the last few years, the number of cases registered for ICSID arbitration has increased significantly. Many of these cases have been settled amicably by the parties. It appears that the ICSID procedures and its rules and regulations have encouraged many of these parties to settle their disputes in this manner.

As of the end of FY1997, no dispute registered with ICSID had ended with violence. It appears that foreign investors from signatory nations and signatory state governments, which are hosts to foreign investments, now realize that ICSID offers a sound procedure and, with its growing body of cases, a solid legal benchmark for dispute resolution within the narrow jurisdiction to which ICSID adheres. ICSID's early expectation that governments and foreign investors might welcome the availability of international procedures for the settlement of investment disputes seems to have been confirmed.

THE FUTURE OF MIGA

Results of More Foreign Direct Investment Will Help

In the first five years of MIGA operations, FDI flows into LDCs increased significantly. MIGA was not the sole reason for this phenomenon but the agency was a major catalyst in turning around one of the developing world's major problems. As LDCs and transition economies become more developed and their private investment environment improves, more FDI will flow into these countries. Many of the political risks still will be prevalent and investment insurance still will be needed.

MIGA's backlog of active guarantee applications is a good indicator of demand for its product. At the end of FY1997, MIGA had a backlog of 1,000 active applications. Another area, which will be in large demand in LDCs in the future, should be infrastructure projects. As these countries expand their economies, they will need to expand and improve their infrastructure. Of the 1,000 active applications mentioned above, 35 percent were in the infrastructure sector.

MIGA's backlog also includes a pipeline of registered projects with many investors and LDCs. These projects involve investors from 50 countries and proposed projects in 120 LDCs. As MIGA country membership increases, this backlog demonstrates a strong future for an agency whose time has come.

More Resources from Members

The full potential of the funding process for MIGA has not been tapped yet. Only 10 percent of a signatory nation's subscribed capital is paid in when the state signs the Convention. Another 10 percent is in the form of promissory notes. MIGA has not had to use funds other than its premium and fee income and the initial cash payment by members. Although the agency has not had to pay out on a claim, the contingency is always present. As the economies of LDCs in which MIGA-guaranteed projects are located improve, the likelihood of significant payouts is remote. However, because the demand for the investment guarantees continues to increase, MIGA will have more premium and fee income. The financial welfare of MIGA seems to be intact for the foreseeable future.

Other investment insurance resources will become available. The World Bank and other financial institutions will furnish added cash. The regional development banks are forming regional MIGA-type insurance units. MIGA's reinsurance, co-insurance, and treaty insurance programs like the ACE Insurance Company, Ltd. of Bermuda project will enhance the global coverage of investment projects. Thus, MIGA will be able to offer more coverage than its present mandated maximum liability dictates.

New Jobs Created in Less Developed Countries

During the eight years of MIGA operations, FY1990–97, the agency has issued 293 investment guarantees against the risk of loss from political acts. These guarantees have amounted to $3.4 billion of political risk coverage and have facilitated $19.9 billion of FDI projects that have created an estimated 38,820 jobs. The synergy of the projects insured by MIGA, coupled with the increased tax and foreign exchange revenues that will be generated by this FDI and the training furnished by most of the investments, will improve the private investment environment in the host LDCs. As these investments generate new projects, a greater number of employment opportunities will be promoted. Such changes should improve the political climates in these countries, thus creating a circular effect, which results in significant flows of FDI into these countries and the excellent chance that the recipient LDCs can begin to export private investment to other LDCs.

Planned Operational Innovations in MIGA's Services

Several innovations in the implementation of MIGA's guarantee services have been planned for the future.[2] These include:

priority to the promotion and issuance of insurance to projects sponsored by companies of developing member countries, especially where MIGA's total insurance exposure is close to country ceilings set by the agency;

sponsorship of the formation of co-insurance syndicates among private insurers prepared to participate in conjunction with MIGA in covering new foreign investments against certain risks;

entering more reinsurance and co-insurance by national agencies in order to minimize MIGA's use of its own insurance capacity to encourage projects; and

cooperation with interested agencies and governments in the creation of "sponsorship funds" that would augment MIGA's financial capacity to insure investments in otherwise restricted project situations while continuing to use MIGA's underwriting services and privileged position.

CONCLUSIONS

ICSID and MIGA are small cogs in the machinery of global, economic development assistance. They rarely are cited in the business and economic literature of academia. Even in the trade literature in this area, they do not merit much space in the coverage of multilateral development institutions.

However, both agencies have gained a solid foothold in the development community. MIGA has accomplished this in only one-third of the time that it has taken ICSID to do so. However, ICSID recently has incurred a significant increase in the registration of arbitration procedures. Because Latin American nations have begun to see the advantages of being signatory nations, ICSID has become a truly global institution in terms of the services that it offers. Throughout its entire history, ICSID has been consistent in one area of operations: its assistance in the formulation of investment legislation and publication of investment laws and treaties of its member nations.

MIGA, in only 10 years of operations, has developed a burgeoning backlog of investment guarantee applications. This, coupled with its expanded co-insurance and reinsurance programs, has given the agency global admiration for its broad coverage of the major political risks involved in foreign investment in LDCs. The projects covered by MIGA insurance have produced a vast amount of new employment in the developing world. Its ancillary programs concerned with investment promotion have increased the positive environment for foreign investment projects located in member country LDCs.

The objectives of both organizations are being fulfilled. They have filled significant gaps: ICSID in the settlement of disputes between foreign private investors and host state governments and MIGA in the guarantee of foreign investments in LDCs against losses from political risks. These agencies both required many years of discussion before they were established. They are now global organizations whose time has come.

ICSID and MIGA have reached the stage when they can be used as models for new institutions needed for other areas. For instance, an agency with rules and regulations similar to those used by ICSID could be established to arbitrate disputes between state governments. The United Nations has the means to do this, but is too political, and the International Court of Justice is too slow and deliberate. A convention could be drafted that could appeal to UN member nations' desire to resolve intergovernmental disputes without resorting to violence. A MIGA-type agency could be established whose function would be to insure the sovereign loans made by international banks to governments. Such an agency might alleviate the problems encountered in the Asian currency crisis of 1997–98. In other words, such agencies could spread the risk among many countries instead of limiting it to a handful of high income nations.

NOTES

1. Phillipe Kahn, "The Law Applicable to Foreign Investments: The Contribution of the World Bank Convention on the Settlement of Investment Disputes," *Indiana Law Journal* 44 (Fall 1968): 32.

2. Multilateral Investment Guarantee Agency, *MIGA: The First Five Years and Future Challenges* (Washington, D.C.: Multilateral Investment Guarantee Agency, 1994), p. 10.

APPENDIXES

Appendix I
MIGA Coverage by Investor and Host Countries
(as of June 30, 1997)

Investor Country	Host Country	MIGA Coverage ($ millions)	Total
U.S.A.	Indonesia	174.00	
	Turkey	142.50	
	Pakistan	134.50	
	China	118.03	
	Argentina	107.50	
	Czech Republic	81.00	
	Peru	69.80	
	Poland	66.00	
	Jamaica	64.30	
	Colombia	63.00	
	Kuwait	50.00	
	Trinidad & Tobago	50.00	
	Uzbekistan	50.00	
	Brazil	45.55	
	Hungary	33.20	
	Philippines	30.00	
	El Salvador	22.05	
	Costa Rica	19.65	

Investor Country	Host Country	MIGA Coverage	Total
	Venezuela	18.00	
	Ecuador	16.00	
	Viet Nam	15.40	
	Saudi Arabia	14.50	
	Guatemala	13.00	
	Chile	11.50	
	Bahrain	5.80	
	South Africa	4.50	
	Egypt	2.20	1,421.98
Netherlands	Brazil	77.00	
	Slovak Republic	69.70	
	Venezuela	53.50	
	Poland	51.80	
	Argentina	50.00	
	Hungary	37.40	
	Russia	32.20	
	Philippines	30.60	
	Colombia	30.00	
	Bulgaria	24.00	
	Honduras	18.00	
	Ecuador	16.00	
	Peru	15.00	
	Kazakhstan	4.60	
	China	4.00	
	South Africa	4.00	517.80
United Kingdom	Russia	69.30	
	Tunisia	64.80	
	Brazil	32.05	
	Pakistan	31.90	
	Venezuela	30.00	
	Argentina	24.00	
	Ecuador	24.00	
	China	14.10	
	Uganda	13.27	
	Papua New Guinea	10.00	
	Paraguay	10.00	
	Bulgaria	4.90	
	Tanzania	3.10	331.42
Canada	Chile	54.80	
	Guyana	49.80	
	Kyrgyz Republic	45.00	

Investor Country	Host Country	MIGA Coverage	Total
	Jamaica	24.00	
	Costa Rica	18.00	
	Argentina	2.00	
	Costa Rica	0.58	194.185
France	Czech Republic	50.00	
	Pakistan	42.07	
	Poland	14.40	
	China	12.60	
	Peru	9.10	
	Bangladesh	9.00	
	Uganda	5.70	
	Sri Lanka	5.40	
	Madagascar	3.60	
	Guinea	2.77	
	Bulgaria	2.70	
	Cameroon	0.40	157.74
Turkey	Russia	40.00	
	Azerbaijan	16.50	
	Kazakhstan	16.50	
	Kyrgyz Republic	14.30	
	Chile	10.00	97.30
Switzerland	Peru	26.90	
	Pakistan	16.70	
	South Africa	12.30	
	Uganda	5.40	61.30
Japan	Bangladesh	26.00	
	Chile	19.80	
	Peru	9.40	
	Pakistan	2.10	
	Indonesia	1.40	58.70
Spain	Peru	19.00	
	Argentina	15.00	
	Algeria	10.00	
	Morocco	9.90	
	Russia	1.20	55.10
South Africa	Mali	50.00	
	Bulgaria	0.648	50.648
Cyprus	Peru	50.00	50.00
Finland	Jamaica	30.00	
	Honduras	11.90	41.90
Norway	Nepal	32.80	32.80

Investor Country	Host Country	MIGA Coverage	Total
Italy	Brazil	21.60	
	Argentina	5.00	
	Russia	5.00	31.60
Belgium	Argentina	15.0	
	Russia	9.90	
	Guinea	2.77	27.67
Sweden	Peru	27.00	27.00
Greece	Romania	15.80	
	Bulgaria	3.70	
	Georgia	3.40	22.90
Norway	Jamaica	20.20	20.20
Luxembourg	Ghana	9.85	
	Chile	5.40	
	Guinea	2.77	18.02
Saudi Arabia	Turkey	4.50	4.50
Argentina	Brazil	3.00	3.00
Norway	Poland	2.70	2.70
Germany	China	2.02	2.02
China	China	0.54	0.54
TOTAL			3,231.023

Source: Multilateral Investment Guarantee Agency, *Annual Reports FY1990–97* (Washington, D.C.: Multilateral Investment Guarantee Agency), various issues.

Appendix II
ICSID Cases 1966–97

12. Société Ouest Africaine des Bétons Industriels v. State of Senegal (ARB/82/1)
13. SEDITEX Engineering Beratungsgesellschaft für die Textilindustrie m.b.H. v. Government of the Democratic Republic of Madagascar (CONC/82/1)
14. Swiss Aluminium Limited and Icelandic Aluminium Company Limited v. Government of Iceland (ARB/83/1)
15. Liberian Eastern Timber Corporation v. Government of the Republic of Liberia (ARB/83/2)
16. Tesoro Petroleum Corporation v. Government of Trinidad and Tobago (CONC/83/1)
17. Atlantic Triton Company Limited v. People's Revolutionary Republic of Guinea (ARB/84/1)
18. Colt Industries Operating Corporation, Firearms Division v. Government of the Republic of Korea (ARB/84/2)
19. Southern Pacific Properties (Middle East) Limited v. Arab Republic of Egypt (ARB/84/3)
20. Maritime International Nominees Establishment v. Government of the Republic of Guinea (ARB/84/4)
21. Ghaith R. Pharaon v. Republic of Tunisia (ARB/86/1)
22. Société d'Etudes de Travaux et de Gestion SETIMEG S.A. v. Republic of Gabon (ARB/87/1)
23. Mobil Oil Corporation, Mobil Petroleum Company, Inc. and Mobil Oil New Zealand Limited v. New Zealand Government (ARB/87/2)
24. Asian Agricultural Products Limited v. Democratic Socialist Republic of Sri Lanka (ARB/87/3)
25. Occidental of Pakistan, Inc. v. Islamic Republic of Pakistan (ARB/87/4)
26. Manufacturers Hanover Trust Company v. Arab Republic of Egypt and General Authority for Investment and Free Zones (ARB/89/1)
27. Vacuum Salt Products Limited v. Government of the Republic of Ghana (ARB/92/1)
28. Scimitar Exploration Limited v. Bangladesh and Bangladesh Oil, Gas and Mineral Corporation (ARB/92/2)
29. American Manufacturing & Trading, Inc. v. Republic of Zaire (ARB/93/1)
30. Philippe Gruslin v. Government of Malaysia (ARB/94/1)
31. SEDITEX Engineering Beratungsgesellschaft für die Textilindustrie m.b.H. v. Government of Madagascar (CONC/94/1)
32. Tradex Hellas S.A. v. Republic of Albania (ARB/94/2)
33. Leaf Tobacco A. Michaelides S.A. and Greek-Albanian Leaf Tobacco & Co. S.A. v. Republic of Albania (ARB/95/1)
34. Cable Television of Nevis, Ltd. and Cable Television of Nevis Holdings, Ltd. v. Federation of St. Kitts and Nevis (ARB/95/2)
35. Antoine Goetz and others v. Republic of Burundi (ARB/95/3)

36. Compañia del Desarrollo de Santa Elena v. Government of Costa Rica (ARB/96/1)
37. Misima Mines Pty. Ltd. v. Independent State of Papua New Guinea (ARB/96/2)
38. Fedax N.V. v. Republic of Venezuela (ARB/96/3)
39. Metalclad Corporation v. United Mexican States (ARB(AF)/97/1)
40. Société d'Investigation de Recherche et d'Exploitation Miniere (SIREM) v. Republic of Burkina Faso (ARB/97/1)
41. Société Kufpec (Congo) Limited v. Republic of Congo (ARB/97/2)
42. Compañia de Aguas del Aconquija S.A. and Compagnie Générale des Eaux v. Argentine Republic (ARB/97/3)
43. Robert Azinian and others v. United Mexican States (ARB(AF)/97/2)
44. Ceskoslovenska obchodni banka, a.s. v. Slovak Republic (ARB/97/4)
45. WRB Enterprises and Grenada Private Power Limited v. Grenada (ARB/97/5)
46. Lanco International, Inc. v. Republic of Argentina (ARB/97/6)
47. Emilio Agustín Maffezini v. Kingdom of Spain (ARB/97/7)
48. Compagnie Française pour le Développement des Fibres Textiles v. République de Cote d'Ivoire (ARB/97/8)
49. Joseph C. Lemire v. Ukraine (ARB(AF)/98/1)

*ARB = arbitration case; CONC = conciliation case; AF = Additional Facility case.

Source: International Centre for Settlement of Investment Disputes, *ICSID Cases* (Washington, D.C.: International Centre for Settlement of Investment Disputes, 1997); International Centre for Settlement of Investment Disputes, *List of ICSID Current Cases* (as of February 1998) (Washington, D.C.: International Centre for Settlement of Investment Disputes, 1998).

Selected Bibliography

Amerasinge, C. F. "The International Centre for Settlement of Investment Disputes and Development through the Multinational Corporation," *Vanderbilt Journal of Transnational Law*. Vol. 9, Fall 1976, pp. 793– 816.

"Asian Agricultural Products Ltd. (AAPL) v. Republic of Sri Lanka, Case No. ARB/87/3," *ICSID REVIEW — Foreign Investment Law Journal*. Vol. 6, pp. 526–97.

Aslam, Abid. "Middle East: PLO, MIGA Sign Political Risk Insurance Accord," *Inter Press Service*. March 4, 1997, p. 2.

August, Ray. *International Business Law: Text, Cases, and Readings*. Englewood Cliffs, N.J.: Prentice-Hall, 1993.

Aytittey, George B. N. "How Africa Ruined Itself," *The Wall Street Journal*. December 9, 1992, p. A20.

_____. "African Thugs Keep Their Continent Poor," *The Wall Street Journal*. January 2, 1998, p. 8.

Baer, John J. "Staying Out of Court," *International Business*. Vol. 10, July/August 1997, p. 10.

Baker, James C. "Settling Foreign Investment Disputes Via ICSID," *Business*. Vol. 40, July-August-September 1990, pp. 43–44.

_____. *International Business Expansion into Less-Developed Countries: the International Finance Corporation and Its Operations*. Binghamton, N.Y.: The Haworth Press, 1993.

_____. "Global Foreign Investment Insurance: The Case of MIGA with Comparisons to OPIC and Private Insurance," *Managerial Finance*. Vol. 21, 1995, pp. 23–39.

____. *International Finance: Management, Markets, and Institutions.* Upper Saddle River, N.J.: Prentice-Hall, 1998.

Baker, James C., and Susan M. Edwards. "Selected Multilateral Financial Institutions: Their Role in the Private Sector and Theories of Their Evolution," *Proceedings of the 1997 Annual Meeting of the Association for Global Business.* Boone, N.C.: Association for Global Business.

Baker, James C., and John K. Ryans, Jr. "A Little Known Solution to Investment Disputes in High Risk Countries," *Akron Business and Economic Review.* Vol. 6, September 1975, pp. 8–12.

Baker, James C., and Lois J. Yoder. "ICSID Arbitration and the U.S. Multinational Corporation," *Journal of International Arbitration.* Vol. 5, 1988, pp. 81–95.

Baker, James C., and Lois J. Yoder. "ICSID and The Calvo Clause: A Hindrance to Foreign Direct Investment in LDCs," *Ohio State Journal on Dispute Resolution.* Vol. 5, 1989, pp. 93–112.

Berger, Klaus Peter. "The New Multilateral Investment Guarantee Agency: Globalizing the Investment Insurance Approach Towards Development," *Syracuse Journal of International Law and Commerce.* Vol. 15, 1988, pp. 13–58.

Bhattacharya, Amar, Peter J. Montiel, and Sunil Sharma. "How Can Sub-Saharan Africa Attract More Private Capital Flows," *Finance & Development.* Vol. 34, June 1997, pp. 3–6.

Bleakley, Fred R. "Foreign Investment by Multinational Grew 40% in 1995, Lifted by Mergers," *The Wall Street Journal.* September 25, 1996, p. A2.

Bleiberg, Robert M. "Ill Wind From Jamaica," *Barron's.* July 15, 1974, pp. 7, 12.

Bond, Stephen R. "Arbitration of International Commercial Disputes under the Auspices of the International Chamber of Commerce," *International Journal of Technology Management.* Vol. 4, 1989, pp. 489–511.

Bremner, Brian, Michael Shari, Ihlwan Moon, Mike McNamee, and Kerry Capell. "Rescuing Asia," *Business Week.* November 17, 1997, pp. 116–22.

Brennglass, Alan C. *The Overseas Private Investment Corporation: A Study in Political Risk.* New York: Praeger, 1983.

Broches, Aron. "The Convention on the Settlement of Investment Disputes: Some Observations on Jurisdiction," *Columbia Journal of Transnational Law.* Vol. 5, 1968, pp. 263–80.

____. "Choice-of-Law Provisions in Contracts with Governments," *Record of the Association of the Bar of the City of New York.* Vol. 26, January 1971, pp. 42–55.

____. "Introductory Remarks," *1972 Administrative Council Annual Meeting.* Washington, D.C.: International Centre for Settlement of Investment Disputes, 1972, p. 3.

____. "On the Finality of Awards: A Reply to Michael Reisman," *ICSID REVIEW — Foreign Investment Law Journal.* Vol. 8, 1993, pp. 92–103.

Brostoff, Steven. "World Bank OKs Political Risk Unit," *National Underwriter.* Vol. 91, April 13, 1987, pp. 6, 115.

Caporaso, James A. "International Relations Theory and Multilateralism: The Search for Foundations," *International Organization.* Vol. 46, 1992, pp. 599–632.

Chang, Duck-Soon. "Arbitration in Korea," *East Asian Executive Reports.* Vol. 14, January 1992, pp. 21–22.

Corkran, Douglas. "Tanzania Opens Its Doors to U.S. Business," *Business America.* Vol. 112, July 1, 1991, p. 11.

Davis, G. Alisha. "Africa's New Dawn," *International Business.* Vol. 10, February 1997, p. 10.

"Decision of the Tribunal of Geneva," *ICSID REVIEW — Foreign Investment Law Journal.* Vol. 1, Fall 1986, pp. 383–91.

Delaume, Georges R. "ICSID Arbitration in Practice," *International Tax and Business Lawyer.* Vol. 2, Winter 1984, pp. 73–74.

____. "ICSID Arbitration Proceedings: Practical Aspects," *Pace Law Review.* Vol. 5, Spring 1985, pp. 563–89.

____. "ICSID Tribunals and Provisional Measures — A Review of the Cases," *ICSID REVIEW — Foreign Investment Law Journal.* Vol. 1, Fall 1986, pp. 392–95.

Delphos International. "Financing," *Business America.* Vol. 112, March 25, 1991, pp. 18–23.

Deshpande, V. S. "International Commercial Arbitration: Uniformity of Jurisdiction," *Journal of International Arbitration.* Vol. 5, June 1988, pp. 115–30.

Diebold, William, Jr. (ed.). "The History and the Issues," *Bilateralism, Multilateralism and Canada in U.S. Trade Policy.* Cambridge, Mass.: Ballinger, 1988.

Drucker, T. C. "The Perspective of Canadian Investors on Accession to ICSID," *News from ICSID.* Vol. 7, Winter 1990, pp. 6–9.

Echeverri-Gent, John. "Between Autonomy and Capture: Embedding Government Agencies in their Societal Environment," *Policy Studies Journal.* Vol. 20, 1992, pp. 342–64.

Escobar, Alejándro A. "Three Aspects of ICSID's Administration of Arbitration Proceedings," *News from ICSID.* Vol. 14, Summer 1997, pp. 4–8.

"Finance: COFACE in Cooperative Agreement with MIGA," *Les Echos.* December 13, 1994, p. n.a.

Foreign Investment Advisory Service. *Foreign Investment Advisory Service.* Washington, D.C.: Foreign Investment Advisory Service, d. n.a.

Grau, Miguel. "Peru: Privatization Programs," *Latin Finance.* No. 49, July 1993, p. 106.

Haendel, Dan. *Foreign Investments and the Management of Political Risk.* Boulder, Colo.: Westview Press, 1979.

Hammerskjold, Dag. Address to the American Bankers' Association Meeting, March 22, 1960.

Hanlon, Michelle L. D. "The Japan Commercial Arbitration Association: Arbitration with the Flavor of Conciliation," *Law & Policy in International Business*. Vol. 22, 1991, pp. 603–26.

Hirst, Alastair. "How the Major Arbitration Institutions Work in Practice, and How They Compare," *Middle East Executive Reports*. Vol. 18, May 1995, p. 1.

Hoellering, Michael F. "Conservatory and Provisional Measures in International Arbitration: AAA's Experience," *Arbitration Journal*. Vol. 16, December 1992, pp. 40–45.

Hofmann, Mark A. "OPIC Loses Bid for Reathorization," *Business Insurance*. Vol. 30, 1996, pp. 1, 77, 78.

Holden, Dennis. "More Debt — or Investment?" *United States Banker*. October 1985, p. 76.

Horlick, Gary. "Dispute Resolution under NAFTA," *Journal of World Trade*. Vol. 27, February 1993, pp. 21–41.

International Centre for Settlement of Investment Disputes. "Articles 27(1) and (2)," *Convention on the Settlement of Investment Disputes Between States and Nationals of Other States*. Washington, D.C.: International Centre for Settlement of Investment Disputes, 1966.

_____. *Convention on the Settlement of Investment Disputes between States and Nationals of Other States*. Washington, D.C.: International Bank for Reconstruction and Development, October 14, 1966.

_____. *Annual Report 1969/70*. Washington, D.C.: International Centre for Settlement of Investment Disputes,

_____. *Additional Facility for the Administration of Conciliation, Arbitration and Fact-Finding Proceedings*. Washington, D.C.: International Centre for Settlement of Investment Disputes, September 1978.

_____. "Investment Promotion Treaties," *ICSID Newsletter*. No. 83-1, January 1983, pp. 3–9.

_____. "Annual Meeting of the Administrative Council of the International Centre for Settlement of Investment Disputes," *Proceedings of ICSID Administrative Council*. Vol. 21, 1987, p. 3.

_____. *1987 Annual Report*. Washington, D.C.: International Centre for Settlement of Investment Disputes,

_____. "New Foreign Investment Legislation Referring to ICSID," *News from ICSID*. Vol. 6, Summer 1989, p. 8.

_____. *ICSID Cases*. Washington, D.C.: International Centre for Settlement of Investment Disputes, November 30, 1996.

_____. *1997 Annual Report*. Washington, D.C.: International Centre for Settlement of Investment Disputes.

_____. *ICSID Bibliography*. Washington, D.C.: International Centre for Settlement of Investment Disputes, April 15, 1997.

_____. "Model Clauses Recording Consent to the Jurisdiction of the International Centre for Settlement of Investment Disputes, ICSID/5." Washington,

D.C.: International Centre for Settlement of Investment Disputes, date n.a.

IFC Annual Report 1996.

IFC Annual Report 1997.

Javits, Benjamin A. *Peace by Investment.* New York: Funk & Wagnalls, 1950.

Kahler, Miles. "Multilateralism with Small and Large Numbers," *International Organization.* Vol. 46, 1992, pp. 681–708.

Kahn, Phillipe. "The Law Applicable to Foreign Investments: The Contribution of the World Bank Convention on the Settlement of Investment Disputes," *Indiana Law Journal.* Vol. 44, Fall 1968, pp. 1–32.

Keohane, Robert O. "Reciprocity in International Relations," *International Organization.* Vol. 40, Winter 1986, pp. 1–27.

Kielmas, Maria. "Political Risk Coverages Come to the West Bank," *Business Insurance.* Vol. 31, May 5, 1997, p. 29.

Kuchenberg, Thomas. "The World Bank: Arbiter Extraordinaire," *The Journal of Law and Economic Development.* Vol. 2, 1968, pp. 259–83.

Lota, Gerd-Peter E. "The Multilateral Guarantee Agency: Benefits," *Credit & Financial Management,* Vol. 88, January 1986, p. 38.

Lyons, Ronan. "OPIC Makes Political Capital," *Project & Trade Finance.* Vol. 146, 1995, pp. 30–31.

MacKenzie, Gregory W. "ICSID Arbitration as a Strategy for Levelling the Host States," *Syracuse Journal of International Law and Commerce.* Vol. 19, 1993, pp. 197–234.

Magid, Per, Rosalyn Higgins, and Marc Lalonde. "AMCO v. Republic of Indonesia: Resubmitted Case Decision on Jurisdiction," *ICSID REVIEW — Foreign Investment Law Journal.* Vol. 3, Spring 1988, pp. 166–90.

Marchais, Bertrand P. "ICSID and the Courts," *News from ICSID.* Vol. 3, Summer 1986, pp. 4–7.

____. "Composition of ICSID Tribunals," *News from ICSID.* Vol. 4, Summer 1987, p. 5.

____. "Setting up the Initial Procedural Framework in ICSID Arbitration," *News from ICSID.* Vol. 5, Winter 1988, pp. 5–9.

Marsden, Keith. "The Role of Foreign Direct Investment," Washington, D.C.: International Finance Corporation, August 1989.

Marsden, Keith, and T. Bélot. *Private Enterprise in Africa: Creating a Better Environment.* Washington, D.C.: World Bank, 1987, pp. viii–ix.

Martin, Josh. "OPIC: Your Link to Global Investment," *Management Review.* Vol. 79, p. 48.

Martin, Lisa. "Interests, Power, and Multilateralism," *International Organization.* Vol. 46, August 1992, pp. 765–92.

Multilateral Investment Guarantee Agency. *Banco de Boston Argentina Project Evaluation Report.* Washington, D.C.: Multilateral Investment Guarantee Agency, December 1, 1997.

____. *Crescent Greenwood, Ltd., Pakistan Project Evaluation Report.* Washington, D.C.: Multilateral Investment Guarantee Agency, November 24, 1997.

____. "Investment Guarantee Guide." Washington, D.C.: Multilateral Investment Guarantee Agency, August 1997.

____. *Kafco Bangladesh Project Monitoring Report.* Washington, D.C.: Multilateral Investment Guarantee Agency, May 29, 1997.

____. *MIGA Annual Report 1990.* Washington, D.C.: Multilateral Investment Guarantee Agency.

____. *MIGA Annual Report 1991.* Washington, D.C.: Multilateral Investment Guarantee Agency.

____. *MIGA Annual Report 1992.* Washington, D.C.: Multilateral Investment Guarantee Agency.

____. *MIGA Annual Report 1993.* Washington, D.C.: Multilateral Investment Guarantee Agency.

____. *MIGA Annual Report 1994.* Washington, D.C.: Multilateral Investment Guarantee Agency.

____. *MIGA Annual Report 1995.* Washington, D.C.: Multilateral Investment Guarantee Agency.

____. *MIGA Annual Report 1996.* Washington, D.C.: Multilateral Investment Guarantee Agency.

____. *MIGA Annual Report 1997.* Washington, D.C.: Multilateral Investment Guarantee Agency.

____. *MIGA Business Profile 1997.* Washington, D.C.: Multilateral Investment Guarantee Agency, 1997.

____. *MIGA: The First Five Years and Future Challenges.* Washington, D.C.: Multilateral Investment Guarantee Agency, 1994.

"MIGA Leverages up Insurance Capacity, Writes Record Cover," *International Trade Finance.* August 11, 1995, p. 11.

Moore, Michael M. "International Arbitration Between States and Foreign Investors — the World Bank Convention," *Stanford Law Review.* Vol. 18, June 1966, pp. 1359–80.

Mullins, Ronald Gift. "World Bank Unit in Deal with Private Reinsurer," *Journal of Commerce.* April 25, 1997, p. 1A.

O'Hare, Patrick. "The Convention on the Settlement of Investment Disputes," *Stanford Journal of International Studies.* Vol. 6, 1971, pp. 146–62.

Parra, Antonio R. "ICSID and New Trends in International Dispute Settlement," *News from ICSID.* Vol. 10, Winter 1993, p. 8.

____. "The Rights and Duties of ICSID Arbitrators," *News from ICSID.* Vol. 13, Winter 1996, pp. 4–11.

Pfefferman, Guy P., and Andrea Madarassy. *Trends in Private Investment in Thirty Developing Countries.* Washington, D.C.: International Finance Corporation, 1989.

Pinto, C. W. "Settlement of Investment Disputes: The World Bank's Convention," *Howard Law Review.* Vol. 13, Spring 1967, pp. 338–41.

"Political Risk Has Receded," *The Mining Journal.* June 24, 1994, p. 466.

"Project Finance," *Institutional Investor.* Vol. 29, October 1995, p. 122.

Ragan, Charles R. "Arbitration in Japan: Using Alternative Methods of Resolving Disputes," *East Asian Executive Reports*. Vol. 14, October 1992, p. 18.

Reisman, Michael. "Repairing ICSID's Control System: Some Comments on Aaron Broches' 'Observations on the Finality of ICSID Awards,'" *ICSID REVIEW — Foreign Investment Law Journal*. Vol. 7, 1992, pp. 196–211.

Rittberger, Volker. "Global Conference Diplomacy and International Policy-Making," *European Journal of Political Research*. Vol. 11, 1983, pp. 167–82.

Ruggie, John Gerard. "Multilateralism: the Anatomy of an Institution," *International Organization*. Vol. 46, 1992, pp. 561–98.

Ryans, John K., Jr., and James C. Baker, "The International Centre for Settlement of Investment Disputes," *Journal of World Trade Law*. Vol. 10, January/February 1976, pp. 65–79.

Sassoon, David M. "Convention on the Settlement of Investment Disputes," *Journal of Business Law*. October 1965, p. 339.

Sauvant, Karl P. "FDI and the Asia Pacific Region," *News from ICSID*. Vol. 12, Summer 1995, pp. 3–5.

Schmidt, John T. "Arbitration Under the Auspices of the International Centre for Settlement of Investment Disputes (ICSID): Implications of the Decision on Jurisdiction in Alcoa Minerals of Jamaica, Inc. v. Government of Jamaica," *Harvard International Law Journal*. Vol. 17, 1976, pp. 90+.

Seppala, Christopher R., and Daniel Gogek. "Multi-party Arbitration Under ICC Rules," *International Financial Law Review*. Vol. 8, November 1989, pp. 32–34.

Shihata, I.F.I. "Increasing Private Capital Flows to LDCs," *Finance & Development*. Vol. 29, December 1984, pp. 6–9.

____. "MIGA and the Standards Applicable to Foreign Investment," *ICSID REVIEW — Foreign Investment Law Journal*. Vol. 1, 1986, pp. 327–39.

____. "Report of the Secretary-General to the ICSID Administrative Council Meeting." Washington, D.C.: International Centre for Settlement of Investment Disputes, December 1988, pp. 2–4.

____. "MIGA and Dispute Settlements," *Middle East Executive Reports*. Vol. 12, April 1989, pp. 8, 22–26.

____. "The Experience of ICSID in the Selection of Arbitrators," *News from ICSID*. Vol. 6, Winter 1989, p. 5.

____. "Introduction by the Secretary-General," *ICSID 1990 Annual Report*. 1990, p. 5.

____. "Report of the Secretary-General to the ICSID Administrative Council." Washington, D.C.: International Centre for Settlement of Investment Disputes, October 1992.

____. "ICSID and Paths to Institutional Cooperation," *News from ICSID*. Vol. 9, Winter 1992, p. 7.

Shipper, Harold D., Jr. (ed.). *International Risk and Insurance: An Environmental-Managerial Approach.* Burr Ridge, Ill.: Irwin McGraw-Hill. (Schroath, Frederick. Ch. 8, "The Political Risk Environment for Risk and Insurance").

Sirefman, Josef P. "The World Bank Plan for Investment Dispute Arbitration," *Arbitration Journal.* Vol. 20, 1965, pp. 168–78.

Snidal, Duncan. "Coordination Versus Prisoners' Dilemma: Implications for International Cooperation and Regimes," *American Political Science Review.* Vol. 79, December 1985, pp. 923–42.

Soley, David A. "ICSID Implementation: An Effective Alternative to International Conflict," *The International Lawyer.* Vol. 19, Spring 1985, pp. 521–44.

Souter, Gavin. "ACE Assumes More Political Risk," *Business Insurance.* Vol. 31, May 5, 1997, pp. 2, 35.

Szasz, Paul C. "A Practical Guide to the Convention on Settlement of Investment Disputes," *Cornell International Law Review.* Vol. 1, 1968, pp. 1–35.

____. "The Investment Disputes Convention and Latin America," *Virginia Journal of International Law.* Vol. 11, March 1971, pp. 256–65.

Teresawa, Yoshio. "New Guarantees for International Investment," *Tokyo Business Today.* February 1989, p. 64.

Third World Legal Studies. *Foreign Investment in the Light of the New International Economic Order.* Windsor, Ontario: Third World Legal Studies, 1983.

Voss, Jurgen. "The Multilateral Investment Guarantee Agency: Status, Mandate, Concept, Features, Implications," *Journal of World Trade Law.* Vol. 21, August 1987, pp. 5–23.

Wallace, Laura. "MIGA: Up and Running," *Finance & Development.* Vol. 29, March 1992, pp. 48–49.

West, Luther C. "Award Enforcement Provisions of the World Bank Convention," *Arbitration Journal.* Vol. 23, 1968, pp. 38–53.

Williams, S. Linn. "Political And Other Risk Insurance: Eximbank, OPIC and MIGA," *Middle East Executive Reports.* Vol. 11, February 1988, pp. 8, 13–18.

____. "Political And Other Risk Insurance: Eximbank, OPIC and MIGA," *Middle East Executive Reports.* Vol. 11, March 1988, pp. 23–25.

____. "Political And Other Risk Insurance: Eximbank, OPIC and MIGA," *Middle East Executive Reports.* Vol. 11, June 1988, pp. 23–24.

Witherell, William H. "Towards an International Set of Rules for Investment: The OECD Initiative," *News from ICSID.* Vol. 12, Winter 1995, pp. 3–6.

World Bank. "Termination of Two Proceedings in Bauxite Cases," *World Bank News Release.* March 17, 1977, p. 1.

Yun Chong Su. "The Convention on the Settlement of Investment Disputes — Commentary and Forecast," *Malaya Law Review.* Vol. 11, December 1969, pp. 287–314.

Ziadé, Nassib G. "ICSID Clauses in the Subrogation Context," *News from ICSID.* Vol. 7, Summer 1990, p. 4.

_____. "Some Recent Decisions in ICSID Cases," *ICSID REVIEW — Foreign Investment Law Journal.* Vol. 6, Fall 1991, pp. 514–25.

Web Sites Used

http://www.worldbank.org/html/extpb/annrep97/overview.htm (November 17, 1997, p. 8).

http://www.asiadevbank.org/glance/regmem.html (November 17, 1997, p. 1).

http://www.africandevelopmentbank.com/BOARD.htm (November 17, 1997, p. 1).

http://www.africandevelopmentbank.com/BROCHUR.htm (November 17, 1997, p. 1).

http://www.ebrd.com/inro/contact/g01.htm (November 17, 1997, p. 1).

http://www.miga.org/mandate.htm (May 9, 1997, p. 1).

Index

ABOUT THE AUTHOR

James C. Baker is Professor of Finance and International Business at Kent State University. He is the author of numerous books and articles on international finance.

ISBN 1-56720-312-4

9 781567 203127

90000>

EAN

HARDCOVER BAR CODE